Index to
Evergreen Review

by
David A. Bower
and
Carol Campbell Strempek

The Scarecrow Press, Inc.
Metuchen, N.J.   **1972**

Table of Contents

Preface

This index, with authors, titles, and subjects intensified in one alphabetical sequence, is a reference guide to the EVERGREEN REVIEW for the years 1957 through 1970. The term "author" implies not only writers, but photographers, cartoonists, artists and illustrators.

In the case of pseudonyms, we used the pseudonym as main entry with a notation that it was a pseudonym, and included cross references from the author's real name, if ascertainable. For the most part, we have used READERS' GUIDE TO PERIODICAL LITERATURE for choice of subject headings. However, when it seemed that READERS' GUIDE subject headings were out-dated or inappropriate to the "personality" of EVERGREEN, contemporary usage was preferred, such as Films instead of Moving-Pictures, Blacks instead of Negroes, etc.

Included at the end of the index is a list of all authors of essays, stories, plays, poems, and the like, and all artists, photographers, illustrators, translators, and cartoonists that have appeared in the magazine, so that any reader interested only in, for example, EVERGREEN poetry or cartoons may use this list to find all the poetry or all the cartoons in the main index.

Because of EVERGREEN's popularity (for whatever reason) there were many issues missing from supposedly "complete holdings." We did, however, manage to locate all the issues through the facilities of Mugar Library of Boston University, Simmons College Library, and Widener at Harvard. We would especially like to thank Paul Gurney, former Interlibrary Loan Librarian at B.U., Adeane Bregman, Reference Librarian, and Robert Watts, Director of Simmons College Library, for their kind help.

David A. Bower
Carol Campbell Strempek

Boston. June, 1971

v

PART I: Index

A

A [novel excerpt] A. Warhol.
58:26-31+, Sept '68.

ABEL, Lionel
Brecht [review essay] 14:
134-40, Sept/Oct '60.

The ABILITY to function [essay]
N. Hentoff. 79:45-7, Je '70.

ABORTION
Notes from the underground:
abortion. J. Nathan. 46:23-5,
Apr '67.

ABOUT Evergreen Review No.
32 [essay] 33:32. Aug/Sept '64.

ABOUT LeRoi Jones [review
essay] C. Brown. 75:65-70,
Feb '70.

ABOUT Zhivago and his poems
[essay] F. O'Hara. 7:230-8,
winter '59.

ABRAMOV, Fyodor
The new life; a day on a col-
lective farm [novel] 30:1-64,
May/Je '63.

ACCIDENT [poem] L. Barnes.
45:41, Feb '67.

An ACCOUNT of the events preceding the death of Bill Burroughs [essay] A. Morrissett.
29:103-8, Mar/Apr '63.

The ACHIEVEMENT of Lee
Konitz [essay] H. Pekar. 43:
30-2, Oct '66.

ACTORS AND ACTRESSES
see
BOGART, Humphrey
DEAN, James
LAHR, Bert

ADAMOV, Arthur
As we were [play] 4:113-
26, '57.
The endless humiliation
[autobiographical essay] 8:64-
95, spring '59.

ADAMS, George
[photo] 79:38, Je '70; 85:
cover, Dec '70.

The ADAPTABLE Mr. Albee
[essay] J. Lahr. 54:36-9+,
May '68.

The ADDICT in the street:
Hector Rodriguez [essay] J.
Larner. 35:11-15, Mar '65.

ADELMAN, Bob
[photo] 30: cover, 58-63,
May/Je '63.

ADULT animals [cartoons] P.
Wende. 41:33-7, Je '66.

The ADVENTURES of Phoebe
Zeit-Geist [comic strip] M.
O'Donoghue and F. Springer,
38:58-61, Nov '65; 39:54-7,
Feb '66; 40:50-3, Apr '66; 41:
57-61, Je '66; 42:58-62, Aug
'66; 43:66-73, Oct '66; 44:48-51,
Dec '66; 45:48-52, Feb '67; 46:
92-7, Apr '67; 47:33-40, Je '67;
49:31-9, Oct '67.

The ADVENTURES of Tom &

7

Dick Smith [comic strip] P.
Wende. 45:84-8, Feb '67.

AFRICA [poem] P. Brown.
10:55, Nov/Dec '59.

AFTER a Saturday night with
Lady Day and Hart Crane and
Mrs. Brady's daughter, he
spends a Sunday morning in the
park, alone [poem] P. Gleeson.
9:132, summer '59.

AFTER all these years [story]
B. Amidon. 83:35-6, Oct '70.

AFTER Budapest [interview] J.
Sartre. 1:5-23, '57.

AFTER Eliot: some notes toward a reassessment [essay]
P. Roche. 39:84-92, Feb '66.

AFTER the drowning of his sister's husband [poem] Archilochos. 25:91, Jl/Aug '62.

AFTER the war is over [car-
toon] A. Sens. 18:83-5, Jl/
Aug '61.

AGAINST borders [poem] E.
Evtushevko. 25:23-4, Jl/Aug
'62.

AGAINST interpretation [essay]
S. Sontag. 34:76-80+, Dec '64.

AGHWEE the sky monster
[story] K. Ōe. 54:44-8+, May
'68.

AIR raid warning of twelfth November [poem] Ho-Chi-Minh.
43:45, Oct '66.

AL Fatah speaks: a conversation with "Abu Amar" [inter-
view] A. Schleifer. 56:44-6+,
Jl '68.

ALAIN Robbe-Grillet [essay]

R. Barthes. 5:113-26, summer
'58.

ALBEE, Edward
The zoo story (a play in one
scene - 1958) 12:28-52, Mar/
Apr '60.

ALBEE, EDWARD
(photograph of) 54:36, May
'68.

ALBEE, EDWARD - CRITICISM
AND INTERPRETATION
The adaptable Mr. Albee.
J. Lahr. 54:36-9+, May '68.
The zoo story
Hold that tiger. J. Tallmer.
18:109-13, May/Je '61.

ALCORN, John S.
[illus] 81:52, Aug '70.

ALEX
[cartoon] 36:30, Je '65.

ALGERIAN WAR
Declaration concerning the
right of insubordination in the
Algerian War. 15:1-4, Nov/
Dec '60.
France: of patriotism, ref-
uge and scoundrels. J. Barry.
24:36-50, May/Je '62.
France: technology, politics,
and the average man. J. Barry.
25:80-90, Jl/Aug '62.
France: the decline of an
American dream - 1. J. Barry.
23:48-62, Mar/Apr '62.

ALLAIS, Alphonse
A real Parisian affair [story]
13:98-102, May/Je '60.

ALLAIS, ALPHONSE
Alphonse Allais: literary
assassin. F. Caradec. 13:
97-8, May/Je '60.
(photograph of) 13:95, May/
Je '60.

ALLEN Ginsberg meets the
Swedish cyclist [story] G.
Harding. 74:22-5+, Jan '70.

ALLEN, WOODY - CRITICISM
AND INTERPRETATION
Play it again, Sam
Broadway comedy: images of
impotence. J. Lahr. 78:39-
40+, May '70.

ALPHONSE Allais: literary
assassin [essay] F. Caradec.
13:97-8, May/Je '60.

AMAR, ABU [pseud]
Al Fatah speaks: a conversation with "Abu Amar" [inter-
view] A. Schleifer. 56:44-6+,
Jl '68.

AMERICAN construction sculpture [essay] I. Sandler. 8:
136-46, spring '59.

The AMERICAN frag [poem]
L.-P. Fargue. 19:63, Jl/Aug
'61.

AMERICAN INDIANS
From the third eye...white
man still speaks with forked
tongue. R. Wolf. 78:91-93,
May '70.
Red man, white man, man on
the moon. F. Turner. 80:22-
26+, Jl '70.

AMERICAN INDIANS - FILMS
From the third eye... Hollywood's last stand. T. Seligson.
85:78-9, Dec '70.

The AMERICAN musical: the
slavery of escape [essay] J.
Lahr. 58:22-5+, Sept '68.

AMERICAN pastime [story] D.
Weber. 84:23-5+, Nov '70.

AMI
[cartoon] 9:171, summer '59.

AMIDON, Bill
After all these years [story]
83:35-6, Oct '70.
Cannonball catcher [story]
76:25-6+, Mar '70.

AMNESIA in Memphis [poem]
G. Corso. 3:77, '57.

AMOR, Guadalupe
My mother's bedroom [auto-
biographical excerpt] 7:121-6,
winter '59.

AMRAM, David
In memory of Jack Kerouac
[reminiscence] 74:41+, Jan '70.

An ANALYSIS of Alain Resnais'
film Hiroshima mon amour [re-
view essay] A Hodeir. 12:102-
113, Mar/Apr '60.

ANAND, Mulk Raj
The great delight [essay]
9:172-97, summer '59.

ANAND, MULK RAJ - CRITI-
CISM AND INTERPRETATION
The great delight
Letter to the editor: The
great delight and the big lie. J.
Campbell. 14:155-9, Sept/Oct
'60.

ANATHEMA [poem] P. Myers.
49:52-53, Oct '67.

ANATOMY of the beasts: heroes,
perverts, and saints [review]
C. Hernton. 46:34-5+, Apr '67.

AND you think you could?
[poem] V. Mayakovsky. 20:
89, Sept/Oct '61.

The ANDALUSIAN smile: reflections on Luis Buñuel [essay]
J. Price. 40:24-9+, Apr '66.

ANDERSCH, Alfred
The crocodile [story] 19:

86-95, Jl/Aug '61.
The night of the giraffe [story]
16: 32-55, Jan/Feb '61.
Spilt beer [autobiographical
essay] 21: 47-53, Nov/Dec '61.

ANDERSON, Benny
Tarzan. The Government. Re-
frigerators [story] 41: 42-5,
Je '66.

ANDREWS, Lyman
The death of Mayakovsky
(1893-1930) [poem] 50: 70-1,
Dec '67.

ANGELINA-in-the-wilderness or,
the last freedom [story] L.
Skir. 59: 58-61, Oct '68.

The ANGRY young film makers
[essay] A. Vogel. 6: 163-83,
autumn '58.

The ANIMAL that died but eyes
still alive [novel excerpt] A.
Tutuola. 5: 107-112, summer '58.

ANIMALS of all countries [poem]
J. Ashbery. 8: 97, spring '59.

ANIMALS of all countries (II)
[poem] J. Ashbery. 8: 99,
spring '59.

ANIMALS of all countries (III)
[poem] J. Ashbery. 8:100,
spring, '59.

An ANNIVERSARY unnoticed
[essay] R. Seaver. 36: 53-6,
Je '65.

ANNUL in me my manhood
[poem] Brother Antoninus. 2:
19-20, '57.

ANTHOLOGY of Mexican poetry
[review] J. Schuyler. 7: 221,
winter '59.

ANTI-WAR DEMONSTRATIONS

see
VIETNAMESE WAR, 1957 -
PROTESTS, DEMONSTRA-
TIONS, ETC. AGAINST.

ANTONINUS, Brother
Annul in me my manhood
[poem] 2: 19-20, '57.
Out of the ash [poem] 2: 20,
'57.
A penitential psalm [poem]
2: 18, '57.
The south coast [poem] 2:
17, '57.

ANTONINUS, BROTHER
(photograph of) 2: between
pages 64 and 65, '57.

ANTONIONI, MICHAELANGELO -
CRITICISM AND INTERPRE-
TATION
Zabriskie point
From the third eye... An-
tonioni: where does Zabriskie
point? K. Carroll. 81: 74-6,
Aug '70.

ANZAI, Hitoshi
Morning: phone rings [poem]
84: 51, Nov '70.

An APODEICTIC outline [satire]
S. Taylor. 13: 150-7, May/Je
'60.

APPLEJACK [review] J.
Tallmer. 24: 95-106,
May/Je '62.

APPLYING black power:
a speculative essay. N.
Hentoff. 44: 44-7+,
Dec '66.

APPREHENSIONS [poem] R.
Duncan. 16: 56-67, Jan/Feb
'61.

ARAB STATES - FOREIGN RE-
LATIONS
see

ISRAELI-ARAB WAR, 1967-

ARAFAT, YASIR
        see
AMAR, ABU [pseud]

ARBUS, Diane
    [photo] 29: cover, Mar/Apr
'63.

ARCHILOCHOS
    After the drowning of his
    sister's husband; English version
    by Willis Barnstone [poem] 25:
    91, Je/Aug '62.
    On a lewd servant; English
    version by Willis Barnstone
    [poem] 25: 91, Je/Aug '62.
    On the male organ; English
    version by Willis Barnstone
    [poem] 25: 91, Jl/Aug '62.

ARCHITECTURE, MEXICAN
    Felix Candela: shells in archi-
    tecture. E. McCoy. 7: 127-
    33, winter '59.

ARCINIEGA, RICARDO POZAS
        see
POZAS ARCINIEGA, RICARDO

ARIKHA, Avigdor
    [illus.] 47: 46; 49, Je '67.

ARMSTRONG, LOUIS
    Louis Armstrong: style be-
    yond style. M. Williams. 24:
    111-20, May /Je '62.
    (photograph of) 24: 111; 112,
    May/Je '62.

ARNAUD, Georges
    Sweet confessions [play] 3:
    135-59, '57.

ARNAUD, Noël
    Remy de Gourmont; man of
    masks [essay] 13: 106-7, May/
    Je '60.

ARNAUD, NOËL
    (photograph of) 13: 95, May/

Je '60.

ARNETT, Carroll
    La Dene and the Minotaur
    [story] 27: 18-29, Nov/Dec '62.

ARONOWITZ, Alfred
    From the third eye... Pop
    freak and passing fancies [re-
    view essay] 77: 86-8, Apr '70.

ARP, Hans
    Kaspar is dead [poem] 21:
    35, Nov/Dec '61.

ARRABAL, Fernando
    Fernando Arrabal Ruiz, my
    father [reminiscence] F. Arra-
    bal. 71: 47, Oct '69.
    Picnic on the battlefield
    [play] 15: 76-90, Nov/Dec '60.

ARRABAL, FERNANDO
    (photograph of) 15: 63,
    Nov/Dec '60.

ARRABAL, FERNANDO - CRITI-
    CISM AND INTERPRETATION
    Dialogue with Arrabel. A.
    Morrissett. 15: 70-5, Nov/
    Dec '60.
    A new comic style: Arrabal.
    G. Serreau. 15: 61-9, Nov/
    Dec '60.

ARREOLA, Juan Jose
    Nine sketches: Freedom;
    Moles, Insects; Gravity; The
    toad; Epithalamium; The en-
    counter; The map of lost ob-
    jects; The boa [prose-poems]
    7: 134-8, winter '59.

ART
        see
CONSTRUCTIVISM
DECADENCE IN ART
DESTRUCTIVISM (Art)
EROTIC ART
NEW YORK SCHOOL (Art)
SAN FRANCISCO SCHOOL (Art)
SURREALISM (Art)

ART, MEXICAN
The cactus curtain; an open
letter on conformity in Mexico
art. J. Cuevas. 7: 111-20,
winter '59.
see also
ART, NAHUATL
PAINTING, MEXICAN

ART, NÁHUATL
A Náhuatl concept of art. M.
León-Portilla. 7: 157-67, winter
'59.

ART, POLITICAL
see
ART, RUSSIAN

ART, PRE-COLUMBIAN
see
ART, NÁHUATL

ART, RUSSIAN
Russian revolutionary posters,
1917-1929 [illustrations] S. Congrat-Butler. 46: 74-9, Apr '67.

ART AND INDUSTRY
see
BUSINESS AND THE ARTS

ART AND SOCIETY
Breaking through the circle
of self: art and social action.
N. Hentoff. 55: 45-7, Je '68.

ART CRITICISM
Against interpretation. S.
Sontag. 34: 76-80+, Dec '64.

ART GALLERIES
The importance of a wall:
galleries. K. Sawyer. 8: 122-
35, spring '59.

ARTAUD, Antonin
Letters from Rodez. 11:
60-84, Jan/Feb '60.
No more masterpieces [essay]
5: 150-9, summer '58.
Spurt of blood [play] 28: 62-
6, Jan/Feb '63.

Three letters. 28: 52-61,
Jan/Feb '63.

ARTAUD, ANTONIN
Artaud at Rodez. C. Maro-
witz. 53: 64-7+, Apr '68.
(photographs of) 11: 61-2,
Jan/Feb '60; 53: 64, Apr '68.

ARTAUD, ANTONIN-CRITICISM
AND INTERPRETATION
Close to Antonin Artaud. M.
Saillet. 13: 79-83, May/Je '60.

ARTICLE [review essay] D.
Newlove. 85: 23-9+, Dec '70.

ARTIE [story] P. Southgate.
9: 120-8, summer '59.

ARTIST of the outrageous [re-
view essay] J. Lahr. 75: 31-
4+, Feb '70.

ARTISTS
see
ARCHITECTS
PAINTERS
SCULPTORS

ARTISTS - POLITICAL ACTIVI-
TIES
Breaking through the circle
of self: art and social action.
N. Hentoff. 55: 45-7, Je '68.

The ARTIST'S studio [cartoon]
A. Sens. 25: 102, Jl/Aug '62.

The ARTS and business [essay]
J. Lahr. 68: 63-5+, Jl '69.

ARUEGO
[cartoon] 54: 35, May '68.

AS the dark snow continues to
fall [poem] W. Merwin. 35:
50, Mar '65.

AS we were [play] A. Adamov.
4: 113-26, '57.

13   ASHBERY, John

ASHBERY, John
 The poems [13 poems] 8: 97-
101, spring '59.

ASHBERY, JOHN - CRITICISM
 AND INTERPRETATION
      The poems
 Poets and painters in collabo-
ration. F. Porter. 20: 121-6,
Sept/Oct '61.

ASHTON, Dore
 An Eastern view of the San
Francisco school [essay] 2: 148-
59, '57.
 Mark Tobey [essay] 11: 29-36,
Jan/Feb '60.
 Philip Guston [essay] 14: 88-
91, Sept/Oct '60.

ASPECTS of Japanese culture
[essay] D. Suzuki. 6: 40-56,
autumn '58.

AT Apollinaire's grave [poem]
A. Ginsberg. 8: 59-62, spring
'59.

AT night all cats are grey
[story] P. Boyle. 33: 13-15+,
Aug/Sept '64.

AT the moment of love and blue
eyelids [poem] P. Carroll. 8:
63, spring '59.

ATHILL, Diana
 An unavoidable delay [story]
12: 61-73, Mar/Apr '60.

The ATOM bomb and the future
of man [essay] K. Jaspers. 5:
37-57, summer '58.

ATOMIC WEAPONS AND DIS-
 ARMAMENT
 The moral unneutrality of
science. C. P. Snow. 17: 1-
2, Mar/Apr '61.

AUBADE [poem] B. Boyd. 6:
57, autumn '58.

AUBADE [poem] K. Shapiro.
50: 63, Dec '67.

AUGHATANE [story] J. Williamson. 16: 84-101, Jan/Feb
'61.

AUTHORS
         see
ALLAIS, Alphonse
BECKETT, Samuel
BRÉE, Germaine
CAHN, Edgar
DAUMAL, René
ELLMAN, Richard
ESSLIN, Richard
FARGUE, Léon-Paul
FÉNÉON, Félix
GARRETT, Leslie
JONES, LeRoi
KANE, Cheikh Hamidou
KEROUAC, Jack
KRIM, Seymour
LANG, Daniel
LIPTON, Lawrence
MAILER, Norman
MAY, Rollo
ORWELL, George
SCHWOB, Marcel
TERKEL, Studs
THURBER, James
YACOUBI, Ahmed
          see also
BLACK AUTHORS
DRAMATISTS
POETS

The AUDIENCE [play] F. García
Lorca. 6: 93-107, autumn '58.

AUTO eroticism [pictorial sa-
tire] M. O'Donoghue and T.
Lafferty. 55: 33-9, Je '68.

The AUTOMATION of caprice
[play] M. O'Donoghue. 33: 38-
41, Aug/Sept '64.

AUTOMOBILES
 A car for Bonnie. J.-F.
Held. 58: 62-4, Sept '68.
 The classless cars. J.-F. Held.
54: 57-61, May '68.

see also
CAMARO
FERRARI
MERCEDES
MINI-COOPER S
MORGAN
ROLLS-ROYCE
VOLKSWAGEN

AVEDON, Richard
[photographs] 81: cover, 34-41, Aug '70.

AVEDON, RICHARD - CRITI-
CISM AND INTERPRETATION
The silent theater of Richard
Avedon. J. Lahr. 81: 34+,
Aug '70.

- B -

BABII Yar [poem]   E. Evtushenko. 22: 57-9, Jan/Feb '61.

BABII YAR (Kiev, Russia)
Note on "Babii Yar." 22:
60, Jan/Feb '62.

The BABY [story] Y. Kemal.
14: 96-124, Sept/Oct '60.

BACH, Eric
[photo] 53: 49-55, Apr '68.

BACHMANN, Ingeborg
Early noon [poem] 21: 54-5,
Nov/Dec '61.

BACH'S music moves curtains
[poems] J. Sabines.   7: 139,
winter '59.

BACK roads to far towns; after
Bashō [poem] L. Ferlinghetti.
78: 68, May '70.

BAJA CALIFORNIA
"Lower" California. L. Ferlinghetti.   24: 61-71, May/Je
'62.

BAKER, FRED - CRITICISM

AND INTERPRETATION
Events
Events: an interview with
Fred Baker. K. Carroll. 79:
41-3, Je '70.

BALL/ta-moore [poem]   C.
Webb.   57: 21, Aug '68.

BALLAD [poem] D. Posner. 32:
43, Apr/May '64.

BALLAD for anyone listening
[poem] N. Rosten.   38: 69,
Nov '65.

The BALLAD of the black cloud
[poem] G. Grass.   32: 69, Apr/
May '64.

BALLETS
see
STRAVINSKY, I. - CRITICISM
AND INTERPRETATION
Agon

WEILL, K. - CRITICISM AND
INTERPRETATION
The seven deadly sins.

BANK day [story] D. Woolf.
14: 14-27, Sept/Oct '60.

The BANQUET [story] W. Gombrowicz.   44: 41-3+, Dec '66.

BARBARELLA [comic strip] J.
Forest.   37: 35-43, Sept '65;
38: 37-45, Nov '65; 39: 33-43,
Feb '66.

BARE bearers [poem] T. Fiofori.   56: 27, Jl '68.

BARKER, Danny
A memory of King Bolden
[essay] 37: 66-74, Sept '65.

BARNES, Lakenan
Accident [poem] 45: 41,
Feb '67.

BARNIER, L.
Julien Torma, author by
neglect [essay] 13: 118-9, May/
Je '60.
(photograph of) 13: 96, May/
Je '60.

BARNSTONE, Willis, translator
see
ARCHILOCHOS. After the
drowning of his sister's husband.
_____. On a lewd servant.
_____. On the male organ.
JULIAN the Apostate. Calculation.

BARRY, Joseph
France: of patriotism, refuge
and scoundrels [essay] 24: 36-
50, May/Je '62.
France: technology, politics,
and the average man [essay] 25:
80-90, Jl/Aug '62.
France: the decline of an
American dream-1 [essay] 23:
48-62, Mar/Apr '62.
Letter from Paris [essay] 26:
101-9, Sept/Oct '62.

BARTHES, Roland
Alain Robbe-Grillet [essay]
5: 113-26, summer '58.

BASIE, WILLIAM ("Count") -
CRITICISM AND INTERPRE-
TATION
Count Basie: style beyond
swing. M. Williams. 38: 62-
5, Nov '65.

BATAILLE, Georges
Madame Edwarda [story] 34:
63-7, Dec '64.

BATHS
see
ST. JAMES BATHS

BAURET, Jean-François
Portfolio of photographs. 78:
41-5, May '70.

The BEARD [play] M. McClure.
49: 64-79, Oct '67.

THE BEARD (play)
Notes from the underground:
San Francisco censorship. J.
Nathan. 45: 16-20, Feb '67.

BEAST parade [poem] L.
Kandel. 41: 47, Je '66.

A BEAST'S repast [portfolio of
photographs with text] S. Dali
and W. Bokelberg. 44: 33-40,
Dec '66.

BEAT POETRY
San Francisco letter. K.
Rexroth. 2: 5-14, '57.

BEATNIKS
The upbeat beatnik. A.
Buchwald. 14: 153-4, Sept/Oct
'60.

BECK, JACK W.
[illus] 32: 74, Apr/May '64;
33: 34, Aug/Sept '64; 34: 62,
Dec '64.

BECK, Julian
Notes from the underground:
Theater and revolution [essay]
54: 14-15+, May '68.
Report from Times Square
[essay] 24: 121-5, May/Je '62.
Sunday sermon and acrostic
[poem] 33: 48, Aug/Sept '64.

BECKER, Paul
Harlem [poem] 44: 92, Dec
'66.

BECKETT, Samuel
The calmative [story] 47:
46-9+, Je '67.
Cascando [play] 30: 47-57,
May/Je '63.
Dante and the lobster [story]
1: 24-36, '57.
Echo's bones [poem] 1: 179-
92, '57.

Embers (a play for radio)
10: 28-41, Nov/Dec '59.
The end [story] 15: 22-41,
Nov/Dec '60.
The expelled [story] 22: 8-20,
Jan/Feb '62.
From an abandoned work
[story] 3: 83-91, '57.
From an unabandoned work
[poem] 14: 58-65, Sept/Oct '60.
Imagination dead imagine
[essay] 39: 48-9, Feb '66.
Krapp's last tape [play] 5:
13-24, summer '58.
Lessness [story] 80: 35-6,
Jl '70.
Play [play] 34: 42-7, Dec
'64.
Text for nothing I [story] 9:
21-4, summer '59.
Words and music [play] 27:
34-43, Nov/Dec '62.

BECKETT, SAMUEL - CRITI-
  CISM AND INTERPRETATION
Where now? who now? M.
Blanchot. 7: 222-9, winter '59.
          Endgame
King Lear or Endgame. J.
Kott. 33: 52-65, Aug/Sept '64.
          Film
Article. D. Newlove. 85:
23-9+, Dec '70.

BECKETT, Samuel, translator
          see
PINGET, R. The old tune.

BEGINNING of a poem of These
States [poem] A. Ginsberg.
49: 46-9, Oct '67.

BEHAN, Brendan
The big house: a play for
radio. 20: 40-63, Sept/Oct '61.

Where we all came into town
[essay] 18: 18-32, May/Je '61.

BEHAVIOR MODIFICATION
The drugged classroom. N.
Hentoff. 85: 31-3, Dec '70.

BEHIND the brick wall [story]
T. Déry. 29: 88-102, Mar/
Apr '63.

BEHIND the iron (theater) curtain [essay] A. Schneider. 79:
91-4, Je '70.

BEHOLD the new journalism--
it's coming after you! [review
essay] N. Hentoff. 56: 49-51,
Jl '68.

BEIDERBECKE, BIX
Bix Beiderbecke and the
white man's burden. M. Williams. 19: 108-13, Jl/Aug '61.
(photograph of) 19: 109,
Jl/Aug '61.

Un BEL de [story] J. Oppenheimer. 28: 86-94, Jan/Feb
'63.

BELIEF and technique for
modern prose [essay] J.
Kerouac. 8: 57, spring '59.

BELLES-LETTRES [notations]
F. Fénéon. 13: 105, May/Je
'60.

BENTLEY, Eric
Letter to the editor [cor-
rection to his essay, "The
science fiction of Bertolt
Brecht"] 42: 94, Aug '66.
The science fiction of Bertolt
Brecht [essay] 41: 28-32+, Je
'66.

BENTLEY, Eric, translator
          see
BRECHT, B. The elephant
calf...

BERGER, Patricia
Eighteenth birthday [poem]
56: 48, Jl '68.

BERKELEY in time of plague
[poem] J. Spicer. 2: 52, '57.

BERKSON, Bill
see
O'HARA, Frank and Bill Berkson

BERLIN
Berlin, border of the divided
world. U. Johnson. 21: 18-
30, Nov/Dec '61.
Berlin impressions. G.
Corso. 16: 69-83, Jan/Feb '61.

The BERLIN Antigone [story]
R. Hochhuth. 32: 70-3, Apr/
May '64.

BERLIN, border of the divided
world, [essay] U. Johnson. 21:
18-30, Nov/Dec '61.

BERLIN impressions [essay]
G. Corso. 16: 69-83, Jan/Feb
'61.

A BERRY feast [poem] G.
Snyder. 2: 110-14, '57.

BERTHA [play] K. Koch.   15:
42-5, Nov/Dec '60.

BERTRAND, R.
The erotic drawings of
Bertrand. 76: 39-45, May '70.

BESS, Donovan
Miller's "Tropic" on trial
[essay] 23: 12-37, Mar/Apr '62.

The BETRAYED kingdom [story]
R. Brautigan. 76: 51, Mar '70.

BEVERLOO, Cornelius van
see
CORNEILLE [pseud]

BEYOND the novel [essay] E.
M. Cioran.   17: 80-92, Mar/
Apr '61.

BHAKTIVEDANTA, Swami
Notes from the underground:
International Society for Krishna
Consciousness.   J. Nathan. 45:
7-16, Feb '67.

BIANCIARDI, Luciano
The same old soup [story]
55: 16-21+, Je '68.

BIELER, Manfred
Wedding march [story] 40:
54-5, Apr '66.

The BIG house; a play for
radio. B. Behan.   20: 40-63,
Sept/Oct '61.

The BIG sale [poem] R. Wells.
82: 27, Sept '70.

BIG Sur and the good life
[essay] H. Miller. 2: 36-45,
'57.

BILLIE Holiday: actress with-
out an act [review essay] M.
Williams.   26: 115-25, Sept/
Oct '62.

BILLY Graham and friend
[essay] D. Rader.   74: 31-5+,
Jan '70.

BINDERS keepers [pictorial
satire] M. O'Donoghue and T.
Lafferty.   62: 33-9, Jan '69.

A BIRD in the word [poem] R.
Saggese. 53: 62, Apr '68.

BIRDS of paradise and humming-
birds [poem] J. Ashbery.   8:
100-1, spring '59.

BIRTH CONTROL
see
CATHOLIC CHURCH AND
BIRTH CONTROL

BISCHOF, Werner
[photo]17: cover, May/Apr'61.

BISHOP, Jordan
Notes from the underground:
Revolution in the Rockies:
Woodstock West [essay] 80:
71-2, Jl '70.
Schools, jails, and the god-

dam system [essay] 81: 53-5+,
Aug '70.

BIX Beiderbecke and the white
man's burden [review essay] M.
Williams. 19: 108-13, Jl/Aug
'61.

BLACK AUTHORS
    The Black writer and the new
censorship. J. Lester. 77:
19-21+, Apr '70.

BLACK blood: a South African
diary [essay] A. Giggins. 34:
28-32+, Dec '64.

BLACK Dada nihilismus [poem]
L. Jones. 29: 85-7, Mar/Apr
'63.

BLACK eye [story] D. Newlove.
77: 57-9+, Apr '70.

BLACK IDENTITY
    Uninventing the Negro. N.
Hentoff. 38: 34-6+, Nov '65.

BLACK jasmine [story] K.
Singh. 37: 54-8, Sept '65.

BLACK LEADERS
        see
BROWN, H. Rap
CLEAVER, Eldridge
KING, Martin Luther
MALCOLM X
NEWTON, Huey P.

The BLACK man is making new
gods [poem] L. Jones. 50:
49, Dec '67.

BLACK PANTHERS
    Jean Genêt and the Black
Panthers. M. Manceaux. 82:
35-7+, Sept '70.

BLACK people! [poem] L.
Jones. 50: 49, Dec '67.

BLACK POETRY

Poems by Black children.
T. Seligson.   79: 27-9, Je '70.

BLACK power, white power
[illus] T. Ungerer.   50: 47,
Dec '67.

BLACK POWER
    Applying black power: a
speculative essay. N. Hentoff.
44: 44-7+, Dec '66.
    Chicago, honkies, and Camus.
J. Newfield. 50: 58-60, Dec
'67.
    The coming of black power.
N. Hentoff. 57: 59-61, Aug
'68.
    The last stand of the dis-
pensables. N. Hentoff. 70:
59-62, Sept '69.
    The new movement. N.
Hentoff. 42: 66-73, Aug '66.

BLACK studies: bringing back
the person [essay] J. Jordan.
71: 39-41+, Oct '69.

The BLACK writer and the new
censorship [essay] J. Lester.
77: 19-21+, Apr '70.

BLACKBURN, Paul
    '50s teenagers and '50s rock
(by Frank Zappa, as told to
Richard Blackburn) [essay] 81:
43-6, Aug '70.
    The flies [poem] 19: 54,
Jl/Aug '61.
    Listening to Sonny Rollins at
the Five-Spot [poem] 48: 41,
Aug '67.
    Poem 25: 78, Jl/Aug '62.
    Poor dog [poem] 51: 85,
Feb '68.
    Sirventes [poem] 10: 83-6,
Nov/Dec '59.
    Song for a cool departure
[poem] 4: 143-4, '57.
    Two poems [Here they go;
Torch ballad for John Spicer: d.
8/17/65] 43: 80-1, Oct '66.

BLACKS - SOCIAL CONDITIONS
Last exit before the Great
Society. N. Hentoff. 37: 59-
65, Sept '65.

BLAKE, Quentin
[cartoon] 49: 95, Oct '67.

BLANCHOT, Maurice
Where now? Who now?
[essay] 7: 222-9, winter '59.

BLASER, Robin
Poem. 41: 138, '57.

BLECHMAN, R. O.
Cold war [cartoon] 27: 87-9,
Nov/Dec '62.

BLOK, Alexander
The twelve; English version
by Anselm Hollo [poem] 19: 31-
43, Jl/Aug '61.

BLOOD and fire [story] D.
Rader. 84: 53-5, Nov '70.

The BLOOD of a wig [story]
T. Southern. 49: 22-4+, Oct
'67.

BLOOD orange [poem] J. Prévert. 14: 70, Sept/Oct '60.

The BLUE bouquet [story] O.
Paz. 18: 99-101, May/Je '61.

BLUES
Recording with Big Joe. M.
Williams. 25: 118-27, Jl/Aug
'62.

BLUES for Sister Sally [poem]
L. Kandel. 45: 46-7, Feb '67.

BOBBER, Richard
[illus] 58: 58, Sept '68.

BOBO, the priest [story] D.
Richie. 46: 67+, Apr '67.

BOGART, HUMPHREY

The death of Sam Spade.
J. Goldberg. 28: 107-16, Jan/
Feb '63.
(photograph of) 81: 36,
Aug '70.

BOISE, Ron
Eleven pieces of sculpture
depicting themes from the Kama
Sutra [portfolio of photographs]
36: between pages 64 and 65,
Je '65.

BOISE, RON - CRITICISM AND
INTERPRETATION
Sculpture by Ron Boise: the
Kama Sutra theme. A. Watts.
36: 64-5, Je '65.

BOKELBERG, Werner
[photo] 44: 33-40, Dec '66.

BOLDEN, BUDDY
A memory of King Bolden.
D. Barker. 37: 66-74, Sept '65.

BOLIVIA - POLITICS AND
GOVERNMENT
see
GUERILLAS - BOLIVIA

BOLIVIAN campaign diary. C.
Guevara. 57: 32-5+, Aug '68.

BÖLL, Heinrich
In this country of ours
[essay] 21: 102-9, Nov/Dec '61.

BONITZER, Pascal, Michel
Delahaye, and Sylvie Pierre
An interview with Nagisa
Oshima. 80: 31-3+, Jl '70.

BONNARD
[illus] 13: 43, 65, 68, 78,
128, 130, 138, May/Je '60.

BONNIE and Clyde [interview]
A. Penn. 55: 61-3, Je '68.

BONUS, Jack
[illus] 76: 34-5, Mar '70;

77: 43, Apr '70.

The BOOK [story] R. Creeley
20: 64-8, Sept/Oct '61.

BOOK bust in Brighton [essay]
76: 18+, Mar '70.

BOOK of the migrant [poem]
M. Calvillo. 7: 153-6, winter
'59.

BORDER crossing [essay] J.
Schultz. 30: 99-112, May/Je
'63.

BORGES, Jorge Luis
    Houses like angels [poem]
29: 57, Mar/Apr '63.

BORIS MacCreary's abyss [poem]
H. Gregory. 8: 103-9, spring
'59.

BORN, A.
    [cartoons] 53: 74, Apr '68;
55: 72, 95, Je '68; 56: 73, 80,
94, Jl '68; 57: 73, Aug '68; 60:
66, Nov '68.

BORZIC, Jean
    Science: an administrative
question [satire] 13: 160-8,
May/Je '60.

BOSQUET, Michel
    The last hours of Ché Guevara
[essay] 51: 37-8+, Feb '68.

BOSTON [essay] D. Rader. 59:
18-19+, Oct '68.

BOSTON courtroom scene [tran-
script excerpt] 28: 81-4, Jan/
Feb '63.

The BOSTON trial of "Naked
Lunch" [transcript excerpt] 36:
40-9+, Je '65.

BOUCHÉ, H. P.
    Léon-Paul Fargue; explorer.

[essay] 13: 115-16, May/Je '60.

BOUCHÉ, H. P.
    (photograph of) 13: 96, May/
Je '60.

The BOURGEOIS poet [poems]
K. Shapiro. 32: 50-5, Apr/
May '64.

BOWSER, Larry
    [cartoon] 51: 82, Feb '68.

BOYD, Bruce
    Aubade [poem] 6: 57, autumn
'58.

BOYLE, Kay
    The long walk at San Fran-
cisco State [essay] 76: 21-3+,
Mar '70.
    No one can be all things to
all people [essay] 81: 63-7,
Aug '70,

BOYLE, Patrick
    At night all cats are grey
[story] 33: 13-15+, Aug/Sept
'64.
    Go away, old man, go away
[story] 27: 95-106, Nov/Dec '62.
    Shaybo [story] 45: 21-3+,
Feb '67.

BRAMLEY, Peter
    [illus] 54: 32, May '68; 58:
56-7, Sept '68; 74: 62, Jan '70;
76: 24, Mar '70.

BRANDRETH, R.
    The specialists [cartoon] 56:
46, Jl '68.
    [cartoon] 48: 86-7, 95, 98,
Aug '67; 49: 50, 86, 93, Oct
'67; 51: 80, 104, Feb '68; 52:
101, Mar '68; 55: 46, Je '68;
58: 66, Sept '68; 60: 73, 78,
Nov '68; 75: 71, Feb '70; 78:
37, 78, May '70.

BRASSAÏ
    Paris la nuit, a portfolio of

photographs [text by Henry
Miller] 24: 12-22, May/Je '62.
[photo] 24: cover, May/Je
'62.

BRAUTIGAN, Richard
   The betrayed kingdom [story]
76: 51, Mar '70.
   Complicated banking problems
[story] 84: 41, Nov '70.
   The menu [essay] 42: 30-2+,
Aug '66.
   Trout fishing in America
[novel excerpt] 31: 12-27, Oct/
Nov '63.
   Trout fishing in America-2
[novel excerpt] 33: 42-7, Aug/
Sept '64.

BRAZIL'S Cinema Nôvo: an interview with Glauber Rocha.
M. Delahaye.   73: 29-32+, Dec
'69.

BREAK your mother's back
[story] J. Hickey.   4: 139-42,
'57.

BREAKING through the circle of
self: art and social action
[essay] N. Hentoff.   55: 45-7,
Je '68.

BRECHT [review] L. Abel. 14:
134-40, Sept/Oct '60.

BRECHT, Bertolt
   The elephant calf or the
provability of any and every
contention; English version by
Eric Bentley [play] 29: 27-39,
Mar/Apr '63.
   The Prince of Homburg
[poem] 12: 53, Mar/Apr '60.

BRECHT, BERTOLT
   Brecht's last years.   M.
Kesting.   21: 56-67, Nov/Dec
'61.

BRECHT, BERTOLT - CRITI-
   CISM AND INTERPRETATION

Brecht. L. Abel.   14: 134-
40, Sept/Oct '60.
   The science fiction of Bertolt
Brecht.   E. Bentley.   41: 28-
32+, Je '66.
   The seven deadly sins
   The seven deadly sins.   J.
Tallmer. 9: 200-7, summer '59.

BRECHT, Stefan S.
   Notes from the underground:
Nude restaurant [review] 53:
98-100, Apr '68.
   Notes from the underground:
Sun Ra [review] 54: 88-90,
May '68.

BRECHT'S last years [essay]
M. Kesting.   21: 56-67, Nov/
Dec '61.

BRÉE, GERMAINE - CRITI-
   CISM AND INTERPRETATION
         Camus
   On a study of Camus.   W.
Fowlie. 8: 198-9, spring '59.

BRENNAN, Garnet E.
   Marijuana witchhunt [essay]
55: 55-6+, Je '68.

BRENNAN, GARNET E., draw-
ing of 55: 54, Je '68.

BRESLIN, JIMMY - CRITI-
   CISM AND INTERPRETATION
   The newspaper as literature.
Literature as leadership.   S.
Krim. 48: 31-2+, Aug '67.

BRIDE of a Samurai [story] S.
Tanino. 43: 24-8+, Oct '66.

The BRIDGE [poem] L. Jones.
12: 59-60, Mar/Apr '60.

BRIDGE to the innermost
forest [poem] J. Broughton.
2: 107, '57.

BRIGGS, George
   you too can be john wayne

BRIGGS, George

BRIGGS, George

BRIGGS, George

BRIGGS, George

BRIGGS, George

[poem] 77: 43, Apr '70.

BRITISH GUIANA
Down the Demerera. J. Tallmer. 15: 120-2, Nov/Dec '60.

BROADWAY comedy: images of impotence [review essay] J. Lahr. 78: 39-40+, May '70.

The BROKEN water jar [poem] O. Paz. 7: 41-4, winter '59.

BROOK, Peter
"The great masturbator" [interview] 53: 41-2+, Apr '68.

BROOK, PETER
(photograph of) 53: 43, Apr '68.

BROOK, PETER - CRITICISM AND INTERPRETATION
Tell me no lies
"We want to be humane, but we're only human." J. Lahr. 53: 36-40+, Apr '68.

BROTHER Antoninus
see
ANTONINUS, Brother

The BROTHERS [story] R. Coover. 23: 41-7, Mar/Apr '62.

BROUGHTON, James
Bridge to the innermost forest [poem] 2: 107, '57.
The madman's house [poem] 2: 109, '57.
Nativity 1956 [poem] 2: 106, '57.
Papa had a bird (a creation myth) [poem] 24: 91-2, May/Je '62.
Please do not feed the senators [poem] 2: 108, '57.

BROUGHTON, JAMES

(photograph of) 2: between pages 64 and 65, '57.

BROUGHTON, W. S.
Threnody [poem] 31: 45-7, Oct/Nov '63.

BROWN, Cecil M.
About Le Roi Jones [review essay] 75: 65-70, Feb '70.
I never raped one either, but I try not to let it bother me [story] 78: 47-9+, May '70.
The Minister of Information raps: an interview with Eldridge Cleaver. 59: 44-6+, Oct '68.

BROWN, Dean
[photo] 74: 17, Jan '70.

BROWN, Donna
[illus] 56: 14, Jl '68.

BROWN, H. RAP
Notes from the underground: H. Rap Brown. J. James. 57: 16-17+, Aug '68.
(photograph of) 57: 17, Aug '68.

BROWN, Helen and Jane Seitz
Flower power: an interview with a hippie. 49: 54-7, Oct '67.

BROWN, P. (Pete) R.
Africa [poem] 10: 55, Nov/Dec '59.
Few [poem] 38: 25, Nov '65.
Lips [poem] 38: 25, Nov '65.
Sitting reading Rilke [poem] 20: 63, Sept/Oct '61.
Small poem. 10: 55, Nov/Dec '59.
Thoughtful [poem] 18: 32, May/Je '61.
Waking [poem] 20: 63, Sept/Oct '61.

BRUCE, LENNY
Lenny Bruce: 1926-66. J. Tallmer. 44: 22-3, Dec '66.

(photograph of) 44: 22,
Dec '66.

BRUNOFF, Laurent de
[illus] 9: 198-9, summer '59.

BRUNOT, James
The cure [story] 9: 166-70,
summer '59.
The M. team [story] 49: 80-
5, Oct '67.

BRYAN, Frederick van Pelt
Opinion: United States District Court, Southern District of
New York, civil 147-87. Grove
Press, Inc. and Readers' Subscription, Inc., plaintiffs, --
against--Robert K. Christenberry, individually and as Postmaster of the City of New York,
defendant. 9: 37-68, summer
'59.

BÜCHNER, GEORG - CRITI-
CISM AND INTERPRETATION
Georg Büchner. M. Ham-
burger. 1: 68-98, '57.

BUCHWALD, Art
The upbeat beatnik [essay]
14: 153-4, Sept/Oct '60.

The BUCK is my benison [poem]
J. Grady. 31: 82, '57.

BUCKLEY, WILLIAM F.
Mr. Buckley. D. Phelps.
37: 32-4+, Sept '65.

BUDDHISM
see
ZEN BUDDHISM

BUDNIK, Dan
[photo] 39: 23, Feb '66.

BUKOWSKI, Charles
The day we talked about
James Thurber [story] 74: 55-
7+, Jan '70.
Men's crapper [poem] 50:

75, Dec '67.
Soup, cosmos and tears
[poem] 79: 37, Je '70.

BULATOVIC, Miodrag
The lovers [story] 27: 60-74,
Nov/Dec '62.

BUNK Johnson blowing [poem]
M. Rukeyser. 51: 77, Feb
'68.

BUNKE, TAMARA
see
TANIA [pseud]

BUÑUEL, LUIS - CRITICISM
AND INTERPRETATION
The andalusian smile: re-
flections on Luis Buñuel. J.
Price. 40: 24-9+, Apr '66.

BURNS, Jim
The colour of... [poem] 38:
24-5, Nov '65.
The end bit [poem] 38: 25,
Nov '65.

BURROUGHS, William S.
Comments on The night be-
fore thinking [essay] 20: 31-6,
Sept/Oct '61.
Day the records went up
[story] 60: 46-50+, Nov '68.
Deposition: testimony con-
cerning a sickness [essay] 11:
15-23, Jan/Feb '60.
"Exterminator!" [story] 46:
54-5, Apr '67.
Introduction to Naked lunch,
The soft machine, Novia ex-
press [essay] 22: 99-102, Jan/
Feb '62.
"Johnny 23" [story] 52:
26-7, Mar '68.
Naked lunch [novel excerpt]
16: 18-31, Jan/Feb '61.
Nova express [novel ex-
cerpt] 29: 109-16, Mar/Apr
'63.
Novia express [novel ex-
cerpt] 22: 103-9, Jan/Feb '62.

Outskirts of the city [excerpt from his novel, Novia express] 25: 73-8, Jl/Aug '62.

Points of distinction between sedative and consciousness-expanding drugs [essay] 34: 72-4, Dec '64.

They just fade away [novel excerpt] 32: 62-3+, Apr/May '64.

BURROUGHS, WILLIAM S.
An account of the events preceding the death of Bill Burroughs. A. Morrissett. 29: 103-8, Mar/Apr '63.

BURROUGHS, WILLIAM S. -
CRITICISM AND INTERPRETATION
Cut-ups: a project for disastrous success. By. Gysin. 32: 56-61, Apr/May '64.
                Naked lunch
The cannibal feast. E. Seldon. 22: 110-13, Jan/Feb '62.

BURROWS, E. G.
Paternity [poem] 3: 92, '57.
View from an airliner [poem] 3: 93-94, '57.

BUSINESS AND THE ARTS
The arts and business. J. Lahr. 68: 63-5+, Jl '69.

BUSKIRK, ALDEN van
                see
VAN BUSKIRK, ALDEN

BUT whose Turkey? [essay] A. Seymour. 85: 74-7, Dec '70.

BUTOR, Michel
Delphi [essay] 18: 114-26, May/Je '61.

BY the motel pool [excerpt from the novel Numbers] J. Rechy. 50: 30-2+, Dec '67.

BYE bye blackbird [essay] J. Tallmer. 10: 117-31, Nov/Dec '59.

- C -

CABALLERO
[cartoons] 50: 76, Dec '67; 52: 102, Mar '68; 53: 72, Apr '68; 55: 20, Je '68; 56: 24, Jl '68.

CABOCHONS [story] J. Ferry. 13: 72, May/Je '60.

The CACTUS curtain; an open letter on conformity in Mexican art [essay] J. Cuevas. 7: 111-20, winter '59.

CADOO, Emil J.
[photographs] 28: cover, 67-72, Jan/Feb '63; 32; cover, 33-42, Apr/May '64; 33: 33, Aug/Sept '64; 34: 33, Dec '64.

CADOO, Emil J., Massin, and Michel Rivgauche.
Homage à Piaf [song and photographs] 38: 28-33, Nov '65.

CAHN, EDGAR - CRITICISM AND INTERPRETATION
Our brother's keeper
From the third eye... white man still speaks with forked tongue. R. Wolf. 78: 91-3, May '70.

CAIN'S book [novel excerpt] A. Trocchi. 4: 48-74, '57; 8: 109-18, spring '59; 12: 16-23, Mar/Apr '60; 19: 44-54, Jl/Aug '61.

CALCULATION [poem] Julian the Apostate. 25: 91, Jl/Aug '62.

CALDWELL, John F.
[cartoons] 77: 75, Apr '70;

79: 69, 86, Je '70; 80: 58, Jl
'70; 85: 68, Dec '70.

CALIFORNIA
Big Sur and the good life.
H. Miller. 2: 36-45, '57.

CALIFORNIA. STATE COLLEGE,
SAN FRANCISCO
The long walk at San Francisco State. K. Bayle. 76: 21-
3+, Mar '70.

CALIFORNIA. UNIVERSITY.
BERKELEY
The strike: student power in
Berkeley [essay] L. Rapoport.
46: 80-2, Apr '67.

CALISHER, Hortense
Fathers and satyrs [story]
44: 24-7+, Dec '66.

The CALL [poem] A. Crozier.
38: 24, Nov '65.

CALMAN
[cartoon] 49: 61, Oct '67.

The CALMATIVE [story] S.
Beckett. 47: 46-9+, Je '67.

CALVILLO, Manuel
Book of the migrant [poem]
7: 153-6, winter '59.

CAMARO (automobile)
Due apologies from behind
the wheel of a big V8. J. Held.
56: 62-5, Jl '68.

CAMDEN, N. J. [poem] M.
Rumaker. 80: 37, Jl '70.

The CAMERA as fountain pen
[essay] A. Michelson. 48: 56+,
Aug '67.

CAMPBELL, Joseph
Letter to the editor: the
great delight and the big lie. 14:
155-9, Sept/Oct '60.

CAMPUS drug raid [poem] R.
Jones. 58: 56-7, Sept '68.

CAMUS, Albert
Reflections on the guillotine
[essay] 3: 5-55, '57; 12:
special supplement, Mar/Apr
'60.

CANADA, Stephen
Paris VC [poem] 51: 114,
Feb '68.

CANDELA, FELIX
Felix Candela: shells in
architecture. E. McCoy. 7:
127-33, winter '59.

The CANNIBAL feast [review]
E. Seldon. 22: 110-13, Jan/
Feb '62.

CANNONBALL catcher [story]
B. Amidon. 76: 25-6+, Mar
'70.

CANZLER
[cartoon] 74: 64, Jan '70.

CAPITAL PUNISHMENT
Reflections on the guillotine.
A. Camus. 3: 5-55, '57; 12:
special supplement, Mar/Apr
'60.

CAPRICCIO to Djuna [poem] M.
O'Donoghue. 47: 66-7, Je '67.

CAPTAIN America's restaurant
[essay] N. Hentoff. 74: 59-61,
Jan '70.

A CAR for Bonnie [essay] J-F.
Held. 58: 62-4, Sept '68.

The CAR with the pointed helmet [essay] J. Held. 59: 62-5,
Oct '68.

CARADEC, F.
Alphonse Allais: literary
assassin [essay] 13: 97-8, May/
Je '60.

CARADEC, F.
(photograph of) 13:95, May/
Je '60.

CARROLL, Kent E.
Events: an interview with
Fred Baker. 79:41-3, Je '70.
Film and revolution: an interview with Jean-Luc Godard.
83:47-50+, Oct '70.
From the third eye... An-
tonioni: where does Zabriskie
point? [review essay] 81:74-
6, Aug '70.
Taboos and film: an interview with Vilgot Sjoman. 82:
49-53, Sept '70.
"Woodstock:" an interview
with Michael Wadleigh and Bob
Maurice. 81:27-9+, Aug '70.

CARROLL, Paul
At the moment of love and
blue eyelids [poem] 8:63,
spring '59.
Death is a letter that was
never sent [review] 19:114-16,
Jl/Aug '61.
Dinner party [poem] 26:99-
100, Sept/Oct '62.
George swimming at Barnes
Hole, but it got too cold [poem]
10:53-4, Nov/Dec '59.

CARSON, L. M. Kit
Easy rider: a very American
thing. An interview with Dennis
Hopper. 72:24-7, Nov '69.
From the third eye... Mucking with the real [review essay]
82:77-9, Sept '70.
Notes from the underground:
have you seen it all, Dennis
Hopper? [review] 81:16-18, Aug
'70.

CARSON McCullers 2/19/17-
9/29/67 [poem] M. Rumaker.
50:97, Dec '67.

CARTAGENA [poem] G. Snyder.
9:130, summer '59.

CARTIER-BRESSON, Henri
[photo] 23: cover, Mar/Apr
'62.

CARTOON SHOWS (television)
A purple dog, a flying
squirrel, and the art of television. M. Williams. 20:114-20,
Sept/Oct '66.

CASCANDO [play] S. Beckett.
30:47-57, May/Je '63.

The CASE of James Dean
[essay] E. Morin. 5:5-12,
summer '58.

CASSAVETES, John
A way of life: an interview
with John Cassavetes. A. Labarthe. 64:45-7, Mar '69.

CASTRO, Fidel
El Ché vive! [speech ex-
cerpt] 51:34-5, Feb '68.

CASTRO, FIDEL
Four days with Fidel. K.
Karol. 51:51-2+, Feb '68.

CATALOGUE of small defeats
[review] D. Rader. 83:24-6,
Oct '70.

The CATCH [story] K. Ôe. 45:
53-72, Feb '67.

The CATECHISM [story] R.
Daumal. 20:94-8, Sept/Oct
'61.

CATENACCI, Edward N.
Hey, Leroy! [poem] 59:72,
Oct '68.

The CATHARSIS of anguish;
days following the assassination
of President Kennedy [poem] P.
Roche. 32:21-5, Apr/May '64.

CATHOLIC CHURCH
see

27   CATHOLIC CHURCH

PAUL, IV, pope

CATHOLIC CHURCH AND
   BIRTH CONTROL
The tyranny of Warrendale.
P. Tyler.   69:31-3+, Aug '69.

CATHOLIC CHURCH - HAITI
On the use of Catholic religious prints by the practitioners of Voodoo in Haiti. M.
Leiris. 13:84-94, May/Je '60.

CAT'S air [poem] M. McClure.
2:46, '57.

CAZ
[cartoon] 79:73, 84, Je '70;
80:51, 66, Jl '70; 84:56, 74,
Nov '70.

CELAN, Paul
A death fugue; English version by Jerome Rothenberg.
[poem] 21:45-6, Nov/Dec '61.

CÉLINE, Louis-Ferdinand [pseud]
The nymphettes of Sieg-
maringen [autobiographical excerpt from Castle to castle]
60:36-40+, Nov '68.

CÉLINE, LOUIS-FERDINAND
   [pseud]
A talk with Louis-Ferdinand
Céline. R. Stromberg. 19:102-
7, Jl/Aug '61.

CENDRARS, Blaise
The transsiberian express;
English version by Anselm
Hollo. [poem] 33:20-31, Aug/
Sept '64.

CENSORSHIP
About Evergreen Review No.
32. 33:32, Aug/Sept '64.
Defense of the freedom to
read. H. Miller. 9:12-20,
summer '59.
Inexcusable thoughts: from
the editors. 35:8-9, May '65.

Notes from the underground:
book bust in Brighton.   76:18+,
Mar '70.
Notes from the underground:
San Francisco censorship. J.
Nathan. 45:16-20, Feb '67.
     see also
TRIALS (Obscenity)

CENSORSHIP - AUSTRALIA
Matilda waltzes but still
keeps her maidenhead. J. Williamson. 35:86-8, Mar '65.

CENSORSHIP - FILMS
Notes from the underground:
now you see it, now you don't.
H. Greer. 79:16-18+, Je '70.

CENSORSHIP - ITALY
Written address to an Italian
judge. J. Kerouac. 31:108-
10, Oct/Nov '63.

CESC
[cartoons] 44:43, Dec '66.
48:97, Aug '67; 49:57, Oct '67;
50:110, Dec '67; 52:99, Mar
'68; 59:70, Oct '68.

CHAMULA INDIANS
Juan Perez Jolote, part I
[narrative] R. Pozas Arciniega.
7:91-104, winter '59.

CHANCES R [poem] A. Gins-
berg. 46:57, Apr '67.

CHANT song [poem] J. Pré-
vert. 13:62-3, May/Je '60.

CHARACTERS IN FILMS
           see
SPADE, SAM

CHARHADI, Driss Ben Hamid
   [pseud]
The orphan [autobiographical
excerpt] 26:23-34, Sept/Oct
'62.
The whore [novel excerpt]
30:30-42, May/Je '63.

monologue; The wanderings of
the tribe.   7:59-61, winter '59.

CHWAST, Seymour
 [illus] 54:44-6, May '68; 60:
58-9, Nov '68; 75:46, Feb '70.

CICELLIS, Kay
 Exposure [story] 34:36-41,
Dec '64.

CINEMA VÉRITÉ
 From the third eye... mucking with the real. L. Carson.
82:77-9, Sept '70.
 Turning the camera into the
audience. N. Hentoff. 53:47-
8+, Apr '68.

CIORAN, E. M.
 Beyond the novel [essay] 17:
80-92, Mar/Apr '61.
 On a certain experience of
death [essay] 6:108-23, autumn '58.

The CIRCUS [poem] J. Ash-
bery. 8:98, spring '59.

CIRCUS [collection of poems]
L. Kandel. 41:46-9, Je '66.

The CITY of lost angels [essay]
J. Rechy. 10:10-27, Nov/Dec
'59.

CITY of night [novel excerpt] J.
Rechy. 24:23-24, May/Je '62.
_____26: 38-48, Sept/
Oct '62.

CIVIL RIGHTS
                see
OMNIBUS CRIME CONTROL
 AND SAFE STREETS ACT,
 1968
WOMEN'S RIGHTS

CLAIR, René
 The Chinese princess [story]
13:67-8, May/Je '60.

CLAIR, RENÉ
 (photograph of) 13:67, May/
Je '60.

CLARKE, Austin C.
 What happened? [story] 85:
21-2+, Dec '70.

The CLASSLESS cars [essay]
J. Held. 54:57-61, May '68.

The CLEAN woman [cartoon]
A. Sens. 36:61, Je '65.

CLEAR winter (clair hiver)
[poem] P. Reverdy. 11:26,
Jan/Feb '60.

CLEAVER, ELDRIDGE
 The Minister of Information
raps: an interview with Eldridge
Cleaver. C. Brown. 59:44-
6+, Oct '68.

CLEAVER, ELDRIDGE
 (photograph of) 59:44, Oct
'68.

CLICHY [song] J. McDonald.
 85:41, Dec '70.

CLIFFORD, Joan
 Night in the subway [poem]
8:102, spring '59.

CLOSE to Antonin Artaud
[essay] M. Saillet. 13:79-83,
May/Je '60.

CLOSING the olympics [car-
toons] Siné. 15:94-5, Nov/Dec
'60.

CLOWNISH TV-I: Dick Van Dyke
[review essay] M. Williams.
45:101-4, Feb '67.

CLOWNISH TV-II: Red Skelton
[review essay] M. Williams.
46:68-71, Apr '67.

COCAINE
Drug notes. M. McClure.
25:103-17, Jl/Aug '62.

COGNIZANT [poem] H. Davis.
23:93, Mar/Apr '62.

COHEN, Edward M.
Fishman Paper Box Co.,
Inc. [story] 37:27-9+, Sept '65.

The COIN [story] G. Gadgil.
6:141-9, autumn, '58.

COLD MOUNTAIN
see
HAN-SHAN

COLD night [poem] Ho-Chi-
Minh. 43:45, Oct '66.

COLD war [cartoon] R. Blechman. 27:87-9, Nov/Dec '62.

COLEMAN Hawkins: some notes
on a phoenix [essay] M. Williams. 36:75-8, Je '65.

COLEMAN, ORNETTE - CRI-
TICISM AND INTERPRETA-
TION
Genesis of the new music-
III: Ornette Coleman. A.
Spallman. 47:78-80, Je '67.
The jazz avant garde: who's
in charge here? M. Williams.
41:64-8, Je '66.
Ornette Coleman: the mean-
ing of innovation. M. Williams.
15:123-33, Nov/Dec '60.

COLEMAN, ORNETTE
(photograph of) 15:125,
Nov/Dec '60.

COLLEGE OF "PATAPHYSICS"
An apodeictic outline. S.
Taylor. 13:150-7, May/Je '60.
Opus pataphysicum. I.
Sandomir. 13:169-80, May/Je
'60.
Report to the corps of prov-
editors on some concrete his-

torical problems concerning
pataphysical activity posed by
the fiftieth anniversary of the
death of Jarry. N. Kamenev.
13:181-5, May/Je '60.
Science: an administrative
question. J. Borzic. 13:160-8,
May/Je '60.

COLLEGE PROFESSORS AND
INSTRUCTORS - TENURE
Freeing the university:
abolish tenure. N. Hentoff.
73:39-41+, Dec '69.

COLLEGE STUDENTS
Higher education for what?
N. Hentoff. 78:65-7, May '70.

COLLEGES AND UNIVERSITIES
The universities: a crisis of
legitimacy. N. Hentoff. 62:
47-9, Jan '69.

COLLEGES AND UNIVERSITIES
- BLACK STUDIES
Black studies: bringing back
the person. J. Jordan. 71:
39-41+, Oct '69.

COLLINS, Lee
Jazz: from Lee Collins'
story as told to Mary Collins
and John W. Miner [autobi-
ographical excerpt] 35:66-71,
Mar '65.

COLLINS, Mary
see
COLLINS, Lee. Jazz: from
Lee Collins' story.

The COLOUR of... [poem] J.
Burns. 38:24-5, Nov '65.

COLTRANE, JOHN - CRITI-
CISM AND INTERPRETATION
Genesis of the new music-I:
Coltrane. A. Spellman. 45:
81-3, Feb '67.
The jazz avant garde: who's
in charge here? M. Williams.

41:64-8, Je '66.

COLTRANE, JOHN
(photograph of) 45:81, Feb
'67.

COLUMBIA UNIVERSITY
Columbia's new course-re-
bellion I. N. Hentoff. 58:
65-7+, Sept '68.
Up against the wall! D.
Radar. 57:22-5+, Aug '68.

COLUMBIA'S new course-re-
bellion I [essay] N. Hentoff.
58:65-7+, Sept '68.

COMEDIANS
see
BRUCE, LENNY
LAHR, BERT
SKELTON, RED
VAN DYKE, DICK

The COMING of black power
[essay] N. Hentoff. 57:59-61,
Aug '68.

COMMANDER Lowell (1887-
1950) [poem] R. Lowell. 8:
39-41, spring '59.

COMMENTS on the The night
before thinking [essay] W. Burroughs. 20:31-6, Sept/Oct '61.

The COMMONPLACE of Song My
[essay] N. Hentoff. 76:59-61,
Mar '70.

COMMUNAL LIVING
Passage to more than India.
G. Snyder. 52:41-3+, Mar '68.

COMMUNICATION
Man's total communication
system. R. Fuller. 83:39-41+,
Oct '70.
see also
MASS MEDIA

COMMUNITY CONTROL OF

SCHOOLS
The dimensions of community
control. N. Hentoff. 64:31-2+,
Mar '69.

COMMUNIST CHINA
see
CHINA (People's Republic)

The COMPANY of men [poem]
C. Olson. 8:119-20, spring '59.

The COMPLAINT of my family
[poem] W. Merwin. 35:50,
Mar '65.

COMPLICATED banking prob-
lems [story] R. Brautigan.
84:41, Nov '70.

CONDAK, Cliff
[illus] 75:20, Feb '70.

A CONEY Island of the mind
[poem excerpt] L. Ferlinghetti.
2:30-2, '57.

CONGRAT-BUTLAR, Stefan
Russian revolutionary posters,
1917-1929 [illustrations and
notes] 46:74-9, Apr '67.

The CONQUEST of the sky
[poem] J. Ashbery. 8:97,
spring '59.

CONROY, Frank
Spring for Alison [story] 12:
90-101, Mar/Apr '60.

CONSTRUCTIVISM
American construction sculpture. I. Sandler. 8:136-46,
spring '59.

The CONTINUING position of
India; a special statement on
India's foreign policy by its
permanent delegate to the United
Nations [essay] A. Lall. 7:
14-21+, winter '59.

CRANE, Jim
The danger is from within
[cartoon] 26:35, Sept/Oct '62.
[cartoons] 28:95, Jan/Feb '63;
31:89, Oct/Nov '63.

CREATION (literary, artistic,
etc.)
How to proceed in the arts;
a detailed study of the creative
act. L. Rivers and F. O'Hara.
19:97-101, Jl/Aug '61.

CREELEY, Robert
The book [story] 20:64-68,
Sept/Oct '61.
The hole [poem] 39:70, Feb
'66.
She went to stay [poem] 6:
39, autumn, '58.
The three ladies [poem] 5:
25, summer '58.

CREWS, Judson
Little home scene [poem]
28:85, Jan/Feb '63.

CRITICISM
                see
ART CRITICISM
LITERARY CRITICISM

The CROCODILE [story] A.
Andersch. 19:86-95, Jl/Aug '61.

CROSS, Elizabeth
                see
CROSS, Guy and Elizabeth Cross

CROSS, Guy and Elizabeth Cross
Ep (epidermal) art [photo-
graphs] 46:42-7, Apr '67.

CROZIER, Andrew
The call [poem] 38:24,
Nov '65.
Drill poem. 38:24, Nov '65.

CRUZ, Victor Hernandez
Papo got his gun! [poem] 48:
73-80, Aug '67.

CUBA
Cuba libre. L. Jones. 15:
139-59, Nov/Dec '60.
Letter from Havana. L.
Martin. 83:24, Oct '70.
Notes from the underground:
Impressions of Cuba. M.
Randall. 49:20-1+, Oct '67.
Notes from the underground:
sugar cane and the "free-world"
press. R. Seaver. 77:16+,
Apr '70.

CUBA - INVASION, 1970
Last stop at La Maquina.
L. Martin. 79:90, Je '70.

CUBA - REVOLUTION, 1959
Where it all began: the land-
ing in Cuba. C. Guevara. 51:
39-41+, Feb '68.

CUBA libra [essay] L. Jones.
15:139-59, Nov/Dec '60.

CUEVAS, José Luis
The cactus curtain; an open
letter on conformity in Mexican
art [essay] 7:111-20, winter '59.
Recollections of childhood
[essay with 12 lithographs] 29:
40-56, Mar/Apr '63.

CUEVAS, JOSÉ LUIS
(photograph of) 7:112,
winter '59.

cummings, e. e.
Poem. 8:38, spring '59.

cummings, e. e. - CRITICISM
AND INTERPRETATION
                95 poems
e. e. cummings. W. Wil-
liams. 7:214-6, winter '59.

CUNLIFFE, Dave
Who are the angels? [poem]
38:25, Nov '65.

The CURE [story] J. Brunot.
9:166-70, summer '59.

The CURSE of the cat woman
[poem] E. Field. 34:21-2,
Dec '64.

CURTIS
[cartoon] 78:82, May '70.

CUSTOM [novel excerpt] J.
Schultz. 24:85-90, May/Je '62.

CUTTING edge [story] J. Purdy.
1:99-109, '57.

CUT-UPS: a project for disastrous success [essay] B.
Gysin. 32:56-61, Apr/May '64.

CYBERNATION
Last exit before the Great
Society. N. Hentoff. 37:59-
65, Sept '65.

CZECHOSLOVAKIA - OCCUPA-
TION, 1968-
The socialism that came in
from the cold. J. P. Sartre.
84:27-32+, Nov '70.

- D -

DAGERMAN, Stig
The games of night [story]
15:47-56, Nov/Dec '60.

DAHL, Ronald
Poem. 35:43, Mar '65.

The DAILY newspaper in 1980
[essay] N. Hentoff. 40:62-3+,
Apr '66.

DAKAR [poem] J. Stowers.
47:54, Je '67.

DALI, Salvador and Werner
Bokelberg
A beast's repast [portfolio of
photographs with text] 44:33-
40, Dec '66.

The DANCING ape... [poem] J.
Spicer. 2:52, '57.

The DANCING boy [story] W.
Eastlake. 85:35-7+, Dec '70.

The DANGER is from within
[cartoon] J. Crane. 26:35,
Sept/Oct '62.

DANGEROUS passage [story]
I. Grey. 11:101-15, Jan/Feb
'60.

DANSE mabraque [story] L.
Fargue. 13:116-7, May/Je '60.

DANTE and the lobster [story]
S. Beckett. 1:24-36, '57.

D'ARCY, MARTIN CYRILL,
(photograph of) 81:38, Aug
'70.

DARTON, Eric
Dear Algernon [poem] 60:
41, Nov '68.

DAUGHTERS OF THE AMERI-
CAN REVOLUTION
see
GENERALS OF THE DAUGH-
TERS OF THE AMERICAN
REVOLUTION

DAUMAL, René
The catechism [story] 20:94-
8, Sept/Oct '61.
The great magician [story]
13:123-5, May/Je '60.
An idiomatic tale [story] 13:
126, May/Je '60.
[illus] 13:148, May/Je '60.

DAUMAL, RENÉ
René Daumal, experimental
mystic. L. Etienne. 13:122-3,
May/Je '60.
(photograph of) 13:96, May/
Je '60.

DAVIS, Douglas M.
The new eroticism [essay]
58:48-55, Sept '68.

DAVIS, Hank
Cognizant [poem]   23:93,
Mar/Apr '62.

DAVIS, MILES - CRITICISM
AND INTERPRETATION
Miles Davis: conception in
search of a sound. M. Williams. 34:88-91, Dec '64.

DAVIS, Paul
[illus] 56:56, Je '68; 74:30,
Jan '70; 80:38-9, Jl '70.

DAVIS, STUART
Stuart Davis: a memoir.
B. O'Doherty.   39:22-7, Feb
'66.
(photograph of) by Dan
Budnik 39:23, Feb '66.

DAWSON
[cartoon] 76:70, Mar '70.

The DAY Rap Brown became a
press agent for Paramount
[essay] A. Vogel. 67:43-5+,
Je '69.

DAY the records went up
[story] W. Burroughs. 60:46-
50+, Nov '68.

The DAY we talked about James
Thurber [story] C. Bukowski.
74:55-7+, Jan '70.

The DEAD man's float in the
moon [story] D. Newlove. 53:
33-5+, Apr '68.

DEAN, JAMES
The case of James Dean. E.
Morin. 5:5-12, summer, '58.
(photograph of) 5:cover,
summer '58.

DEAR Algernon [poem] E.
Darton. 60:41, Nov '68.

DEATH (Philosophy)

A little treatise on dying.
J. Kott.   48:61-3, Aug '67.
On a certain experience of
death. E. M. Cioran.   6:108-
23, autumn '58.
Todos santos, día de muertos.
O. Paz.   7:22-37, winter '59.

A DEATH fugue [poem] P.
Celan.   21:45-6, Nov/Dec '61.

DEATH is a letter that was
never sent [review] P. Carroll.
19:114-6, Jl/Aug '61.

The DEATH of Horatio Alger
[story] L. Jones.   36:28-9+,
Jan '65.

The DEATH of Mayakovsky
(1893-1930) [poem] L. Andrews.   50:70-1, Dec '67.

The DEATH of Sam Spade
[essay] J. Goldberg.   28:107-
16, Jan/Feb '63.

DEATH ROW
                 see
PRISONERS, CONDEMNED

DEBATE [poem] J. García
Térres 7:89, winter '59.

DEBRAY, Régis
A message to my friends
[essay] 51:48-9+, Feb '68.

DEBRAY, RÉGIS
I was arrested with Debray.
G. Roth.   51:44-7+, Feb '68.
(photograph of) 51:48, Feb
'68.

DECADENCE IN ART
What do you think of your
blue-eyed artist now, Mr.
Death? D. Rader. 80:38-41+,
Jl '70.

DECADES of dream-walking
[essay] J. Lahr. 74:37-9+,
Jan '70.

DÉCAUDIN, Michel
Félix Fénéon, Soft spoken anarchist [review] 13:103, May/Je '60.

DECAUDIN, MICHEL
(photograph of) 13:95, May/Je '60.

DECLARATION concerning the right of insubordination in the Algerian War [essay] 15:1-4, Nov/Dec '60.

DEFENCE of the freedom to read [letter to Trygve Hirsch, barrister-at-law, Oslo, Norway] H. Miller. 9:12-20, summer '59.

DE GRAZIA, Edward
The swings [play] 26:50-66, Sept/Oct '62.

DELAHAYE, Michael
Brazil's Cinema Nôvo: an interview with Glauber Rocha. 73: 29-32+, Dec '69.
Lola in L. A. : an interview with Jacques Demy. 65:29-31+, Apr '69.

DELAHAYE, Michael and Jean Narboni
An interview with Roman Polanski. 66:27-9+, May '69.

DELAHAYE, Michael
see also
BONITZER, Pascal; Michel Delahaye; and Sylvie Pierre.
COMOLLI, Jean and Michel Delahaye.

DELANEY, Shelagh
Pavan for a dead prince [poem] 30:16-23, May/Je '63.
Tom Riley [story] 16:102-8, Jan/Feb '61.

DELPHI [essay] M. Butor. 18: 114-26, May/Je '61.

DÉMERON, Pierre
A voyeur in the labyrinth: an interview with Alain Robbe-Grillet. 43:46-9+, Oct '66.

DEMOCRACY
On bringing democracy to America. N. Hentoff. 69:46-7+, Aug '69.

DEMOCRATIC NATIONAL CONVENTION, 1968
Pigs, Prague, Chicago, other Democrats, and the sleeper in the park. J. Schultz. 60:26-35+, Nov '68.

DEMY, JACQUES
Lola in L. A. : an interview with Jacques Demy. M. Delahaye. 65:29-31+, Apr '69.

DENBY, Edwin
Three sides of Agon [review essay] 7:168-76, winter '59.

DENT, Thomas
Early morning scene [poem] 30:72-81, May/Je '63.

DE OCA, Marco Antonio Montes
see
MONTES de OCA, Marco Antonio

DEPOSITION: testimony concerning a sickness [essay] W. Burroughs. 11:15-23, Jan/Feb '60.

DÉRY, Tibor
Behind the brick wall [story] 29:88-102, Mar/Apr '63.

DESCLOZEAUX
[cartoons] 74:32, 38, 66, Jan '70; 75:73, 77, 84, 87, Feb '70; 76:69, Mar '70; 78:74, 84, May '70.

The DESERT [story] M. Rumaker. 2:65-105, '57.

DESIRE for Spring [poem] K. Koch. 5:104, summer '58.

DESIRE game [novel excerpt] U. Molinaro. 40:46-9, Apr '66.

DESMOND, PAUL - CRITICISM AND INTERPRETATION
Mulligan and Desmond at work. M. Williams. 28:117-26, Jan/Feb '63.

DESTOUCHES, Louis Ferdinand
see
CÉLINE, Louis-Ferdinand [pseud]

DESTRÉ, Sabine
A note on Story of 0 [essay] 31:31-2, Oct/Nov '63

DESTRÉ, Sabine and Ghnassia
The French revolution--1968 [pictorial] 57:41-9, Aug '68.

DESTRUCTIVISM (art)
Notes from the underground: Destruction in art. J. Nathan. 46:21-3, Apr '67.

DE VINCENT, George
Poverty, U. S. A. [portfolio of photographs] 35:60-5, Mar '65.
[photo] 48:73-80, Aug '70.

The DIALECTIC of solitude [essay] O. Paz. 20:100-13, Sept/Oct '61.

DIALOGUE with Arrabal. A. Morrissett. 15:70-5, Nov/Dec '60.

The DIAMOND [story] A. Pieyre de Mandiargues. 22:61-80, Jan/Feb '62.

DICK VAN DYKE [review essay] M. Williams. 45:101-4, Feb '67.

DIEPPE to Newhaven 1961

[autobiographical essay] C. Miller. 26:89-97, Sept/Oct '62.

The DIMENSIONS of community control [essay] N. Hentoff. 64:31-2+, Mar '69.

DINNER party [poem] P. Carroll. 26:99-100, Sept/Oct '62.

DINNER with the King of England [story] R. Coover. 27:110-8, Nov/Dec '62.

DI PRIMA, Diane
Spring thoughts for Freddie [memoir] 55:65-9+, Je '68.

DIRECT communication (poet to secretary) [poem] M. Horovitz. 40:49, Apr '66.

DIRECTORS
see
FILM DIRECTORS
THEATRICAL DIRECTORS

DISCARDING the dream [essay] R. Terrell. 78:35-7+, May '70.

DISSENTERS
From dissent to what kind of resistance? N. Hentoff. 52:31-2+, Mar '68.

DO they or don't they? Why it matters so much [essay] P. Tyler. 78:25-7+, May '70.

DO you know Gorky? Kline? Pollock? [story] B. Friedman. 47:26-7+, Je '67.

DOCUMENTARY FILMS
The tyranny of Warrendale. P. Tyler. 69:31-3, Aug '69.

DODDS, "Baby"
His story (as told to Larry Gara): New Orleans beginnings [and] Jazz on the river [autobiographical essay] 1:110-48, '57.

The Oliver band [autobi-
ographical essay] 4:80-100, '57.

DODGSON, Charles Lutwidge
see
CARROLL, Lewis [pseud]

DOG [poem] L. Ferlinghetti.
2:33-5, '57.

The DOGCHAIN gang [poem]
S. Rice. 84:25, Nov '70.

DOOLITTLE, Hilda
see
H. D.

DOPE [poem] J. Wieners. 42:
41, Aug '66.

DORN, Edward
Driving across the prairie
[reminiscense] 68:35-7+, Jl
'69.
A fate of unannounced years
[poem] 14:125, Sept/Oct '60.
Vaquero [poem] 5:103,
summer '58.

DOROSHOW, JACK (Flawless
Sabrina)
Notes from the underground:
Miss All-American. J. Nathan.
47:19-21, Je '67.

The DOUBLE standard of justice
[essay] B. Seale. 79:48-9,
Je '70.

DOUGLAS, William O.
Redress and revolution
[essay] 77:41-3+, Apr '70.

DOUGLASS, Ann
[photographs] 64:30-1, Mar
'69; 71:38, Oct '69.

DOWDEN, George
Filthy pictures seized in
London [poem] 49:28-30, Oct '67.
On the death of the pilot
Francis Gary Powers [poem]
17:78-9, Mar/Apr '61.

DOWN the Demerera [essay] J.
Tallmer. 15:120-2, Nov/Dec
'60.

DOWN the ladder awhile [story]
H. Gold. 39:28-32, Feb '66.

DRAGTIME and drugtime; or
film à la Warhol [review essay]
P. Tyler. 46:27-31+, Apr '67.

DRAMA
see
HAPPENINGS
OFF-BROADWAY THEATER
THEATER

DRAMA - technique
21 points to the Physicists.
F. Dürrenmatt. 34:34-5, Dec
'64.
Writing for the theatre. H.
Pinter. 33:80-2, Aug/Sept '64.

DRAMAS
single works
See name of author for full
entry.
Alice in wonderland. Carroll,
Lewis.
The apple. Gelber, Jack.
Che! Raphael, Lennox.
The connection. Gelber, Jack.
Endgame. Beckett, Samuel.
Fortune and men's eyes. Her-
bert, John.
God bless. Feiffer, Jules
Indians. Kopit, Arthur.
King Lear. Shakespeare,
William.
Last of the red hot lovers.
Simon, Neil.
Little Murders. Feiffer, Jules.
Macbeth (modern version)
Shakespeare, William.
Operation sidewinter. Shepard,
Sam
Play it again, Sam. Allen, Woody.
The serpent. Van Itallie, Jean
Claude.
Tango. Mrozek, Slawomir.
Waiting for Godot. Beckett,
Samuel.

The White House murders.
  Feiffer, Jules.

DRAMATISTS
        see
ALBEE, Edward
ALLEN, Woody
ARRABAL, Fernando
ARTAUD, Antonin
BECKETT, Samuel
BRECHT, Bertolt
FEIFFER, Jules
GELBER, Jack
GREGORY, André
HERBERT, John
KOPIT, Arthur
MROZEK, Slawomir
ORTON, Joe
PINTER, Harold
RAPHAEL, Lennox
SHAKESPEARE, William
SHEPARD, Sam
SIMON, Neil
VAN ITALLIE, Jean Claude

DREAMS; a radio play.   G.
Eïch.   21:80-92, Nov/Dec '61.

DREXLER, ROSALYN - CRITI-
  CISM AND INTERPRETATION
      One or another
  Catalogue of small defeats.
D. Rader.   83:24-6, Oct '70.

DRIGGS, Frank S.
  Jimmy Rushing's story as
told to Frank Driggs.   40:64-
9, Apr '66.

DRILL poem.   A. Crozier.
38:24, Nov '65.

DRIVE, we'll do the rest
[essay] J. Held.   55:70-3, Je
'68.

DRIVEN mod [pictorial satire]
M. O'Donoghue [and] T. Lafferty.   51:53-9, Feb '68.

DRIVING across the Prairie
[reminiscence] E. Dorn.   68:
35-7+,   Jl '69.

DRIVING with Flora [cartoons]
P. Flora.   34:81-7, Dec '64.

DRUG ADDICTS
        see
NARCOTIC ADDICTS

DRUG notes [essay] M. Mc-
Clure.   25:103-17, Jl/Aug '62.

The DRUGGED classroom
[essay] N. Hentoff.   85:31-3,
Dec '70.

DRUGS
        see
BEHAVIOR MODIFICATION
COCAINE
DRUG USE IN EDUCATION
HALLUCINOGENIC DRUGS
HEROIN
NARCOTIC ADDICTS
PEYOTE
SEDATIVE DRUGS

DRUGS - PSYCHOLOGICAL
  EFFECTS
        see
HALLUCINOGENIC DRUGS

DUBERMAN, Martin
  History [play] 65:49-55,'
Apr '69.
  On becoming an historian
[essay] 65:57-9+, Apr '69.

DUBERMAN, MARTIN
  (photograph of) 65:56, Apr
'69.

DUBUFFET, Jean
  Monsieur Juva's flint statues
[essay] 13:73-8, May/Je '60.
  Zoologie [illus] 13:34, May/
Je '60.

DUBUFFET, JEAN
  (photograph of) 13:73, May/
Je '60.

DUE apologies from behind the
wheel of a big V8 [essay] J.
Held.   56:62-5, Jl '68.

DUHEME, Jacqueline
[illus] 44:27, Dec '66.

DUKE Ellington: one of a kind
[essay] R. Stewart. 44:52-4+,
Dec '66.

DUMARÇAY, Philippe
[illus] 13:57, 109, 136,
162, May/Je '60.

DUNCAN, Robert
Apprehensions [poem] 16:
56-67, Jan/Feb '61.
The fear that precedes...
[poem] 2:22, '57.
A poem beginning with a line
by Pindar. 11:134-42, Jan/
Feb '60.
The structure of rime [poem]
2:23-9, '57.
This place, rumored to have
been Sodom...[poem] 2:21-2, '57

DUNCAN, ROBERT
(photograph of) 2:between
64 and 65, '57.

DUPREE, Louis
Massa's in the cold cold
brown 4 April 1968 [poem] 55:
53, Je '68.
The relationship of religious
ritual to orgasm frequency
among the tribal women of
Fungoolistan, by Manfreud Meed
[satire] 49:62-3, Oct '67.

DURAN, Manuel
Three poems: The possessed;
Still life; The power and the
glory. 7:85-6, winter '59.

DÜRRENMATT, Friedrich
The tunnel [story] 17:32-42,
Mar/Apr '61.
21 points to the Physicists
[essay] 34:34-5, Dec '64.

DYLAN, BOB
Hayden-Marat/Dylan-Sade:
defining a generation. J. Newfield. 52:23-5, Mar '68.

DYLAN, BOB
(drawing of) 52:22, Mar '68.

- E -

E. E. Cummings [review] W. C.
Williams. 7:214-6, winter '59.

The EAGLE bar [poem] J.
Wieners. 42:41, Aug '66.

EARLY morning scene [poem]
T. Dent. 30:72-81, May/Je '63.

EARLY noon [poem] I. Bachmann. 21:54-5, Nov/Dec '61.

EARNSHAW, Anthony
see
THACKER, Eric and Anthony
Earnshaw.

An EASTERN view of the San
Francisco school [essay] D.
Ashton. 2:148-59, '57.

EASTLAKE, William
The bamboo bed [story] 70:
25-7+, Sept '69.
A child's garden of verses
for the revolution [poems] 81:
47-51, Aug '70.
The dancing boy [story] 85:
35-7+, Dec '70.
The hanging at Prettyfields
[story] 63:29-31+, Feb '69.
Jack Armstrong in Tangier
[story] 42:24-7+, Aug '61
The last Frenchman in Fez
[story] 50:44-6+, Dec '67.
Now Lucifer is not dead
[story] 60:22-4+, Nov '68.
Portrait of an artist with
twenty-six horses [story] 5:
74-85, summer '58.
Something big is happening
to me [story] 25:8-21, Jl/Aug
'62.
Three heroes and a clown
[story] 10:87-98, Nov/Dec '59.

EASTLAKE, WILLIAM - CRI-
TICISM AND INTERPRETA-

TION
The Bronc people
One of the truly good men.
D. Woolf. 8:194-6, spring '59.

EASY rider: a very American
thing: an interview with Dennis
Hopper. L. Carson. 72:24-7+,
Nov '69.

EATHERLY, CLAUDE
(photograph of) 81:37, Aug
'70.

ECCE Homo [portfolio of color
plates] G. Grosz. 40:33-6,
Apr '66.

ECHO'S bones [poems] S.
Beckett. 1:179-92, '57.

ECOLOGY
Keeping ecology alive. N.
Hentoff. 77:31-2+, Apr '70.

EDINBURGH happening [essay]
J. Gelber. 31:55-61, Oct/Nov
'63.

EDUCATION OF CHILDREN
The mystery that isn't: how
do you get those slum savages
to learn? N. Hentoff. 54:40-
3, May '68.
see also
BEHAVIOR MODIFICATION

EDUCATION--U. S.
Public independent education.
N. Hentoff. 83:55-7, Oct '70.

EDUCATORS as dropouts: New
York City's schools [essay] N.
Hentoff. 43:19-23+, Oct '66.

EFBE
cartoon 54:87, May '68.

EGYPT - FOREIGN RELATIONS
see
ISRAELI-ARAB WAR, 1947-

EH Joe [play] S. Beckett. 62:

43-6, Jan '69.

EÏCH, Günter
Dreams; a radio play. 21:80-
92, Nov/Dec '61.

EIGHTEENTH birthday [poem]
P. Berger. 56:48, Jl '68.

The EIGHTH [novel excerpt] G.
Elsner. 36:19-23+, Je '65.

EIKO + Jim [Story] M.
Rumaker. 23:94-109, Mar/Apr
'62.

EISENHOWER, DWIGHT DAVID
(photograph of) 81:35, Aug
'70.

EL Ché vive! [speech excerpt]
F. Castro. 51:34-5, Feb '68.

EL Paso del Norte [essay] J.
Rechy. 6:127-40, autumn '58.

ELEGY, as if I meant it [poem]
J. Palcewski. 46:36-7, Apr '67.

The ELEPHANT calf or the
provability of any and every
contention [play] B. Brecht.
29:27-39, Mar/Apr '63.

ELIOT, THOMAS STEARNS -
CRITICISM AND INTERPRE-
TATION
After Eliot: some notes
toward a reassessment. P.
Roche. 39:84-92, Feb '66.

ELISCU, Lita
Notes from the underground:
Wild 90 [review] 53:15+, Apr
'68.
Vietnam déjà vu: a film review of Godard's La Chinoise.
56:66-8, Jl '68.

ELISE Cowen; a brief memoir
of the fifties. L. Skir. 48:
70-2+, Aug '67.

ELLINGTON, DUKE - CRITICISM
AND INTERPRETATION
Duke Ellington: one of a kind.
R. Stewart.   44:52-4+, Dec '66.
Some comments in apprecia-
tion of Ellington.   M. Williams.
17:106-14, Mar/Apr '61.

ELLINGTON, DUKE
(photograph of) 17:107, Mar/
Apr '61.   44:52, Dec '66.

ELMAN, Richard M.
The Kerensky complex
[essay] 39:44-7+, Feb '66.
The memorial [story] 35:44-
50, Mar '65.
Turn on Guatemala! [story]
59:20-2+, Oct '68.

ELMAN, RICHARD - CRITICISM
AND INTERPRETATION
James Joyce
A portrait of the Irish as
James Joyce.   H. Gregory.   11:
186-93, Jan/Feb '60.

ELSNER, Gisela
The eighth [novel excerpt]
36:19-23+, Je '65.

EMBERS (a play for radio). S.
Beckett.   10:28-41, Nov/Dec
'59.

The EMPRESS' new clothes
[essay] K. Tynan.   73:43-7+,
Dec '69.

EMSHWILLER, ED - CRITI-
CISM AND INTERPRETATION
Relativity
Notes from the underground:
Relativity--a cosmic dream.   P.
Tyler.   48:21+, Aug '67.

The END [story] S. Beckett.
15:22-41, Nov/Dec '60.

The END bit [poem] J. Burns.
38:25, Nov '65.

The END of an ethnic dream

[poem]   J. Wright.   47:41,
Je '67.

The END of the underground
[essay] J. Lahr.   65:45-8+,
Apr '69.

The ENDLESS humiliation [auto-
biographical essay] A. Adamov.
8:64-95, spring '59.

ENDLESS journeys (Voyages sans
fin) [poem] P. Reverdy.   11:26,
Jan/Feb '60.

ENGLISH LANGUAGE
The excluded words. W.
Young.   32:28-32+, Apr/May
'64.

"ENIF"
[cartoon] 70:83, Sept '69.

ENRIQUE VARGAS' GUT
THEATER (Spanish Harlem)
The street scene: playing for
keeps.   J. Lahr.   59:48-51+,
Oct '68.

ENZENSBERGER, Hans Magnus
Foam; English version by
Jerome Rothenberg [poem] 19:
64-71, Jl/Aug '61.
A poem for the affluent society [poem] 21:93, Nov/Dec
'61.
Portrait of a house detective
[poem] 36:72, Je '65.

EP (epidermal) art [photo-
graphs] G. Cross and E. Cross.
46:42-7, Apr '67.

EPANORTHOSIS on the moral
clinamen [satirical verse] I.
Sandomir.   13:186, May/Je '60.

EPITAPH for a Canadian kike
[reminiscence] S. Krim.   77:66-
73, Apr '70.

EREBUS [novel excerpt] R.
Hunter.   67:23-5+, Je '69.

ERECTING a sacrilegious cross
on a Saturday on Washburn
Campus [poem] H. W. Stan-
ford. 16:109, Jan/Feb '61.

ERNST, Max
[illus] 13:192, May/Je '60.

EROTIC ART
The new eroticism D.
Davis. 58:48-55, Sept '68.
see also
PORNOGRAPHY

The EROTIC society [essay]
M. Girodias. 39:64-9, Feb '66.

EROTICISM
A little treatise on erotics.
J. Kott. 43:54-5, Oct '66.
A voyeur in the labyrinth:
an interview with Alain Robbe-
Grillet. P. Demeron. 43:46-
9+, Oct '66.

ERSMAN, CHRISTINA
(photograph of) 83:cover,
Oct '70.

ESHLEMAN, Clayton
Hand (reading the Human
Universe of Charles Olsen)
[poem] 62:29, Jan '69.

ESKIMO LITERATURE
Notes on Eskimo literature.
L. Kemp. 33:72-3, Aug/Sept
'64.

ESPIONAGE
see
PHILBY, K.

ESPINASSE, Françoise
An interview with Fernando
Arrabal. 71:43-6+, Oct '69.

ESSENTIALS of spontaneous
prose [essay] J. Kerouac. 5:
72-3, summer '58.

ESSLIN, MARTIN - CRITICISM

AND INTERPRETATION
Brecht: the man and his work
Brecht. L. Abel. 14:134-
40, Sept/Oct '60.

ETHIOPIA
Journal of a painter in
Ethiopia. Corneille. 10:56-67,
Nov/Dec '59.

ÉTIEMBLE
One China or two? [essay]
8:24-34, spring '59.

ETIENNE, Luc
René Daumal, experimental
mystic [essay] 13:122-3, May/
Je '60.

ETIENNE, LUC
(photograph of) 13:96, May/
Je '60.

ETHICS
see
MORAL ATTITUDES

EVEN the sun was afraid [poem]
C. Bukowski. 63:44-5, Feb '69.

EVENTS [photographs from the
film] F. Baker. 79:41-3,
Je '70.

EVENTS: an interview with Fred
Baker. K. Carroll. 79:41-3,
Je '70.

EVERGREEN drops in on a
dropout [pictorial satire] 43:33-
40, Oct '66.

EVERGREEN unclassified
[satire] 47:73-7, Je '67.

EVERGREEN REVIEW
About Evergreen Review
No. 32. 33:32, Aug/Sept '64.

The EVERLY BROTHERS
(photograph of) 81:39, Aug
'70.

EVERSON, William
see
ANTONINUS, Brother

EVTUSHENKO, Evgeny
Babii Yar [poem] 22:57-9,
Jan/Feb '62.
Interview. 26:85-8, Sept/
Oct '62.
Three poems; English ver-
sions by Anseln Hollo. I saw
him; Against borders; The
hoods. 25:22-6, Jl/Aug '62.

EVTUSHENKO, EVGENY
Note on "Babii Yar." 22:
60, Jan/Feb '62.

EXCEPT for the heat [story]
J. Malone. 24:52-7, May/Je
'62.

The EXCLUDED words [essay]
W. Young. 32:28-32+, Apr/
May '64.

EXISTENTIALISM
On a certain experience of
death. E.M. Cioran. 6:108-
23, autumn '58.

EXIT 3 [story] M. Rumaker.
5:127-49, summer '58.

An EXPEDITION in search of
little fish [story] R. Walford.
65:17-9+, Apr '69.

The EXPELLED [story] S.
Beckett. 22:8-20, Jan/Feb
'62.

EXPLOITS and opinions of
Doctor Faustroll, Pataphysician
[story excerpts] A. Jarry. 13:
128-38, May/Je '60.

EXPOSURE [story] K. Cicellis. 34:36-41, Dec '64.

"EXTERMINATOR!" [story] W.
Burroughs. 46:54-5, Apr '67.

The EYE of Mexico [special
issue devoted to young Mexican
painters, poets, and prose
writers] 7:winter '59.

- F -

FAG money [poem] J. Nuttall.
38:25-6, Nov '65.

FAKE it new [review] A. Hollo.
26:110-4, Sept/Oct '62.

The FALL and rise of Beckett's
bum: Bert Lahr in Godot [essay]
J. Lahr. 10:29-32+, Sept '69.

FALL in New England [poem]
P. Southgate. 52:95, Mar '68.

The FALL of Jerusalem [essay]
A. Schleifer. 50:26-9+, Dec
'67.

A FAMILY [poem] M. Randall.
46:84-6, Apr '67.

FAMILY matters [poem] G.
Grass. 36:93, Je '65.

A FAR cry from Africa (re-
membering the Mau-Mau re-
bellion) [poem] D. Walcott.
8:36, spring '59.

The FAR-off sound [poem] J.
Grady. 3:80, '57.

FAREWELL letter [to Fidel
Castro] C. Guevara. 51:43,
Feb '68.

FARGUE, Léon-Paul
The American frag [poem]
19:63, Jl/Aug '61.
Danse mabraque [story] 13:
116-7, May/Je '60.

FARGUE, LÉON-PAUL
Léon-Paul Fargue, explorer.
H. Bouchè. 13:115-6, May/Je
'60.
(photograph of) 13:96, May/Je
'60.

FASHION
The Empress' new clothes.
K. Tynan.   73:43-7+, Dec '69.

FASHION or passion: the NAC
and the avant-garde [reply to
A. Vogel] P. Tyler.   48:55,
Aug '67.

FAT Phil's day [story] H.
Selby.   48:52-3, Aug '67.

A FATE of unannounced years
[poem] E. Dorn.   14:125,
Sept/Oct '60.

FATHERS and Satyrs [story]
H. Calisher.   44:24-7+, Dec
'66.

FAUST, Jan
[illus] 85:20, Dec '70.

The FEAR that precedes...
[poem] R. Duncan.   2:22, '57.

FEELING the chill in the 70s
[review] N. Hentoff. 77:16,
Apr '70.

FEHR
[cartoon] 69:23, Aug '69.

FEIFFER, Jules
[illus] 79:20-5, Je '70.

FEIFFER, JULES - CRITI-
CISM AND INTERPRETATION
Jules Feiffer: satire as sub-
version.   J. Lahr. 63:33-4+,
Feb '69.
God bless and Little murders
Jules Feiffer: satire as sub-
version.   J. Lahr.   63:33-4+,
Feb '69.
The White House murder case
Spectacles of disintegration.
J. Lahr.   79:31-3+, Je '70.

FEIFFER, JULES
(photograph of) 63:32, Feb
'69.

FEINSTEIN, Harold
[photo] 1:cover '57.
Portfolio of [8] photographs.
1:between 98 and 99, '57.

FELIX Candela: shells in architecture [essay] E. McCoy. 7:
127-33, winter '59.

FÉNÉON, Félix
Belles-lettres [notations] 13:
105, May/Je '60.
Our times [notations] 13:104-
5, May/Je '60.

FÉNÉON, FÉLIX
Félix Fénéon: Soft spoken
anarchist.   M. Décaudin. 13:
103, May/Je '60.

FÉNÉON, FÉLIX
(drawing of) 13:95, May/Je
'60.

FERGUSON, A.
[cartoon] 66:73, May '69;
70:86, Sept '69.

FERLINGHETTI, Lawrence
Back roads to far towns;
after Bashó [poem] 78:68, May
'70.
A Coney Island of the mind
[poem excerpt] 2:30-2, '57.
Dog [poem] 2:33-5, '57.
He [poem] 12:24-7, Mar/
Apr '60.
Hidden door [poem] 15:91-3,
Nov/Dec '60.
Horn on "Howl" [essay] 4:
145-58, '57.
"Lower" California [essay]
24:61-71, May/Je '62.
The man who rode away
[poem] 27:90-2, Nov/Dec '62.
One thousand fearful words
for Fidel Castro [poem] 18:59-
63, May/Je '61.
Salute! [poem] 54:39, May '68.

FERLINGHETTI, LAWRENCE
(photograph of) 2:between

pages 64 and 65, '57.

FERNANDO Arrabal Ruiz, my
father [reminiscence] F. Arrabal.   71:47, Oct '69.

FERRARI (automobile)
Lady Ferrari.   J. -F. Held.
57:66-9, Aug '68.

FERRY, Jean
Cabochons [story]   13:72,
May/Je '60.
Checkmate of a promising
literary career [story]   13:69-
72, May/Je '60.

FERRY, JEAN
(photograph of)   13:69, May/
Je '60.

FESTIVAL of life [story] E.
Sanders.   76:37-8, Mar '70.

FEW [poem] P. Brown.   38:
25, Nov '65.

FICTION
see
ESKIMO LITERATURE
LITERATURE AND POLITICS
NOVEL, PHILOSOPHY OF
NOVEL, THEORY OF THE
WRITING

FICTION-TECHNIQUE
Belief and technique for
modern prose. J. Kerouac.
8:57, spring '59.
Cut-ups: a project for disastrous success.   B. Gysin.
32:56-61, Apr/May '64.
Essentials of spontaneous
prose J. Kerouac.   5:72-3,
summer '58.
A fresh start for fiction.
A. Robbe-Grillet.   3:97-104,
'57.
From realism to reality. A.
Robbe-Grillet.   39:50-3+, Feb
'66.

I write therefore I am.   J.
Fowles.   33:16-7+, Aug/Sept
'64.
Journey through time-space:
an interview with William S.
Burroughs. D. Odier. 67:39-
41+, Je '69.

FIELD, Edward
The giant Pacific octopus
[poem]   41:62, Je '66.
Graffiti [poem] 26:49, Sept/
Oct '62.
Old movies [4 poems: She;
Frankenstein; the Curse of the
cat woman; A film scenario]
34:18-25, Dec '64.
Poem for the left hand
[poem]   5:71, summer '58.
Prick lore [poem] 56:55, Jl
'68.
Sweet Gwendolyn + the
counters [poem] 45:97, Feb '67.
Two poems; after Constantine
Cavafy.   18:94, May/Je '61.

FIESTAS
see
HOLIDAYS, MEXICAN

FIFTY-third Street [poem] D.
McKain.   68:64, Jl '69.

'50s teenagers and '50s rock
(by Frank Zappa, as told to
Richard Blackburn) 81:43-6,
Aug '70.

FILM and revolution: an interview with Jean-Luc Godard. K.
Carroll.   83:47-50+, Oct '70.

FILM DIRECTORS, American
see
BAKER, Fred
CASSAVETES, John
DASSIN, Jules
EMSHWILLER, Ed
HOLZMAN, David
HOPPER, Dennis
KLEIN, William
MAILER, Norman

NELSON, Ralph
NICHOLS, Mike
PENN, Arthur
ROCCO, Pat
ROOKS, Conrad
WADLEIGH, Michael
WARHOL, Andy

FILM DIRECTORS, Argentinian
see
SOLANAS, Fernando

FILM DIRECTORS, Brazilian
see
ROCHA, Glauber

FILM DIRECTORS, Canadian
see
KING, Allan

FILM DIRECTORS, Czecho-
slovakian
see
JIRES, Jaromil

FILM DIRECTORS, English
see
BROOK, Peter

FILM DIRECTORS, French
see
DEMY, Jacques
GODARD, Jean-Luc
RESNAIS, Alain

FILM DIRECTORS, Greek
see
PAPATAKIS, Nico

FILM DIRECTORS, Hungarian
see
JANCSÓ, Miloós

FILM DIRECTORS, Irish
see
BECKETT, Samuel

FILM DIRECTORS, Italian
see
ANTONIONI, Michelangelo
PASOLINI, Paolo

FILM DIRECTORS, Japanese
see
MISHIMA, Yukio
OSHIMA, Nagisa

FILM DIRECTORS, Polish
see
POLANSKI, Roman

FILM DIRECTORS, Senegalese
see
SEMBENE, Ousmane

FILM DIRECTORS, Spanish
see
BUÑUEL, Luis

FILM DIRECTORS, Swedish
see
BERGMAN, I.
SJOMAN, Vilgot

FILM DIRECTORS, Yugoslavian
see
ZILNIK, Zelimir

The FILM in a divided Germany
[review essay] E. Patalas. 21:
110-8, Nov/Dec '61.

A FILM is a film: some notes
on Jean-Luc Godard [essay] J.
Price. 38:46-53, Nov '65.

A FILM is not a painting [reply
to A. Vogel] R. Schickel. 48:
56, Aug '67.

A FILM scenario: Lower East
side; the George Bernstein
story [poem] E. Field. 34:22-
25, Dec '64.

FILMS
single works
See name of director for full
entry.
Black god, white devil. Rocha,
Glauber.
Bonnie and Clyde. Penn, Arthur
Catch 22. Nichols, Mike.
Chappaqua. Rooks, Conrad

La Chinoise. Godard, Jean-Luc
David Holzman's diary. Holz-
  man, David
Early works. Zilnik, Zelimir
Easy rider. Hopper, Dennis
Events. Baker, Fred
Faces. Cassavetes, John
Film. Beckett, Samuel
Hiroshima, mon amour.
  Resnais, Alain
La hora de los hornos.
  Solanas, Fernando
The hour of the wolf.
  Bergman, Ingmar
I am curious (blue). Sjoman,
  Vilgot
I am curious (yellow).
  Sjoman, Vilgot
The joke. Jires, Jaromil
The last movie. Hopper,
  Dennis
Mandabi. Sembene, Ousmane
Mister freedom. Klein,
  William
Mondo Rocco. Rocco, Pat
Nude Restaurant. Warhol, Andy
Relativity. Emshwiller, Ed
Soldier blue. Nelson, Ralph
Tell me lies. Brook, Peter
Teorama. Pasolini, Paolo
Thanos and Despina. Papa-
  takis, Nico
Trash. Warhol, Andy
Uptight. Dassin, Jules
The vampire killers.
  Polanski, Roman
Warrendale. King, Allan
Wild 90. Mailer, Norman
Woodstock. Wadleigh, Michael
Zabriskie Point. Antonioni,
  Michelangelo

FILMS - ACTORS
          see
BOGART, Humphrey
DEAN, James

FILMS AND FILM-MAKING
  The angry young film makers.
A. Vogel. 6:163-83, autumn '58.
  The tyranny of Warrendale.
P. Tyler. 69:31-3+, Aug '69.

We: a manifesto by film
worker Dziga Vertov. 83:50-1,
Oct '70.

    see also
CENSORSHIP - FILMS
CINEMA VERITÉ
DOCUMENTARY FILMS
SEX IN FILMS

FILMS AND FILMMAKING -
  AFRICA
  Mandabi: confronting Africa
[review essay] J. Lester. 78:
55-8+, May '70.

FILMS AND FILMMAKING -
  BRAZIL
  Brazil's Cinema Nôvo: an
interview with Glauber Rocha.
M. Delahaye. 73:29-32+, Dec
'69.

FILMS AND FILMMAKING -
  CHINA (People's Republic)
  A hundred flowers of the
same kind. K. Karol. 45:42-5,
Feb '67.

FILMS AND FILMMAKING -
  FRANCE
  Mister Freedom: an interview
with William Klein. A. Segal.
77:49-50, Apr '70.

FILMS AND FILMMAKING -
  GERMANY
  The film in a divided
Germany. E. Patalas. 21:
110-8, Nov/Dec '61.

FILMS AND FILMMAKING -
  U. S.
  The day Rap Brown became
a press agent for Paramount.
A. Vogel. 67:43-5+, Je '69.
  Easy Rider: a very American
thing. An interview with Dennis
Hopper. L. Carson. 72:24-
7+, Nov '69.
  The new American cinema:
five replies to Amos Vogel. 48:
54-6+, Aug '67.

13 confusions.   A. Vogel.
47:50-3+, Je '67.
A way of life: an interview
with John Cassavetes.   A.
Labarthe.   64:45-7, Mar '69.

FILTHY pictures siezed in
London [poem] G. Dowden.
49:28-30, Oct '67.

FINOCHIO, RICHARD (HARLOW)
Notes from the underground:
Miss All-American.   J. Nathan.
47:19-21, Je '67.

FINOCHIO, RICHARD (HARLOW)
(photograph of) 50:65-9,
Dec '67.

FIOFORI, Tam
Three poems: Mama, mama,
look at sis!; Wear you off my
mind; Bare bearers.   56:27,
Jl '68.

FISHMAN Paper Box Co. , Inc.
[story] E. Cohen.   37:27-9+,
Sept '65.

A FISH'S life [novel excerpt]
R. Queneau.   13:36-45, May/
Je '60.

FISH waif [pictorial] M.
O'Donoghue and E. Bach. 53:49-
55, Apr '68.

FITTING [story] Lin Yatta.
66:23-4, May '69.

FITZSIMMONS, Thomas and
Rikutaro Fukuda
Tradition and the machine
[essay] 38:86-94, Nov '65.

The 5-day rain [poem] D.
Levertov.   9:35, summer '59.

FLAMMONDE, Paris
Why President Kennedy was
killed [essay] 62:41-2+, Jan '69.

The FLIES [poem] P. Blackburn.   19:54, Jl/Aug '61.

FLORA, Paul
Driving with Flora [cartoons]
34:81-7, Dec '64.
Flora in flight [cartoons]
25:67-72, Jl/Aug '62.
Flora in Venice [cartoons]
27:50-9, Nov/Dec '62.
Travel with Flora [cartoons]
26:75-9, Sept/Oct '62.
[cartoon] 24:51, May/Je
'62; 30:42, 57, 69, May/Je
'63; 31:54-5, Oct/Nov '63.
[illus] 26:cover, Sept/Oct
'62.

FLOWER power: an interview
with a hippie.   H. Brown and
J. Sertz. 49:54-7+, Oct '67.

The FLOWERS and the fire
[story] R. Brooke.   62:51-3+,
Jan '69.

FLOWERS on your way [poem]
J. Ashbery.   8:99, spring '59.

The FLUTE of the fellow
prisoner [poem] Ho-Chi-Minh.
43:44, Oct '66.

The FLY [story] E. Cherrytree.   58:42-7, Sept '68.

FLY away, little dove [essay]
L. Kemp.   7:190-213, winter
'59.

The FLYMAN [story] D. Woolf.
6:81-92, autumn '58.

FOAM [poem] H. Enzensberger.
19:64-71, Jl/Aug '66.

FOLK MUSIC, MEXICAN
see
CORRIDO (Mexican Ballad)

FOLK SINGERS
Horses don't write songs.

J. Hendricks. 64:61-2, Mar '69.

FOLKSONG [story] M. Thomas. 22:39-47+, Jan/Feb '62.

FOND farewell to the Chicago Review [poem] P. Whalen. 9: 131, summer '59.

FOOTBALL [play] J. Swan. 59:36-43, Oct '68.

FOR a picture by Mike Nathan [poem] P. Whalen. 34:74, Dec '64.

FOR C [poem] P. Whalen. 5: 58-9, summer '58.

FOR Charles Olson [poem] M. Rumaker. 76:27, Mar '70.

FOR Darwin's centenary [cartoon] Siné. 12:54-5, Mar/Apr '60.

FOR modern man (1914-1964, RIP) [poem] M. Horovitz. 38: 26-7, Nov '65.

FOR Ray Bremser [poem] S. Krim. 49:21, Oct '67.

FOREST, Jean-Claude
  Barbarella [comic strip] 37: 35-43, Sept '65; 38:37-45, Nov '65; 39:33-43, Feb '66.

FOREST, Jean-Claude
  [illus] 37:cover, Sept '65; 38:cover, Nov '65.

FORMENTERA photographs L. Waldman. 45:33-6, Feb '67.

FORMOSA
  see
CHINA (Republic of)

FORT Lauderdale beer bust [book excerpt] W. Taggart and W. Haines. 52:29-30+, Mar '68.

FOSTER, Charles
  The troubled makers [story] 4:9-28, '57.

FOUR days with Fidel [essay] K. Karol. 51:51-2+, Feb '68.

FOUR SEASONS RESTAURANT
  The most expensive restaurant ever built. B. Friedman. 10: 108-16, Nov/Dec '59.

FOURSOME [play] E. Ionesco. 13:46-53, May/Je '60.

FOWLER, Gene
  San Francisco poem. 48:50-1, Aug '67.

FOWLES, John
  I write therefore I am [essay] 33:16-7+, Aug/Sept '64.

FOWLIE, Wallace
  On a study of Camus [review] 8:98-9, spring '59.
  Rimbaud's desert as seen by Pasolini [review essay] 74:27-9+, Jan '70.

FOX
  [cartoon] 81:22, Aug '70; 82:64, Sept '70.

FRAGMENT III [poem] H. Heissenbüttel. 21:101, Nov/Dec '61.

FRAGMENTS from a diary [poem] A. Ginsberg. 42:28-9, Aug '66.

FRAGMENTS of a journal. E. Ionesco. 59:24-6+, Oct '68.

FRANCE
  France: of patriotism, refuge and scoundrels. J. Barry. 24: 36-50, May/Je '62.
  France: technology, politics, and the average man. J. Barry. 25:80-90, Jl/Aug '62.

France: the decline of an American dream - 1. J. Barry. 23:48-62, Mar/Apr '62.
see also
ALGERIAN WAR
PARIS

FRANK Fleet and his electronic sex machine [comic strip] 65: 36-43, Apr '69; 68:38-45, Jl '69; 69:38-45, Aug '69; 70:50-7, Sept '69; 71:33-7, Oct '70; 72: 34-7, Nov '69; 73:48-51, Dec '69; 74:48-53, Jan '70; 75:54-9, Feb '70; 76:52-7, Mar '70; 77: 60-5, Apr '70; 78:59-64, May '70; 79:58-63, Je '70; 80:42-7, Jl '70; 81:56-61, Aug '70; 82: 42-7, Sept '70; 84:42-7, Nov '70.

FRANK, Robert
[photo] 4:cover, '57; 15:cover, Nov/Dec '60; 74:40, 42-7, Jan '70.

FRANKENSTEIN [poem] E. Field. 34:20-1, Dec '64.

FRANKENTHALER, Helen
[paintings] 12:between page 79 and 80, Mar/Apr '60.

FRANZ Kline talking [dialogue] F. O'Hara. 6:58-64, autumn '58.

FRASER, CHRISTINE
(photograph of) 41:cover, 63, Je '66.

FREAK show and finale [poem] L. Kandel. 41:49, Je '66.

FREDDY [play] P. Southgate. 25:27-39, Jl/Aug '62.

FREED, Arthur
Portfolio of photographs. 77: 33-9, Apr '70.

FREEING the university: abolish

tenure [essay] N. Hentoff. 73: 39-41+, Dec '69.

FREEWHEELIN' Frank [narrative] F. Reynolds. 47:22-5+, Je '67.
_____: part II. 48: 64-8, Aug '67.

FRENCH LITERATURE
see
'PATAPHYSICS

The FRENCH revolution - 1968 [pictorial] S. Destre and Ghnassia. 57:41-9, Aug '68.

FRENZY for two [play] E. Ionesco. 36:31-9+, Je '65.

A FRESH start for fiction [essay] A. Robbe-Grillet. 3: 97-104, '57.

FRIEDMAN, B. H.
Do you know Gorky? Kline? Pollock? [story] 47:26-7+, Je '67.
The most expensive restaurant ever built. [essay] 10: 108-16, Nov/Dec '59.
Thurber's Ross: a minority report [review] 9:216-9, summer '59.

FRIEDMAN, Benno
[photo] 57:30-1, Aug '68.

FRITZ, Virginia
[illus] 53:60, Apr '68; 59: 20, Oct '68; 72:62, Nov '69.

FROM a Brooklyn apartment [poem] D. Tipton. 72:51, Nov '69.

FROM an abandoned work [story] S. Beckett. 3:83-91, '57.

FROM an unabandoned work [poem] S. Beckett. 14:58-65, Sept/Oct '60.

FROM dissent to what kind of
resistance? [essay] N. Hentoff.
52:31-2+, Mar '68.

FROM one smartass to another
[review] J. Holmes. 80:75-
9, Jl '70.

FROM realism to reality [essay]
A. Robbe-Grillet. 39:50-3+,
Feb '66.

FROM the darkness [story] S.
Mrozek. 29:9-11, Mar/Apr '63.

FROM the Petrograd journal -
1917 [poem] F. King. 29:17-
8, Mar/Apr '63.

FROM the third eye... Antonioni:
where does Zabriskie point?
[review essay] K. Carroll. 81:
74-6, Aug '70.

FROM the third eye... Behind
the iron (theater) curtain [essay]
A. Schneider. 79:91-4, Je '70.

FROM the third eye... from one
smartass to another [review]
J. Holmes. 80:75-9, Jl '70.

FROM the third eye... Hollywood's last stand [review essay]
T. Seligson. 85:78-9, Dec '70.

FROM the third eye... Mike
Nichols: the downhill racer [re-
view] N. Hentoff. 83:69-70,
Oct '70.

FROM the third eye... mucking
with the real [review essay] L.
Carson. 82:77-9, Sept '70.

FROM the third eye... Papatakis: tiger in a think tank
[essay] P. Tyler. 83:70-4,
Oct '70.

FROM the third eye... a parable
of political rebellion [review]

D. Rader. 78:91, May '70.

FROM the third eye... Pop freak
and passing fancy [review essay]
A. Aronowitz. 77:86-8, Apr '70.

FROM the third eye... Two steps
toward humanity [reviews] A.
Vogel. 77:88-9, Apr '70.

FROM the third eye... white men
still speaks with forked tongue
[review essay] R. Wolf. 78:
91-3, May '70.

FROST + bite [poem] G. Grass.
32:68, Apr/May '64.

FRUMKIN, Gene
    Variations on the taste of
dried apricots [poem] 19:95,
Jl/Aug '61.

FUENTES, Carlos
    The life line [story] 7:75-84,
winter '59.

FUKUDA, Rikutaro
            see
FITZSIMMONS, Thomas and
    Rikutaro Fukuda

FULLER, R. Buckminster
    Man's total communication
system [essay] 83:39-41+, Oct
'70.

The FUNAMBULISTS [story] J.
Genêt. 32:44-9, Apr/May '64.

FUNERAL rites [novel excerpt]
J. Genêt. 68:47-9+, Jl '69.

FUNK for sale [review] M.
Williams. 10:136-40, Nov/Dec
'59.

- G -

GI protest: the Presidio aftermath [book excerpt] F. Gardner.
75:47-9+, Feb '70.

The GLP arrives! [essay] D.
Newlove. 44:17-9+, Dec '66.

GADGIL, Gangadhar
   The coin [story] 6:141-9,
autumn '58.

GALLERIES
         see
ART GALLERIES

GAMBLING [poem] Ho-Chi-
Minh. 43:44, Oct '66.

GAME life, London 1967 (to
Colin MacInnes) [poem] C.
Hernton. 63:35, Feb '69.

GAMES, Nature of
   The theatre of sports. J.
Lahr. 72:39-41+, Nov '69.

The GAMES of night [story]
S. Dagerman. 15:47-56, Nov/
Dec '60.

GARA, Larry
   [Baby Dodds] his story (as
told to Larry Gara) [autobi-
ographical essay] 1:110-48, '57.

GARCÍA LORCA, Federico
   The audience [play] 6:93-
107, autumn '58.
   The unfaithful wife; English
version by John Frederick
Nims. [poem] 30:43-4, May/
Je '63.

GARCÍA LORCA, FEDERICO
   Lover of Lorca. A. Voznesensky. 31:48-52, Oct/Nov
'63.

GARCÍA TÉRRES, Jaime
   Debate [poem] 7:89, winter
'59.
   The park at Montsouris: a
savage elegy [poem] 7:87-9,
winter '59.

GARDENS - Japan

         see
RYOANJI GARDEN

GARDNER, Fred
   GI protest: the Presidio
aftermath [book excerpt] 75:
47-9+, Feb '70.

GARIBAY, Ricardo
   German drinking beer [story]
22:89-92, Jan/Feb '62.

GARNER, Bob
   Hades and the 400 [story]
79:35-6, Je '70.
   The war machine [story] 52:
45-6+, Mar '68.

GARRETT, Leslie
   The only man in Paris with-
out a woman [story] 68:23-5+,
Jl '69.

GARRETT, LESLIE - CRITI-
   CISM AND INTERPRETATION
         The beasts
   Anatomy of the beasts: heroes,
perverts, and saints. C. Hernton. 46:34-5+, Apr '67.

GARRISON, JAMES
   Why President Kennedy was
killed. P. Flammonde. 62:
41-2+, Jan '69.

GARRO, Elena
   A solid house [play] 7:62-
74, winter '59.

GASCAR, Pierre
   The spider-child of Madras
[story] 9:91-5, summer '59.

GAY liberation: all the sad
young men [essay] D. Rader.
84:18-20+, Nov '70.

GAY LIBERATION FRONT
   Notes from the underground:
gay liberation: all the sad young
men. D. Rader. 84:18-20+,
Nov '70.

GELBER, Jack
  Edinburgh happening [essay]
31:55-61, Oct/Nov '63.
  Neal vs. Jimmy the fag
[story] 34:58-61, Dec '64.

GELBER, JACK - CRITICISM
  AND INTERPRETATION
    The apple
Applejack. J. Tallmer. 24:
95-106, May/Je '62.
    The connection
Who else can make so much
out of passing out?: the sur-
prising survival of an anti-play.
N. Hentoff. 11:170-7, Jan/
Feb '60.

GELBER, JACK
  (photograph of) 24:97, May/
Je '62.

GENERALS OF THE DAUGH-
  TERS OF THE AMERICAN
  REVOLUTION
  (photograph of)   81:36, Aug
'70.

GENERATION GAP
  A generation without a
future? N. Hentoff.   67:47-
50, Je '69.

A GENERATION without a
future? [essay] N. Hentoff.
67:47-50, Je '69.

GENESIS of the new music--I:
Coltrane [review essay] A.
Spellman.   45:81-3, Feb '67.

GENESIS of the new music--II:
Cecil Taylor [review essay] A.
Spellman.   46:72-3+, Apr '67.

GENESIS of the new music--
III: Ornette Coleman [review
essay] A. Spellman. 47:78-80,
Je '67.

GENÊT, Jean
  From: Funeral rites [novel

excerpt] 68:47-9+, Jl '69.
  The funambulists [story] 32:
44-9, Apr/May '64.
  Jean Genêt and the Black
Panthers [interview] M. Mance-
aux. 82:35-7+, Sept '70.
  Our lady of the flowers
[novel excerpt] 18:33-58, May/
Je '61.

GENTLEMAN alone [poem] P.
Neruda. 22:36-7, Jan/Feb '62.

GEORG Büchner [essay]M. Hamburger. 1:68-98, '57.

GEORGE swimming at Barnes
Hole, but it got too cold [poem]
P. Carroll.   10:53-4, Nov/Dec
'59.

GERMAN drinking beer [story]
R. Garibay. 22:89-92, Jan/Feb
'62.

GERMAN LANGUAGE AND
  LITERATURE
  The words behind the slogans.
W. Höllerer. 21:119-26, Nov/
Dec '61.

GERMANY (Federal Republic)
  In this country of ours. H.
Böll.   21:102-9, Nov/Dec '61.

GETTING to the nitty-gritty:
sex, race, and racism [essay]
N. Hentoff. 36:68-74, Je '65.

GHNASSIA
  [photo] 57:41-9, Aug '68.

The GHOUL-priest [story] A.
Ueda. 60:58-62, Nov '68.

The GIANT Pacific octopus
[poem] E. Field.   41:62, Je '66.

GINSBERG, Allen
  At Apollinaire's grave [poem]
8:59-62, spring '59.
  Beginning of a poem of These

States [poem] 49:46-9, Oct '67.
 Chances R [poem] 46:57,
Apr '67.
 Fragments from a diary
[poem] 42:28-9, Aug '66.
 Howl [poem] 2:137-47, '57.
 Kral Majales [poem] 40:22-
3, Apr '66.
 Lysergic acid [poem] 18:80-
4, May/Je '61.
 Mandala [poem] 18:84, May/
Je '61.
 Memory gardens [poem] 80:
27-9, Jl '70.
 Notes written on finally re-
cording Howl [essay] 10:132-5,
Nov/Dec '59.
 Sather gate illumination
[poem] 11:96-9, Jan/Feb '60.
 Siesta in Xbalba and return
to the states [poem] 4:29-47,
'57.

GINSBERG, ALLEN
 A conversation between Ezra
Pound and Allen Ginsberg. N.
Reck. 55:26-9+, Je '68.

GINSBERG, ALLEN - CRITI-
   CISM AND INTERPRETATION
Kaddish and other poems 1958-60
 Death is a letter that was
never sent. P. Carroll. 19:
114-6, Jl/Aug '61.

GINSBERG, ALLEN
 (photograph of) 2:between
64 and 65, '57; 42:cover, Aug
'66; with Peter Orlovsky 81:
cover, 38, Aug '70.

GINSBERG, Louis
 To a mother, buried [poem]
12:74, Mar/Apr '60.

GIRLS [illus] T. Ungerer. 47:
55-60, Je '67.

GIRODIAS, Maurice
 The erotic society [essay]
39:64-9, Feb '66.
 Lolita, Nabokov, and I [essay]

37:44-7+, Sept '65.

GIRODIAS, MAURICE
 Lolita and Mr. Girodias. V.
Nabokov. 45:37-41, Feb '67.

GLEASON, Ralph J.
 The power of non-politics or
the death of the square left
[essay] 49:40-5+, Oct '67.
 San Francisco jazz scene
[essay] 2:59-64, '57.

GLEESON, Patrick Shannon
 After a Saturday night with
Lady Day and Hart Crane and
Mrs. Brady's daughter, he
spends a Sunday morning in the
park, alone [poem] 9:132,
summer '59.
 Room 24 [poem] 9:133,
summer '59.

GLORY hole (Nickel views of
the infidel in Tangiers) [essay]
A. Chester. 35:52-9, Mar '65.

GO away, old man, go away
[story] P. Boyle. 27:95-106,
Nov/Dec '62.

GODARD, JEAN-LUC - CRITI-
   CISM AND INTERPRETATION
 Film and revolution: an interview with Jean-Luc Godard.
K. Carroll. 83:47-50+, Oct
'70.
 A film is a film: some notes
on Jean-Luc Godard. J. Price.
38:46-53, Nov '65.
           La Chinoise
 Vietnam déjà vu. L. Eliscu.
56:66-8, Jl '68.

GOD'S judgment on white
America [speech] Malcolm X.
50:54-7+, Dec '67.

GOING down slow [story] L.
Jones. 43:41-3+, Oct '66.

GOLD, Buddy

GOLD, Buddy

[photo] 82:cover, Sept '70.

GOLD, Herbert
Down the ladder awhile [story]
39:28-32, Feb '66.
The lid [story] 64:39-40+,
Mar '69.

GOLD, Michael
[photo] 83:28, Oct '70.

GOLDBERG, Joe
The death of Sam Spade
[essay with photographs] 28:
107-16, Jan/Feb '63.

GOLDBERG, MICHAEL - CRIT-
ICISM AND INTERPRETATION
Odes
Poets and painters in collab-
oration. F. Porter. 20:121-
6, Sept/Oct '61.

GOLDWYN, SAM
(photograph of) 81:38, Aug
'70.

GOMBROWICZ, Witold
The banquet [story] 44:41-
3+, Dec '66.
On the back stairs [story]
35:26-31+, Mar '65.

GONZALEZ, Luis J. and
Gustavo A. Sánchez Salazar
The story of Tania: Ché's
woman in Bolivia [essay] 60:
18-21+, Nov '68.

A GOOD education: spontaneous
demonstration I [story] M.
Mason. 59:53-4+, Oct '68.

GOOD Joanna [poem] D. Henderson. 81:33, Aug '70.

The GOOD life [cartoons] Siné.
14:66-9, Sept/Oct '60.

GOOD luck to you Kafka/You'll
need it boss [poem] H. Graham.
37:57, Sept '65.

GOOD morning [poem] L.
Hubbell. 26:37, Sept/Oct '62.

GOODBYE [story] J. Schultz.
19:72-82, Jl/Aug '61.

GOODBYE to a tooth [poem]
Ho-Chi-Minh. 43:45, Oct '66.

GOODE, Erich
Marijuana and sex [essay]
66:19-21+, May '69.

GOODMAN, Paul
A statue of Goldsmith [essay]
8:175-82, spring '59.
Why are there no alterna-
tives? [essay] 16:1-5, Jan/
Feb '61.

GOOGIE
[cartoon] 72:57, Nov '69.

GORDON, Bonnie
[illus] 69:28-9, Aug '69;
71:21, Oct '69; 77:22, Apr '70.

GOREY, Edward
The pious infant [story] 35:
22-5, Mar '65.

GOTTLIEB, Saul
Signalling through the flames:
the Living Theatre in Europe
[essay] 45:24-32+, Feb '67.

GOURMONT, Remy de
News from the unfortunate
isles. [story] 13:108-10, May/
Je '60.

GOURMONT, REMY DE
Remy de Gourmont; man of
masks. N. Arnaud. 13:106-
107, May/Je '60.
(drawing of) 13:95, May/Je
'60.

GOVER, Robert
Here goes Kitten [novel ex-
cerpt] 33:18-9, Aug/Sept '64.
One hundred dollar mis-

57

GOVER, Robert

understanding [novel excerpt]
26:12-9, Sept/Oct '62.

GOVERNMENT-inspected meat
[story] D. Rader. 72:29-33+,
Nov '69.

GOVERNMENT, Resistence to
Redress and revolution. W.
Douglas. 77:41-3+, Apr '70.

GRADY, James
The buck is my benison
[poem] 31:82, '57.
The far-off sound [poem] 3:
80, '57.
So why not [poem] 3:81, '57.
Traffic complaint [poem] 3:
81, '57.

GRAFE, Frieda
Rocha's film as carnival
[essay] 73:30+, Dec '69.

GRAFFITI [poem] E. Field.
26:49, Sept/Oct '62.

GRAHAM, BILLY
Billy Graham and friend. D.
Rader. 74:31-5+, Jan '70.
(photograph of) 81:39, Aug
'70.

GRAHAM, Henry
Good luck to you Kafka/You'll
need it boss [poem] 37:57,
Sept '65.

GRASHOW, James
[illus] 81:30, Aug '70.

GRASS, Günter
Family matters [poem] 36:
93, Je '65.
Five poems [crack-up; In the
egg; Frost + bite; The ballad
of the black cloud; To all the
gardeners] 32:67-9, Apr/May
'64.
Unsuccessful raid [poem] 36:
93, Je '65.
The wide skirt [excerpt from

his novel, The toy drum] 21:
36-44, Nov/Dec '61.

GRASS, GÜNTER - CRITICISM
AND INTERPRETATION
Letter from Germany. W.
Höllerer. 15:135-8, Nov/Dec
'60.

GRAY, Pat
Puzzle for Wilhelm Reich
[poem] 37:87, Sept '65.

The GREAT Buddha at Kama-
kura [poem] L. Hubbell. 26:
36-7, Sept/Oct '62.

The GREAT delight [essay] M.
Anand. 9:172-97, summer '59.

The GREAT delight and the big
lie [letter to the editor] J.
Campbell. 14:155-9, Sept/Oct
'60.

The GREAT magician [story]
R. Daumal. 13:123-5, May/Je
'60.

"The GREAT masturbator" [in-
terview] P. Brooks. 53:41-
2+, Apr '68.

GREEN Beret liberalism [essay]
J. Newfield. 57:62-5, Aug '68.

GREEN, Maurice
The possibility of existential
analysis [review essay] 8:184-
93, spring '59.

GREEN, Norman
[illus] 48:28, Aug '67; 49:
64-79, Oct '67; 76:58, Mar '70.

GREEN, Peter
[illus] 77:18, Apr '70; 79:
30, Je '70.

A GREEN thought [story] L.
Michaels. 65:32-5, Apr '69.

GREENBERG, Clement
Jackson Pollock [essay] 3:
95-9, '57.
Letter on Pollock. 5:160,
summer '58.

GREENE, David
Recordings of William Butler
Yeats [review] 8:200-1, spring
'59.

GREER, Herb
Notes from the underground:
now you see it, now you don't
[essay] 79:16-8+, Je '70.

GREGORY, ANDRE - CRITI-
CISM AND INTERPRETATION
Alice in wonderland (adaptation)
Playing with Alice. J. Lahr.
82:59-64, Sept '70.

GREGORY, Horace
Boris MacCreary's abyss
[poem] 8:103-9, spring '59.
Medusa in Gramercy Park
[poem] 22:81-5, Jan/Feb '62.
A portrait of the Irish as
James Joyce [review essay] 11:
186-93, Jan/Feb '60.

GREY, Irene
Dangerous passage [story]
11:101-15, Jan/Feb '60.

GRIDIRON maidens [pictorial
satire] M. O'Donoghue and Chaz.
48:33-40, Aug '67.

GRINGOS [story] M. Rumaker.
38:54-7+, Nov '65.

The GROCER'S assistant. [story]
J. Mitchell. 72:49-52+, Nov '69.

GROSS, John
Our dance [poem] 9:36,
summer '59.

GROSSMAN, Robert
[illus] 52:22, 24, Mar '68;
59:36-43, Oct '68; 65:60, Apr

'69; 67:34-5, 38, Je '69; 72:
38, Nov '69; 73:14, Dec '69;
75:50, 60, Feb '70; 79:44, Je
'70.

GROSZ, George
Portfolio of color plate and
drawings from Ecce Homo. 40:
33-6, Apr '66.
Drawings [from Ecce homo]
16:cover, 68, 71, 73, 75, 76,
79, 80, Jan/Feb '61.
[illus] 40:cover, Apr '66.

GROSZ, GEORGE - CRITICISM
AND INTERPRETATION
Man in the zoo: George
Grosz' Ecce Homo. H. Miller.
40:30-9, Apr '66.

GROUP therapy [cartoon] L.
Myers. 34:26-7, Dec '64.

GROVE PRESS, INC.
Opinion: U. S. District
Court... New York... [for the
plaintiffs] Grove Press, Inc.
and Readers' Subscription, Inc.
... F. Bryan. 9:37-68,
summer '59.

The GROWL [play] M. McClure.
32:75-7+, Apr/May '64.

GRUS
[cartoon] 75:82, Feb '70.

GUARDS carrying pigs [poem]
Ho-Chi-Minh. 43:45, Oct '66.

GUERILLA THEATER
Theater and propaganda. J.
Lahr. 52:33-7, Mar '68.

GUERILLAS--Bolivia
I was arrested with Debray.
G. Roth. 51:44-7+, Feb '68.
A message to my friends.
R. Debray. 51:48-9+, Feb '68.
The story of Tania: Ché's
woman in Bolivia. L. Gonzalez
and G. Sánchez Salazar. 60:18-

-21+, Nov '68.
Ten days in July. K. Howard.
59:33-5+, Oct '68.
Who's who in Ché's diary.
57:36-7, Aug '68.
see also
GUEVARA, CHÉ

GUEST, Barbara
In America, the seasons
[poem] 3:115, '57.
Parachutes, my love, could
carry us higher [poem] 31:
114, '57.
Safe flights [poem] 3:116,
'57.

GUEVARA, Ché
Bolivian campaign diary. 57:
32-5+, Aug '68.
Farewell letter [to Fidel
Castro] 51:43, Feb '68.
Where it all began: the land-
ing in Cuba [book excerpt] 51:
39-41+, Feb '68.

GUEVARA, CHÉ
El Ché vive! F. Castro.
51:34-5, Feb '68.
The last hours of Ché Gue-
vara. M. Bosquet. 51:37-
8+, Feb '68.
Ten days in July. K.
Howard. 59:33-5+, Oct '68.
(photograph of) 51:36, 40,
Feb '68; 57:32, Aug '68.

A GUIDE to all good things in
life [review] A. Vogel. 75:19,
Feb '70.

GUIFFRE, JIMMY - CRITICISM
AND INTERPRETATION
Whatever happened to the
clarinet? M. Williams. 32:
82-3, Apr/May '64.

The GUN [story] B. Roueché.
42:63-4, Aug '66.

GUSTAITIS, Rasa
Hoving, the go go medievalist

[essay] 43:72-9, Oct '66.

GUSTON, PHILIP - CRITICISM
AND INTERPRETATION
Philip Guston. D. Ashton.
14:88-91, Sept/Oct '60.

GUTZEIT, Fred
[illus] 55:57-9, Je '68.

GYSIN, Brion
Cut-ups: a project for disastrous success [essay] 32:56-
61, Apr/May '64.

- H -

H. D.
Sagesse [poem] 5:27-36,
summer '58.

H. Rap Brown [essay] J.
James. 57:16-17+, Aug '68.

HADES and the 400 [story] B.
Garner. 79:35-6, Je '70.

HAINES, William
see
TAGGART, William and William
Haines

HAIRCUTTING
Notes from the underground:
haircut. R. Schechner. 51:24-
6, Feb '68.

HAITI
see
CATHOLIC CHURCH IN HAITI

HALLUCINOGENIC DRUGS
Comments on The night be-
fore thinking. W. Burroughs.
20:31-6, Sept/Oct '61.
The magical mystery trip.
T. Leary. 56:57-61+, Jl '68.
Miserable miracle. H.
Michaux. 1:37-67, '57.
Points of distinction between
sedative and consciousness-
expanding drugs. W. Burroughs.

34:72-4, Dec '64.

HALSMAN, Philippe
[photo] 34:cover, Dec '64.

HAMBURGER, Michael
Georg Buchner [essay] 1:
68-98, '57.

HAMILL, Pete
An American bird [poem]
62:49, Jan '69.

HAMMETT, DASHIELL - CRIT-
    ICISM AND INTERPRETATION
    The Maltese falcon
The death of Sam Spade.   J.
Goldberg.   28:107-16, Jan/Feb
'63.

HAND (reading The Human Universe of Charles Olson) [poem]
C. Eshleman.   62:29, Jan '69.

HANDKE, Russell
Mad love [poem]   75:29,
Feb '70.

The HANGING at Prettyfields
[story] W. Eastlake.   63:29-
31+, Feb '69.

HAN-SHAN
Cold Mountain poems [poems]
6:72-80, autumn '58.

HAN-SHAN - CRITICISM AND
    INTERPRETATION
Preface to the poems of Han-
Shan.   L. Ch'iu-Yin.   6:69-72,
autumn '58.

HAPPENINGS
Edinburgh happening.   J.
Gelber.   31:55-61, Oct/Nov '63.

HAPPY birthday [story] H.
Selby.   69:35-7+, Aug '69.

HAPPY in the weeds [story] W.
Höllerer.   21:68-79, Nov/Dec
'61.

HARDER, Kelsie
[cartoon] 57:75-6, Aug '68.

HARDING, Gunnar
Allen Ginsberg meets the
Swedish cyclist [story) 74:22-
25+, Jan '70.
It's evening when you return.
[poem] 70:44-5, Sept '69.

HARESNAPE, Geoffrey
The tomb [story] 42:42-4+,
Aug '66.

HARLEM [poem] P. Becker.
44:92, Dec '66.

HARLEM, summer 1964
[photo] D. Charles and J.
Mitchell. 34:48-57, Dec '64.

HARLOW
                 see
FINOCHIO, Richard (Harlow)

HARRIS
[cartoon] 68:86, Jl '69; 80:
62, Jl '70; 82:25, Sept '70;
83:59, Oct '70.

HARRISON, Howard
[photo] 65:20-5+, Apr '69.

HARTIGAN, Grace
[painting] 12:between p. 79
and 80, Mar/Apr '60.

HARTIGAN, GRACE - CRITI-
    CISM AND INTERPRETATION
    Salute
Poets and painters in collab-
oration.   F. Porter.   20:121-6,
Sept/Oct '61.

HATCHFELD
[cartoon] 63:53, Feb '69;
65:71, 86, Apr '69.

HAVE you seen it all, Dennis
Hopper [essay] L. Carson.
81:16-18, Aug '70.

HAVEL, Vaclav
War [poem] 48:88, Aug '67.

HAWKINS, COLEMAN - CRITI-
CISM AND INTERPRETATION
Coleman Hawkins: some notes
on a phoenix. M. Williams.
36:75-8, Je '65.

HAYDEN-Marat/Dylan-Sade: defining a generation [essay] J.
Newfield. 52:23-5, Mar '68.

HAYDEN, Tom
Reply to L. Kolakowski
[essay] 47:90-1, Je '67.
Repression and rebellion
[essay] 77:26-9, Apr '70.

HAYDEN, TOM
Hayden-Marat/Dylan-Sade:
defining a generation. J. Newfield. 52:23-5, Mar '68.
(drawing of) 52:24, Mar '68.
(photograph of) 47:90, Je
'67; 81:41, Aug '70.

HAYS, Philip
[illus] 84:22-3, Nov '70.

HE [poem] L. Ferlinghetti. 12:
24-7, Mar/Apr '60.

HE tasted history with a yellow
tooth [poem] A. Trochi. 30:
94-5, May/Je '63.

HEARTS of stone [poem] J.
Williams. 17:43-4, Mar/Apr
'61.

HEDDA
[illus] 84:48, Nov '70.

HEIDI [poem] J. Ashbery. 8:
97, spring '59.

HEIDI (II) [poem] J. Ashbery.
8:99-100, spring '59.

HEIFETZ, Henry
Love poem. 52:82, Mar '68.

HEIMISCHE cookin' [poem] M.
Horovitz. 52:39-40, Mar '68.

HEISSENBÜTTEL, Helmut
Fragment III [poem] 21:101,
Nov/Dec '61.

HELD, Jean-Francis
A car for Bonnie [essay] 58:
62-4, Sept '68.
The car with the pointed helmet [essay] 59:62-5, Oct '68.
The classless cars [essay]
54:57-61, May '68.
Drive, we'll do the rest
[essay] 55:70-3, Je '68.
Due apologies from behind
the wheel of a big V8 [essay]
56:62-5, Jl '68.
Lady Ferrari [essay] 57:66-
9, Aug '68.
The red globules [essay] 53:
56-9, Apr '68.

HELLO out there! [story] E.
Cherrytree. 50:72-81, Dec '67.

HELL'S ANGELS
Freewheelin' Frank F. Reynolds. 47:22-5+, Je '67.
_____. part II.
F. Reynolds. 48:64-8, Aug '67.

HELP wanted! [satire] J.
Marshall. 78:33, May '70.

HENDERSON, David
Boston Road blues [poem]
68:26-9, Jl '69.
Good Joanna [poem] 81:33,
Aug '70.
Ruckus poem [poem] 55:57-9,
Je '68.

HENDRICKS, Jon
Horses don't write songs
[essay] 64:61-2, Mar '69.

HENDRIX, JIMI
Notes from the underground:
Jimi Hendrix: goin' toward
heaven. J. Lester. 85:18-19+,
Dec '70.

HENNESSEY, Brian D.
[photo] 80:cover, Jl '70;
84:cover, Nov '70.

HENRY [poem] T. L. Jackrell.
17:96, Mar/Apr '61.

HENTOFF, Nat
The ability to function [essay]
79:45-7, Je '70.
Applying black power: a
speculative essay. 44:44-7+,
Dec '66.
Behold the new journalism--
it's coming after you! [review
essay] 56:49-51, Jl '68.
Blacks and Jews: an interview with Julius Lester. 65:
21-5+, Apr '69.
Breaking through the circle
of self: art and social action
[essay] 55:45-7, Je '68.
Captain America's restaurant
[essay] 74:59-61, Jan '70.
Circling the colleges: impressions and epiphanies [essay]
66:59-61, May '69.
Columbia's new course--re-
bellion I [essay] 58:65-7+, Sept
'68.
The coming of black power
[essay] 57:59-61, Aug '68.
The commonplace of Song
My [essay] 76:59-61, Mar '70.
Counterpolitics: the decade
ahead [essay] 63:25-7, Feb '69.
The daily newspaper in 1980
[essay] 40:62-3+, Apr '66.
The dimensions of community
control [essay] 64:31-2+, Mar
'69.
The drugged classroom [essay]
85:31-3, Dec '70.
Educators as dropouts: New
York City's schools [essay] 43:
19-23+, Oct '66.
Freeing the university: abolish
tenure [essay] 73:39-41+, Dec
'69.
From dissent to what kind
of resistance? [essay] 52:31-2+,
Mar '68.

From the third eye...Mike
Nichols: the downhill racer
[review] 83:69-70, Oct '70.
A generation without a future?
[essay] 67:47-50, Je '69.
Getting to the nitty-gritty:
sex, race, and racism. [essay]
36:68-74, Je '65.
Higher education for what?
[essay] 78:65-7, May '70.
The joke [review essay] 76:
29+, Mar '70.
Kafka Jones, the singing
fool! [review essay] 50:61-4,
Dec '67.
Keeping ecology alive [essay]
77:31-2+, Apr '70.
Last exit before the Great
Society [essay] 37:59-65, Sept
'65.
The last hurrah? [essay]
81:21-3, Aug '70.
The last stand of the dispensables [essay] 70:59-62,
Sept '69.
The law is an ass (male)
[essay] 84:49-51+, Nov '70.
Mugging the Constitution
[essay] 75:51-3, Feb '70.
The mystery that isn't: how
do you get those slum savages
to learn? [essay] 54:40-3,
May '68.
The new movement [essay]
42:66-73, Aug '66.
The new politics: is there
life before death? [essay] 49:
51-3+, Oct '67.
Notes from the underground:
feeling the chill in the 70s
[review] 77:16, Apr '70.
Notes from the underground:
high school underground [re-
view] 75:16-8, Feb '70.
Notes from the underground:
uncovering news uncoverage
[essay] 76:16-8, Mar '70.
On basic self-defense at
public meetings [essay] 68:69-
71, Jl '69.
On bringing democracy to
America [essay] 69:46-7+, Aug
'69.

On revolutionary profession-
alism [essay] 59:55-7, Oct '68.
Participatory television.
[essay] 71:53-5, Oct '69.
The prison of words: language
and the New Left [essay] 65:
61-3, Apr '69.
Public independent education
[essay] 83:55-7, Oct '70.
A sanity test for self and
society [essay] 60:51-3+, Nov
'68.
The secret companions [essay]
82:55-7, Sept '70.
Something's happening and
you don't know what it is, do
you Mr. Jones? [essay] 41:54-
6, Je '66.
Sounds of silence [essay] 80:
53-5, Jl '70.
Students as media critics: a
new course [essay] 72:53-5,
Nov '69.
Them and us: are peace protests self-therapy? [essay] 48:
46-9+, Aug '67.
Turning the camera into the
audience [essay] 53:47-8+,
Apr '68.
Uninventing the Negro. [essay]
38:34-6+, Nov '65.
The universities: a crisis of
legitimacy [essay] 62:47-9, Jan
'69.
Waiting for Nuremberg [essay]
45:74-80, Feb '67.
We shall overcome--when?
[essay] 39:58-62, Feb '66.
Who else can make so much
out of passing out?: the sur-
prising survival of an anti-play
[review essay] 11:170-7, Jan/
Feb '60.

HERBERT, JOHN - CRITICISM
AND INTERPRETATION
Fortune and men's eyes
Notes from the underground:
like America, beautiful and evil.
D. Rader. 75:16, Feb '70.

HERBERT, Zbigniew

A parable about Russian
emigres [poem] 39:46, Feb '66.

HERE goes Kitten [novel ex-
cerpt] R. Gover. 33:18-9,
Aug/Sept '64.

HERE they go [poem] P. Blackburn. 43:80-1, Oct '66.

HERNTON, Calvin C.
Anatomy of the beasts:
heroes, perverts, and saints
[review] 46:34-5+, Apr '67.
Game life, London 1967 (to
Colin MacInnes) [poem] 63:35,
Feb '69.

HEROIN
Drug notes. M. McClure.
25:103-17, Jl/Aug '62.

HEY, Leroy! [poem] E.
Catenacci. 59:72, Oct '68.

HIBERNATION--after Morris
Graves [poem] J. Spicer. 2:
55, '57.

HICKEY, John
Break your mother's back
[story] 4:139-42, '57.

HIDDEN door [poem] L. Ferlinghetti. 15:91-3, Nov/Dec
'60.

HIGGINS, Aidan
Black blood: a South African
diary [essay] 34:28-32+, Dec
'64.
Sign and ground [story] 30:
85-92, May/Je '63.
Winter offensive [story] 18:
64-79, May/Je '61.

The HIGH bridge above the
Tagus River at Toledo [poem]
W. C. Williams. 3:56, '57.

HIGH school underground [re-
view] N. Hentoff. 75:16-8, Feb
'70.

HIGH yellow put-down minuet
[poem] J. Surgal. 59:47, Oct
'68.

HIGHER education for what?
[essay] N. Hentoff. 78:65-7,
May '70.

HIMES, Chester
     Pinktoes [novel excerpt] 35:
16-8+, Mar '65.

HINDUISM
                    see
INTERNATIONAL SOCIETY FOR
KRISHNA CONSCIOUSNESS

HIPPIES
     Flower power: an interview
with a hippie. L. Rapoport. 49:
54-7+, Oct '67.
     The power of non-politics or
the death of the square left. R.
Gleason. 49:40-5+, Oct '67.
     Thorns of the flower children.
A. Hoffman. 73:21-3, Dec '69.

HIPPIES--Boston
     Notes from the underground:
Boston. D. Rader. 59:18-9+,
Oct '68.

HIS story (as told to Larry
Gara): New Orleans beginnings
[and] Jazz on the river [autobi-
ographical essay] B. Dodds 1:
110-48, '57.

HISTORIANS
     On becoming an historian.
M. Duberman. 65:57-9+, Apr
'69.

HISTORICAL disquisitions [poem]
P. Whalen. 24:58-60, May/Je
'62.

HISTORY [play] M. Duberman.
65:49-55, Apr '69.

A HISTORY of the opera [poem]
S. Hochman. 40:60-1, Apr '66.

HISTORY--PHILOSOPHY
     On becoming an historian. M.
Duberman. 65:57-9+, Apr '69.

HOCHHUTH, Rolf
     The Berlin Antigone [story]
32:70-3, Apr/May '64.
     The Pole who died on time
[essay] 55:30-2+, Je '68.

HO-Chi-Minh
     Prison poems [the leg irons;
the flute of the fellow prisoner;
Twilight; Gambling; The water
ration; Cold night; Air raid
warning of twelfth November;
Goodbye to a tooth; Guards
carrying pigs] 43:44-5, Oct '66.

HOCHMAN, Sandra
     A history of the opera [poem]
40:60-1, Apr '66.

HODEIR, Andre
     An analysis of Alain Resnais'
film Hiroshima mon Amour [re-
view essay] 12:102-13, Mar/Apr
'60.

HOFF, Rowell
     Redstone [poem] 15:46, Nov/
Dec '60.

HOFFMAN, Abbie
     Thorns of the flower children
[essay] 73:21-3, Dec '69.

HOFFMAN, ABBIE
     Should I assume America is
already dead? S. Krim. 68:19-
21+, Jl '69.

HOFFMAN, Phil
     A syllabic poem. 38:85,
Nov '65.

HOLD that tiger [review] J.
Tallmer. 18:109-13, May/Je
'61.

HOFFMANN, Gert
     Our man in Madras [play]

63:55-61, Feb '69.

The HOLE [poem] R. Creeley.
39:70, Feb '66.

HOLIDAY, BILLIE
Billie Holiday: actress without an act. M. Williams. 26:
115-25, Sept/Oct '62.
Bye, bye blackbird. J. Tallmer. 10:117-31, Nov/Dec '59.
(photograph of) 10:119, Nov/
Dec '59; 26:115, 116, Sept/Oct
'62.

HOLIDAY Inn University [essay]
J. Ryan. 83:29-33+, Oct '70.

HOLIDAYS, Mexican
Todos santos, dia de Muertos.
O. Paz. 7:22-37, winter '59.

HOLLAND, Brad
[illus] 55:16, Je '68; 69:24,
Aug '69; 72:28, Nov '69; 74:54,
Jan '70; 78:46, May '70; 82:54,
Sept '70; 83:38-41, Oct '70.

HÖLLERER, Walter
Happy in the weeds [story]
21:68-79, Nov/Dec '61.
Letter from Germany [essay]
15:135-8, Nov/Dec '60.
The words behind the slogans
[essay] 21:119-26, Nov/Dec '61.

HOLLO, Anselm
Fake it new [review] 26:
110-4, Sept/Oct '62.
Lament of the 12th of July
1961 [poem] 22:88, Jan/Feb '62.
The lean rats on the march;
after Heinrich Heine [poem] 31:
28-30, Oct/Nov '63.
Mr. president; for e. e.
cummings, were he still alive
[poem] 45:94, Feb '67.
Requiem for a princess--M.
M. [poem] 27:16-7, Nov/Dec
'62.
A warrant is out for the arrest of Henry Miller [poem] 28:

80, Jan/Feb '63.

HOLLO, Anselm, translator
see
BLOK, A. The twelve.
CENDRARS, B. The transsi-
berian express.
EVTUSHENKO, E. Three poems.
VOZNESENSKY, A. The three-
cornered pear/America.

HOLLYWOOD'S last stand [re-
view essay] T. Seligson. 85:
78-9, Dec '70.

HOLMES, John Clellon
From the third eye... from
one smartass to another [re-
view] 80:75-9, Jl '70.
The last cause [essay] 44:
28-32+, Dec '66.

The HOLY barbarians [review]
S. Krim. 9:208-14, summer
'59.

HOLZMAN, DAVID - CRITICISM
AND INTERPRETATION
David Holzman's diary
From the third eye... muck-
ing with the real. L. Carson.
82:77-9, Sept '70.

HOMAGE to Lucretius [poem]
P. Whalen. 2:116, '57.

HOMAGE to Robert Creeley
[poem] P. Whalen. 2:115, '57.

HOMERUN [memoir] K. Brown.
64:49-51+, Mar '69.

HOMMAGE à Piaf [song and
photographs] E. Cadoo, Massin,
and M. Rivgauche. 38:28-33,
Nov '65.

HOMOSEXUAL FILMS
Notes from the underground:
"It could only happen in Cali-
fornia." D. Rader. 80:72-4,
Jl '70.

HOMOSEXUALITY IN PRISONS
  On Rikers Island.   T. Seligson.   77:45-7+, Apr '70.

HOMOSEXUALS
  Notes from the underground:
Miss All-American.   J. Nathan.
47:19-21, Je '67.
         see also
GAY LIBERATION FRONT

HOMOSEXUALS--DEMONSTRA-
    TIONS
  Notes from the underground:
the road is known.   L. Skir.
82:16-20+, Sept '70.

The HONEY lamb [poem] J.
Williams.   17:44-5, Mar/Apr
'61.

The HOODS [poem] E. Evtu-
shenko.   25:24-6, Jl/Aug '62.

HOPPER, Dennis
  Easy rider: a very American
thing [interview] L. Carson.
72:24-7+, Nov '69.

HOPPER, DENNIS - CRITICISM
    AND INTERPRETATION
         Easy rider
  Easy rider: a very American
thing: an interview with Dennis
Hopper.   L. Carson.   72:24-
7+, Nov '69.
        The last movie
  Have you seen it all, Dennis
Hopper?   L. Carson.   81:16-8,
Aug '70.

HORN, CLAYTON W.
  Horn on "Howl" L. Ferlinghetti.   4:145-58, '57.

HORN on "Howl" [essay] L.
Ferlinghetti.   4:145-58, '57.

HORN, Paula
  London portfolio [photo-
graphs] 22:49-56, Jan/Feb '62.
  [photo] 22:cover, Jan/Feb '62;

24:108, 110, May/Je '62.

HOROVITZ, Michael
  Direct communication (poet
to secretary) [poem] 40:49,
Apr '66.
  For modern man (1914-1964,
RIP) [poem] 38:26-7, Nov '65.
  Heimische cookin' [poem]
52:39-40, Mar '68.

HORSES don't write songs
[essay] J. Hendricks.   64:61-2,
Mar '69.

HOSKIN
  [cartoon] 76:78, Mar '70.

HOSOE, Eikoh
  Portfolio [of photographs]
35:38-42, Mar '65.

HOTEL Park (East 110 St.)
[poem] F. Lima.   27:32-33,
Nov/Dec '62.

HOUSES like angels [poem] J.
Borges.   29:57, Mar/Apr '63.

HOVING, THOMAS P. F.
  Hoving, go go medievalist.
R. Gustaitis.   43:72-9, Oct '66.

HOW the war ended in Vietnam
[satire] F. Rayfield.   49:25-7+,
Oct '67.

HOW to proceed in the arts; a
detailed study of the creative
act [essay] L. Rivers and F.
O'Hara.   19:97-101, Jl/Aug '61.

HOW try finish book crazy
N. Y. eight years too fucking
impossible but: 10 tracks from
a record [journal excerpt] S.
Krim.   75:27-9+, Feb '70.

HOWARD, Kenneth
  Bolivian burlesque [essay]
62:59-61, Jan '69.
  Ten days in July [essay]

59:33-5+, Oct '68.

HOWARD, Richard
Letter from Paris [essay] 8:
171-4, spring '59.

HOWL [poem] A. Ginsberg. 2:
137-47, '57.

HOWL
Notes written on finally recording Howl. A. Ginsberg.
10:132-5, Nov/Dec '59.

HUBBELL, Lindley Williams
(Hayashi Shuseki)
Good morning [poem] 26:37,
Sept/Oct '62.
The great Buddha at Kama-
kura [poem] 26:36-7, Sept/Oct
'62.

HUBERT Humphrey: lesser
evilism in 1972 [essay] J. Newfield. 60:42-5, Nov '68.

HUBERT Selby: symbolic intent
or ideological resistance (or
cocksucking and revolution) S.
Yurick. 71:49-51+, Oct '69.

HUFFAKER
[cartoon] 66:43, May '69.

HUFFAKER, Sandy
[illus] 60:42, Nov '68.

HUFFMAN, Tom
[illus] 47:68, Je '67; 73:55,
Dec '69.

HUIDOBRO, Vincente
She [poem] 20:99, Sept/Oct
'61.

HUMAN poems [book excerpt]
C. Vallejo. 55:23-5, Je '68.

HUMAN Universe [essay] C.
Olson. 5:88-102, summer '58.

HUMANAE VITAE

An open letter to Paul VI on
the pill. E. Arsan. 69:21-3+,
Aug '69.

HUMOR
The language of laughter. J.
Lahr. 57:26-9+, Aug '68.

HUMPHREY, HUBERT
Hubert Humphrey: lesser
evilism in 1972. J. Newfield.
60:42-5, Nov '68.

A HUNDRED flowers of the
same kind [essay] K. Karol.
45:42-5, Feb '67.

HUNGARY--REVOLUTION, 1956
After Budapest [interview
with Jean-Paul Sartre] 1:5-23,
'57.

A HUNGRY mental lion [review]
S. Krim. 11:178-85, Jan/Feb
'60.

HUNTER, Robert
Erebus [novel excerpt] 67:
23-5+, Je '69.

HUNTLEY, Timothy Wade
Bum [story] 68:67-8, Jl '69.

HURRAH for freedom. [story]
J. Lind. 33:34-7+, Aug/Sept
'64.

HYMN to St. Bridget's steeple
[poem] B. Berkson and F.
O'Hara. 24:107, May/Je '62.

HYPERACTIVE CHILDREN
see
DRUG USE IN EDUCATION

- I -

I don't want to die [poem] B.
Vain. 36:50-1, Je '65.

I heard Evtushenko [poem] H.
Norse. 31:62-71, Oct/Nov '63.

I never raped one either, but I try not to let it bother me [story] C. Brown. 78:47-9+, May '70.

I saw him [poem] E. Evtushenko. 24:22-3, Jl/Aug '62.

I see America daily (an oral collage) [poem] H. Norse. 37:30-1, Sept '65.

I was arrested with Debray [essay] G. Roth. 51:44-7+, Feb '68.

I was curious [diary excerpt] V. Sjoman. 56:18-21+, Jl '68.

I write therefore I am [essay] J. Fowles. 33:16-7+, Aug/Sept '64.

ICE-CREAM CONES
   Solving the ice-cream cone problem. H. Selby. 57:56-8, Aug '68.

ICEFLOE [poem] B. Pasternak. 8:37, spring '59.

The IDEA of the New Left [essay] C. Oglesby. 63:52-4+, Feb '69.

An IDIOMATIC tale [story] R. Daumal. 13:126, May/Je '60.

ILLIERS, FRANCE
   The sources of the Loir at Illiers. M. Proust. 19:55-62, Jl/Aug '61.

I'M not complaining [story] M. Thomas. 30:64-9, May/Je '63.

IMAGINATION dead imagine [essay] S. Beckett. 39:48-9, Feb '66.

The IMPACT of surrealism on the New York School [essay and reproductions] J. Myers. 12:75-

85, Mar/Apr '60.

The IMPALPABILITIES [poem] C. Tomlinson. 14:95, Sept/Oct '60.

The IMPORTANCE of a wall: galleries [essay] K. Sawyer. 8:122-35, spring '59.

IMPRESSIONS of Cuba [essay] M. Randall. 49:20-1+, Oct '67.

IN America, the seasons [poem] B. Guest. 3:115, '57.

IN memory of Jack Kerouac [reminiscence] D. Amram. 74:41+, Jan '70.

IN memory of my feelings [poem] F. O'Hara. 6:18-23, autumn '58.

IN San Francisco [poem] C. Plymell. 64:41-3, Jan '69.

IN search of a new mythology [essay] J. Lahr. 62:55-8+, Jan '69.

IN the afternoons [story] M. Mason. 28:101-6, Jan/Feb '63.

IN the comics [poem] L. Kandel. 48:26-7, Aug '67.

IN the egg [poem] G. Grass. 32:68, Apr/May '64.

IN this country of ours [essay] H. Böll. 21:102-9, Nov/Dec '61.

IN town [poem] G. Madonia. 69:57, Aug '69.

INDIA--FOREIGN POLICY
   The continuing position of India; a special statement on India's foreign policy by its permanent delegate to the United

Nations. A. Lall. 7:14-21+,
winter '59.

INDIANS
                see
AMERICAN INDIANS

INEXCUSABLE thoughts: from
the editors. 35:8-9, Mar '65.

INNKEEPING
                see
HOLIDAY INN UNIVERSITY

INSTANT jazz [essay] M.
Williams. 8:164-70, spring '59.

INTERNATIONAL DRAMA CON-
    FERENCE, Edinburgh
Edinburgh happening. J.
Gelber. 31:54-61, Oct/Nov '63.

INTERNATIONAL EXPERIMENTAL
    FILM FESTIVAL, Brussels
The angry young film makers.
A. Vogel. 6:163-83, autumn '58.

INTERNATIONAL SOCIETY FOR
    KRISHNA CONSCIOUSNESS
Notes from the underground:
International Society for Krishna
Consciousness. J. Nathan. 45:
7-16, Feb '67.

INTERRACIAL MARRIAGE
White woman-Black man. J.
Lester. 70:21-3+, Sept '69.
_____(part II) J.
Lester. 71:29-32+, Oct '69.

INTERVIEW with Andrei Voznesensky. E. Sutherland. 28:
37-42, Jan/Feb '63.

An INTERVIEW with Eugene
Ionesco. F. de Towarnicki.
85:49-51+, Dec '70.

An INTERVIEW with Jaromil
Jires. A. Liehm. 76:31-3,
Mar '70.

INTERVIEW with Juan Soriano.
E. Poniatowska. 7:141-52,
winter '59.

An INTERVIEW with Roman
Polanski. M. Delahaye and J.
Narboni. 66:27-9+, May '69.

INTRODUCTION to Naked lunch,
The soft machine, Novia express [essay] W. Burroughs.
22:99-102, Jan/Feb '62.

The INVASION (L'Invasion)
[poem] P. Reverdy. 11:24,
Jan/Feb '60.

INVOCATION and clowns; dance
of the bareback riders. [poem]
L. Kandel. 41:48, Je '66.

IONESCO, Eugène
Foursome [play] 13:46-53,
May/Je '60.
Fragments of a journal. 59:
24-6+, Oct '68.
Frenzy for two [play] 36:31-
9+, Je '65.
An interview with Eugene
Ionesco. F. de Towarnicki.
85:49-51+, Dec '70.
The motor show [play] 32:
64-6, Apr/May '64.
The photograph of the colonel
[story] 3:117-31, '57.
Present past, past present
[excerpts from his memoir] 85:
53-5+, Dec '70.
Slime [story] 41:22-7+, Je
'66.
There is no avant-garde
theater [essay] 4:101-5, '57.
A victim of duty [story] 29:
21-6, Mar/Apr '63.

IONESCO, EUGENE
(photograph of) 13:46, May/
Je '60; 59:24, Oct '68; 85:48,
51, 52, Dec '70.

ISHIKAWA, Masamochi
                see

YADOYA, No Meshimori [pseud]

ISRAEL
        see
JERUSALEM

ISRAELI-ARAB WAR, 1967-
    The fall of Jerusalem. A.
Schleifer. 50:26-9+, Dec '67.
    Peace is a duty in the Near
East as in Vietnam. P. Men-
dès-France. 56:47-8, Jl '68.
        see also
JEWISH-ARAB RELATIONS

IT begins in the wind [novel
excerpt from the novel City of
Night] J. Rechy. 24:33-4,
May/Je '62.

"IT could only happen in California" [review essay] D.
Rader. 80:72-4, Jl '70.

...IT droppeth as the gentle
rain (a ballet) [story] J. Prévert. 13:64-6, May/Je '60.

ITALLIE, Jean Claude van
        see
VAN ITALLIE, Jean Claude

The ITCHY tooth [story] J.
Shuffler. 53:60-3, Apr '68.

IT'S called the blues [poem]
H. Krohn. 52:87, Mar '68.

IT'S evening when you return
[poem] G. Harding. 70:44-5,
Sept '69.

IVANOV, S.
    [illus] 46:cover, Apr '67.

- J -

JACK Armstrong in Tangier
[story] W. Eastlake. 42:24-7+,
Aug '66.

JACKRALL, Thomas L.

    Henry [poem] 17:96, Mar/
Apr '61.
    Power failure [poem] 17:93,
Mar/Apr '61.
    Stretch to health [poem] 17:
94-5, Mar/Apr '61.

JACKSON Pollock [essay] C.
Greenberg. 3:95-6, '57.

JACKSON, Richard
    Pass [poem] 74:56, Jan '70.

JAHN, Janheinz
    On their own feet [story]
20:72-88, Sept/Oct '61.

JAMES, Jud
    Notes from the underground:
H. Rap Brown [essay] 57:16-
7+, Aug '68.

JAMIESON, Douglas
    [illus] 80:27-8, Jl '70.

JANAH, Sunil
    [photo] 9:cover, summer '59.

JANCSÓ, MIKLÓS
    The corruption of power: an
interview with Miklós Jancsó.
J. Comolli and M. Delahaye.
70:47-9+, Sept '69.
    (photograph of) 70:46, Sept
'69.

JAPAN
        see
KYOTO

JAPAN--CULTURE
    Aspects of Japanese culture.
D. Suzuki. 6:40-52, autumn
'58.

JAPAN--RELIGION
        see
ZEN BUDDHISM

JAPANESE LITERATURE
    Tradition and the machine.
T. Fitzsimmons and R. Fukuda.

38:86-94, Nov '65.

JARRY, Alfred
Exploits and opinions of
Doctor Faustroll, Pataphysician
[story excerpts] 13:128-38,
May/Je '60.
[illus] 13:86, 94, 174.
May/Je '60.
The man with the axe [poem]
13:146, May/Je '60.
Poem. 13:146-7, May/Je '60.
The royal toilet [poem] 13:
147, May/Je '60.
Ubu Cocu (Act I) [play] 13:
139-45, May/Je '60.

JARRY, ALFRED
(photograph of) 13:127,
May/Je '60.

JASPERS, Karl
The atom bomb and the future
of man [essay] 5:37-57, summer
'58.

The JAZZ avant garde: who's
in charge here? [essay] M.
Williams. 41:64-8, Je '66.

"JAZZ on a summer's day"
[review essay] J. Tallmer. 14:
126-33, Sept/Oct '60.

JAZZ
Funk for sale. M. Williams.
10:136-40, Nov/Dec '59.
Instant jazz. M. Williams.
8:164-70, spring '59.
The jazz avant garde: who's
in charge here? M. Williams.
41:64-8, Je' 66.
New Orleans beginnings [and]
Jazz on the river. B. Dodds.
1:110-48, '57.
Rehearsal diary. M. Williams.
31:115-27, Oct/Nov '63.
San Francisco jazz scene.
R. Gleason. 2:59-64, '57.
Talking with myself (with
limited apologies to Edmund
Wilson) M. Williams. 33:83-

5, Aug/Sept '64.
Third stream problems. M.
Williams. 30:113-25, May/Je
'63.

JAZZ--BANDS, ORCHESTRAS,
ETC.
Count Basie: style beyond
swing. M. Williams. 38:62-5,
Nov '65.
John Lewis and the Modern
Jazz Quartet. M. Williams.
23:112-25, Mar/Apr '62.
The Oliver band. B. Dodds.
4:80-100, '57.

JAZZ COMPOSERS
see
SCHIFFRIN, Lalo
SCHULLER, Gunther

JAZZ MUSICIANS
see
ARMSTRONG, Louis
BASIE, William ("Count")
BIEDERBECKE, Bix
BOLDEN, Buddy
COLEMAN, Ornette
COLLINS, Lee
COLTRANE, John
DAVIS, Miles
DESMOND, Paul
DODDS, "Baby"
ELLINGTON, Duke
GUIFFRE, Jimmy
HAWKINS, Coleman
KONITZ, Lee
LEWIS, John
MONK, Thelonious
MORTON, "Jelly Roll"
MULLIGAN, Gerry
OLIVER, Joe ("King")
PARKER, Charlie
PETERSON, Oscar
ROLLINS, Sonny
RUSSELL, Pee Wee
SILVER, Horace
SOLAL, Martial
STERN, Bert
STITT, Sonny
TAYLOR, Cecil
YOUNG, Lester

JAZZ OPERAS
see
SCHULLER, GUNTHER - CRIT-
ICISM AND INTERPRETATION
The visitation

JAZZ SINGERS
see
HOLIDAY, Billie
McRAE, Carmen
RUSHING, Jimmy
VAUGHAN, Sarah
WILLIAMS, Joe Lee

JEAN Genet and the Black
Panthers [interview] M.
Manceaux. 82:35-7+, Sept '70.

JEFFERIS, G. and J. L.
Nichols
Light on dark corners [book
excerpt] 52:73-7, Mar '68.

JEFFERY
[cartoon] 55:69, Je '68.

JELLY roll Morton: three-
minute form [review essay] M.
Williams. 12:114-20, Mar/
Apr '60.

JENKYNS, Chris
[illus] 8:cover, spring '59.

JERUSALEM
Leo in Jerusalem--I. L.
Skir. 64:19-23+, Mar '69.

JESSE had a wife [story] J.
Schultz. 52:79-82. Mar '68.

JEWISH-ARAB RELATIONS
Al Fatah speaks: a conversation with "Abu Amar" [inter-
view] A. Schleifer. 56:44-6+,
Jl '68.

JIMI Hendrix: goin' toward
heaven [essay] J. Lester. 85:
18-9+, Dec '70.

JIMMY Rushing's story as told

to Frank Driggs. 40:64-9,
Apr '66.

JIMMY'S home [story] B. Price.
77:23-4, Apr '70.

JIRES, Jaromil
An interview with Jaromil
Jires. A. Liehm. 76:31-3,
Mar '70.

JIRES, JAROMIL - CRITICISM
AND INTERPRETATION
The joke
The joke. N. Hentoff. 76:
29+, Mar '70.

JOHN Lewis and the Modern
Jazz Quartet [review essay]
M. Williams. 23:112-25,
Mar/Apr '62.

"JOHNNY 23" [story] W. Burroughs. 52:26-7, Mar '68.

JOHNS, Jasper
[painting] 12:80, Mar/Apr
'60.

JOHNSON, Guy
[illus] 50:44, Dec '67.

JOHNSON, LYNDON BAINES
Quotations from chairman
LBJ [satire] J. Shepherd and
C. Wren. 51:27-9, Feb '68.

JOHNSON, Paul
Porky [story] 6:24-39,
autumn '58.

JOHNSON, Uwe
Berlin, border of the di-
vided world [essay] 21:18-30,
Nov/Dec '61.
The third book about Achim
[novel excerpt] 29:77-84, Mar/
Apr '63.
Speculations about Jakob
[novel excerpt] 21:31-4, Nov/
Dec '61.

JOHNSON, UWE - CRITICISM
AND INTERPRETATION
Letter from Germany. W.
Höllerer. 15:135-6, Nov/Dec
'60.

The JOKE [review essay] N.
Hentoff. 76:29+, Mar '70.

JOMO [poem] J. Stowers. 65:
26, Apr '69.

JON
[cartoon] 56:17, Jl '68; 60:
20, Nov '68; 62:70, Jan '69;
63:77, Feb '69; 64:26, Mar '69;
65:67, 68, Apr '69; 66:80, May
'69; 67:79, 85, Je '69; 68:73,
Jl '69; 69:61, Aug '69; 70:22,
Sept '69; 71:55, 72, Oct '69;
75:80, Feb '70; 77:21, 79, Apr
'70; 78:73, 77, 87, May '70;
79:75, Je '70; 80:61, 70, Jl
'70; 81:73, Aug '70; 82:72,
Sept '70; 83:60, Oct '70; 84:60,
70, Nov '70; 85:66, Dec '70.
[illus] 80:54, Jl '70.

JONES, JAMES - CRITICISM
AND INTERPRETATION
Notes from the underground:
Maverick head-kick. S. Krim.
48:19-20, Aug '67.

JONES, LeRoi
Black Dada nihilismus [poem]
29:85-7, Mar/Apr '63.
The black man is making
new gods [poem] 50:49, Dec '67.
Black people! [poem] 50:49,
Dec '67.
The bridge [poem] 12:59-60,
Mar/Apr '60.
Cuba libre [essay] 15:139-
59, Nov/Dec '60.
The death of Horatio Alger
[story] 36:28-9+, Je '65.
Going down slow [story] 43:
41-3+, Oct '66.
Letter [on J. Kerouac's Es-
sentials of spontaneous prose]
8:253-4, spring '59.

The new sheriff [poem] 19:
96, Jl/Aug '61.
"They think you're an airplane and you're really a bird
[interview] 50:51-3+, Dec '67.
Three poems: leroy; Black
people!; The black man is
making new gods. 50:48-9,
Dec '67.

JONES, LEROI - CRITICISM
AND INTERPRETATION
About LeRoi Jones. C.
Brown. 75:65-70, Feb '70.

JONES, LEROI
(drawing of) 75:64, Feb '70.
(photograph of) 50:50, Dec
'67.

JONES, Roy
Campus drug raid [poem]
58:56-7, Sept '68.

JONVEL, Jean François
Portfolio of photographs. 75:
35-41, Feb '70.

JORDAN, June
Black studies: bringing back
the person [essay] 71:39-41+,
Oct '69.

JOTTINGS on pianists [essay]
M. Williams. 29:120-7, Mar/
Apr '63.

JOU pu tuan; a seventeenth
century erotic moral novel
[excerpt] Li Yü. 29:58-74,
Mar/Apr '63.

JOURNAL of a painter in
Ethiopia [essay] Corneille. 10:
56-67, Nov/Dec '59.

JOURNALISM
Behold the new journalism--
it's coming after you! N.
Hentoff. 56:49-51, Jl '68.
The newspaper as literature.
Literature as leadership. S.

Krim. 48:31-2+, Aug '67.
see also
NEWSPAPERS
NEWSPAPERS--U. S.
UNDERGROUND PRESS
THE VILLAGE VOICE

JOURNEY through time-space:
an interview with William S.
Burroughs. D. Odier. 67:39-
41+, Je '69.

JUAN Pérez Jolote, part I
[narrative] R. Pozas Arciniega.
7:91-104, winter '59.

JUAREZ, MEXICO
El Paso del Norte. J. Rechy.
6:127-40, autumn '58.

JULES Feiffer: satire as sub-
version [essay] J. Lahr. 63: .
33-4+, Feb '69.

JULIAN the Apostate
Calculation; English version
by Willis Barnstone [poem] 25:
91, Jl/Aug '62.

JULIEN Torma, author by
neglect [essay] L. Barnier. 13:
118-9, May/Je '60.

JUSTINE [novel excerpt] M. de
Sade. 36:57-60+, Je '65.

JUVA
Monsieur Juva's flint statues.
J. Dubuffet. 13:73-8, May/Je
'60. K. E. D.
[cartoon] 60:53, Nov '68.

- K -

A KABUKI play [play] Kan-
jincho. 14:28-57, Sept/Oct '60.

KAFKA Jones, the singing fool!
[review essay] 50:61-4, Dec '67.

KAJAN, Tibor
[cartoon] 65:81, Apr '69.

KAMA SUTRA
Eleven pieces of sculpture
depicting themes from the Kama
Sutra [portfolio of photographs]
R. Boise 36:between pages 64
and 65, Je '65.

KAMENEV, Nicolai Nicolaie-
vitch
Report to the corps of pro-
veditors on some concrete historical problems concerning
pataphysical activity posed by
the fiftieth anniversary of the
death of Jarry. [satirical es-
say] 13:181-5, May/Je '60.

KANAREK, Michael
[illus] 85:56-9, Dec '70.

KANDEL, Lenore
Blues for Sister Sally [poem]
45:46-7, Feb '67.
Circus [collection of poems]
41:46-9, Je '66.
Freak show and finale
[poem] 41:49, Je '66.
In the comics [poem] 48:26-
7, Aug '67.
Invocation and clowns; dance
of the bareback riders [poem]
41:48, Je '66.
Love in the middle of the
air [poem] 41:47, Je '66.
Poem. 31:53, Oct/Nov '63.
Poem for perverts. 35:20-1,
Mar '65.
Seven of velvet [poem] 75:
49, Feb '70.
Spring '61 [poem] 32:78,
Apr/May '64.

KANE, CHEIKH HAMIDOU -
CRITICISM AND INTERPRE-
TATION
Ambiguous adventure
From the third eye... Two
steps toward humanity. A.
Vogel. 77:88-9, Apr '70.

KANE, John
[cartoon] 58:77, Sept '68.

KANGIN SHU
Some 16th century Japanese
love songs; from the Kanginshu
(translated by Bruce Watson)
27:108-9, Nov/Dec '62.

KANJINCHO
A Kabuki play.   14:28-57,
Sept/Oct '60.

KANZAN
see
HAN-SHAN

KAPLAN, Ervin L.
[cartoon] 39:74, 75, Feb '66.

KARLIN, Eugene
[illus] 46:36-7, Apr '67.

KAROL, K. S.
Four days with Fidel [essay]
51:51-2+, Feb '68.
A hundred flowers of the
same kind [essay] 45:42-5,
Feb '67.

KARP, Ivan C.
Looking for money [auto-
biographical essay] 8:42-55,
spring '59.

KASPAR is dead [poem] H.
Arp. 21:35, Nov/Dec '61.

KATZ, Alex
[illus] 25:27-39, Jl/Aug '62.

KAYE, Anthony
Molly's suggestion [story]
12:56-8, Mar/Apr '60.

KEATON, BUSTER
(photograph of) 81:36, Aug '70.

KEEPING ecology alive [essay]
N. Hentoff. 77:31-2+, Apr '70.

KEMAL, Yasar
The baby [story] 14:96-124,
Sept/Oct '60.

KEMP, Lysander
Fly away, little dove [essay]
7:190-213, winter '59.
Notes on Eskimo literature
[essay] 33:72-3, Aug/Sept '64.

KENNEDY, JOHN F., Assassination of
Why President Kennedy was
killed. P. Flammonde. 62:41-
2+, Jan '69.

KENNEDY, JOHN F.
(photograph of) 20:cover,
Sept/Oct '61.

KENNEDY, ROBERT, Assassi-
nation of
The day of the locust.   J.
Newfield. 67:29-33+, Je '69.

KENNEDY, ROBERT
(photograph of) D. Gordon.
67:28, Je '69.

KENWORTHY, Stephen
Love story [poem] 30:70-1,
May/Je '63.

KERENSKY, ALEXANDER
The Kerensky complex. R.
Elman. 39:44-7+, Feb '66.

KEROUAC, Jack
Belief and technique for
modern prose [essay] 8:57,
spring '59.
Essentials of spontaneous
prose [essay] 5:72-3, summer
'58.
The murder of Swinburne
[excerpt from the novel Vanity
of Duluoz] 51:61-3+, Feb '68.
October in the railroad earth
[story] 2:119-36, '57.
Old angel midnight--2 [story]
33:68-71+, Aug/Sept '64.
On the road to Florida
[story] 74:43-7+, Jan '70.
The railroad earth (conclu-
sion) [story] 11:37-59, Jan/Feb
'60.

Satori in Paris: 1 [essay] 39:17-21+, Feb '66.

———————————: 2 [essay] 40:56-9+, Apr '66.

———————————: 3 [essay] 41:50-3+, Je '66.

Seattle burlesque [story] 4: 106-12, '57.

Written address to the Italian judge [essay] 31:108-10, Oct/ Nov '63.

KEROUAC, JACK
In memory of Jack Kerouac. D. Amram. 74:41+, Jan '70.
(photograph of) 74:40, Jan '70.

KEROUAC, JACK - CRITICISM AND INTERPRETATION
Kerouac's sound. W. Tallman. 11:153-69, Jan/Feb '60.
Essentials of spontaneous prose
Letter. L. Jones. 8:253-4, spring '59.

KEROUAC'S sound [essay] W. Tallman. 11:153-69, Jan/Feb '60.

KESTING, Marianne
Brecht's last years [essay] 21:56-67, Nov/Dec '61.

KILL anything that moves [excerpt from The Pursuit of Loneliness] P. Slater. 79:55-7+, Je '70.

The KILLER [story] N. Mailer. 32:26-7+, Apr/May '64.

KING, ALLAN - CRITICISM AND INTERPRETATION
Warrendale
The tyranny of Warrendale. P. Tyler. 69:31-3+, Aug '69.

KING, Franklin M.
From the Petrograd journal-- 1917 [poem] 29:117-8, Mar/Apr '63.

KING Lear or Endgame [essay] J. Kott. 33:52-65, Aug/Sept '64.

KING, MARTIN LUTHER
Discarding the dream. R. Terrell. 78:35-7+, May '70.
The Martin Luther King I remember. J. Lester. 74:16-21+, Jan '70.
(photograph of) 74:17, Jan '70.

KING Oliver
see
OLIVER, Joe

The KING'S X [story] F. Salas. 48:42-5+, Aug '67.

KIRSTEL, Richard
Pas de deux [portfolio of photographs] 70:33-39, Sept '69.

The KISS of death [poem] M. O'Donoghue. 73:33-8, Dec '69.

KLEIN, William
Mister Freedom: an interview with William Klein. A. Segal. 77:49-50, Apr '70.

KLIBAN, B.
[cartoon] 51:75, 88, 97, 118, Feb '68; 52:43, 81, 84, 90, Mar '68; 53:78, 81, 90, Apr '68; 54:91, May '68; 55:67, 79, 86, Je '68; 57:58, 78, 89, Aug '68; 58:68, 71, Sept '68; 59:66, 68, Oct '68; 60:56, 68, Nov '68; 62:74, Jan, '69; 63:79, 80, 85, Feb '69; 64:55, 58, Mar '69; 65:59, 74, 78, Apr '69; 67:58, 82, Je '69; 68:68, 70, 83, Jl '69; 69:65, Aug '69; 72: 32, 59, Nov '69; 77:47, 58, Apr '70; 79:33, 70, 89, Je '70; 80: 41, 65, 72, Jl '70; 81:54, 67, Aug '70; 82:57, Sept '70; 83: 63, Oct '70; 84:65, Nov '70; 85:61, Dec '70.

KLINE, Franz
    Franz Kline talking [dialogue]
F. O'Hara. 6:58-64, autumn '58.
    Three paintings 6:66-8, au-
tumn '58.

KLINE, FRANZ
    (photograph of) 6:65, autumn
'58.

KLOSSOWSKI, Pierre
    Roberte ce soir [novel ex-
cerpt] 27:76-86, Nov/Dec '62.

KNOCK on wood [story] S.
Salvon. 9:25-33, summer '59.

KNOX, Hugh
    Up again [poem] 73:27,
Dec '69.

KOCH, Kenneth
    Bertha [play] 15:42-5, Nov/
Dec '60.
    Desire for spring [poem] 5:
104, summer '58.
    St. -John Perse's new poem
[review] 7:216-19, winter '59.

KOCH, KENNETH - CRITICISM
    AND INTERPRETATION
        Permanently
Poets and painters in collab-
oration. F. Porter. 20:121-6,
Sept/Oct '61.

KOLAKOWSKI, Leszek
    What is the left today?
[essay] 47:30-2+, Je '67.

KONARAK (temple)
    The great delight. M. Anand.
9:172-97, summer '59.

KONITZ, LEE - CRITICISM
    AND INTERPRETATION
    The achievement of Lee
Konitz. H. Pekar. 43:30-2,
Oct '66.

KONITZ, LEE
    (photograph of) 43:30, Oct '66.

KOOSER, Ted
    Poem. 72:62, Nov '69.

KOPIT, ARTHUR - CRITICISM
    AND INTERPRETATION
        Indians
Arthur Kopit's "Indians":
dramatizing national amnesia.
J. Lahr. 71:19-21+, Oct '69.

KOTT, Jan
    King Lear or Endgame
[essay] 33:52-65, Aug/Sept '64.
    A little treatise on dying
[essay] 48:61-3, Aug '67.
    A little treatise on erotics
[essay] 43:54-5, Oct '66.
    The two paradoxes of Othello
[essay] 40:15-21+, Apr '66.

KOUTA
            see
KANGIN SHU

KRAFT, Lee
    [photo] 68:cover, Jl '69.

KRAHN, Fernando
    [cartoon] 57:65, Aug '68;
60:25, 49, Nov '68; 63:31, Feb
'69; 65:76, Apr '69; 66:77,
May '69.

KRAL Majales [poem] A. Ginsberg. 40:22-3, Apr '66.

KRAPP'S last tape [play] S.
Beckett. 5:13-24, summer '58.

KRAUSS, Lester L.
    [photo] 41:40, Je '66.

KRIM, Seymour
    Epitaph for a Canadian kike
[reminiscence] 77:66-73, Apr
'70.
    For Ray Bremser [poem] 49:
21, Oct '67.
    Head kick [essay] 48:19-20,
Aug '67.
    The holy barbarians [review]
9:208-14, summer '59.

How try finish book crazy
N. Y. eight years too fucking
impossible but: 10 tracks from
a record [journal excerpt] 75:
27-9+, Feb '70.

A hungry mental lion [review]
11:178-85, Jan/Feb '60.

The newspaper as literature.
Literature as leadership [essay]
48:31-2+, Aug '67.

Notes from the underground:
Maverick head-kick [essay] 48:
19-20, Aug '67.

An open letter to Norman
Mailer [essay] 45:89-96, Feb
'67.

Should I assume America is
already dead? [essay] 68:19-
21+, Jl '69.

KRIM, SEYMOUR - CRITICISM
  AND INTERPRETATION
Shake it for the world, smartass
  From one smartass to
another.   J. Holmes. 80:75-9,
Jl '70.

KRISTOFORI
  [cartoon] 45:72, 83, 96, 104,
Feb '67; 46:22, Apr '67; 47:84,
88, 94, 104, Je '67; 48:21, 66,
90, Aug '67; 50:87, 95, Dec
'67; 51:108, Feb '68; 52:92,
Mar '68; 53:69, Apr '68; 54:
62, 69, 71, May '68; 55:19, 76,
Je '68; 56:85, 88, Jl '68; 57:54,
61, Aug '68; 58:72, Sept '68;
59:78, Oct '68; 60:39, 68, 70,
Nov '68; 62:53, 63, 77, 80,
Jan '69; 63:82, Feb '69; 64:68,
Mar '69; 65:19, Apr '69; 66:75,
May '69; 67:80, Je '69; 68:80,
Jl '69; 74:70, Jan '70; 76:61,
Mar '70.

KROHN, Herbert
  It's called the blues [poem]
52:87, Mar '68.

KUHL, Jerome
  [illus] 32:64, Apr/May '64;
33:42, Aug/Sept '64.

KUNITZ, Stanley
  Poems recorded by Richard
Wilbur [review] 8:201-2, spring
'59.

KUPFERBERG, Tuli
  101 ways to make love
[satire] 63:36-41, Feb '69.

KYOTO, Japan
  Letter from Kyoto. G.
Synder. 3:132-4, '57.

- L -

LABARTHE, André S.
  A way of life: an interview
with John Cassavetes. 64:45-7,
Mar '69.

The LADDER of success [car-
toon] A. Sens. 22:86-7, Jan/
Feb '62.

LA Dene and the Minotaur
[story] C. Arnett. 27:18-29,
Nov/Dec '62.

LADY CHATTERLEY'S LOVER
  Opinion: U. S. District Court
...New York... [for the plain-
tiffs] Grove Press, Inc. and
Readers' Subscription, Inc....
F. Bryan. 9:37-68, summer
'59.

LADY Ferrari [essay] J. -F.
Held. 57:66-9, Aug '68.

LADY Overboard [poem] D.
Lyttle. 5:105, summer '58.

LAFFERTY, Thom
  [photo] 62:cover, Jan '69;
63:55-61, Feb '69; 70:20, Sept
'69; 71:28-9, Oct '69; 73:52,
Dec '69; 77:44, Apr '70; 82:
30, Sept '70.
                see also
O'DONOGHUE, Michael and T.
  Lafferty

LAHR, BERT - CRITICISM AND
INTERPRETATION
The fall and rise of Beckett's
bum: Bert Lahr in Godot. J.
Lahr. 70:29-32+, Sept '69.

LAHR, BERT
(photograph of) 81:34, Aug
'70.

LAHR, John
The adaptable Mr. Albee.
[essay] 54:36-9+, May '68.
The American musical: the
slavery of escape [essay] 58:
22-5+, Sept '68.
Arthur Kopit's "Indians":
dramatizing national amnesia
[essay] 71:19-21+, Oct '69.
Artist of the outrageous [re-
view essay] 75:31-4+, Feb '70.
The arts and business. [essay]
68:63-5+, Jl '69.
Black theatre: the American
tragic voice [essay] 69:55-63,
Aug '69.
Broadway comedy: images of
impotence [review essay] 78:
39-40+, May '70.
Decades of dream-walking
[essay] 74:37-9+, Jan '70.
The end of the underground
[essay] 65:45-8+, Apr '69.
The fall and rise of Beckett's
bum: Bert Lahr in Godot [essay]
70:29-32+, Sept '69.
In search of a new mythology
[essay] 62:55-8+, Jan '69.
Jules Feiffer: satire as sub-
version. [essay] 63:33-4+, Feb
'69.
The language of laughter
[essay] 57:26-9+, Aug '68.
The language of silence [es-
say] 64:53-5+, Mar '69.
Mystery on stage [essay] 73:
53-7, Dec '69.
The new theater: a retreat
from realism [essay] 60:54-7+,
Nov '68.
The Open Theatre: beyond
the absurd [essay] 66:63-8, May '69.

Pinter the spaceman [essay]
55:49-52+, Je '68.
Playing with Alice [review
essay] 82:59-64, Sept '70.
Putting Shakespeare in a new
environment [review essay] 76:
63-8, Mar '70.
Sex and politics: an interview with Vilgat Sjöman. 56:
22-6+, Jl '68.
The silent theater of Richard
Avedon [essay] 81:34+, Aug '70.
Slawomir Mrozek: the mask
of irony. [essay] 67:53-5+, Je
'69.
Spectacles of disintegration
[review essay] 79:31-3+, Je '70.
The street scene: playing for
keeps [essay] 59:48-51+, Oct
'68.
Theater and propaganda
[essay] 52:33-7, Mar '68.
The theatre of sports [essay]
72:39-41+, Nov '69.
The theater's voluptuary itch
[essay] 56:32-4+, Jl '68.
"We want to be humane, but
we're only human" [review
essay] 53:36-40+, Apr '68.

LALL, Anand
The continuing position of
India; a special statement on
India's foreign policy by its
permanent delegate to the United
Nations [essay] 7:14-21+, winter
'59.
The snake [story] 22:93-8,
Jan/Feb '62.

LAMANTIA, Philip
Still poem 9 [poem] 11:100,
Jan/Feb '60.

LAMBERT, Spencer
The spider and the fly [story]
54:32-5+, May '68.

LAMENT of the 12th of July
1961 [poem] A. Hollo. 22:88,
Jan/Feb '62.

The LANDLORD [story] L. Myers. 44:56-60, Dec '66.

LANDSCAPE [play] H. Pinter. 68:55-61, Jl '69.

LANDSCAPE GARDENING
see
KYOANJI GARDEN

LANDSCAPE with torrent [poem] J. Merrill. 8:96, spring '59.

LANG, DANIEL - CRITICISM AND INTERPRETATION
Casualties of war
From the third eye... Two steps toward humanity. A. Vogel. 77:88-9, Apr '70.

LANGUAGE AND ART
The language of silence. J. Lahr. 64:53-5+, Mar '69.

The LANGUAGE of laughter [essay] J. Lahr. 57:26-9+, Aug '68.

The LANGUAGE of silence [essay] J. Lahr. 64:53-5+, Mar '69.

LARCHER, David
Portfolio of photographs. 54:49-56, May '68.

LARNER, Jeremy
The addict in the street: Hector Rodriguez [essay] 35:11-5, Mar '65.

The LAST cause [essay] J. Holmes. 44:28-32+, Dec '66.

The LAST crusade [poem] Brother Antoninus. 66:45-9, May '69.

LAST exit before the Great Society [essay] N. Hentoff. 37:59-65, Sept '65.

The LAST Frenchman in Fez [story] W. Eastlake. 50:44-6+, Dec '67.

The LAST hours of Che Guevera [essay] M. Bosquet. 51:37-8+, Feb '68.

The LAST hurrah? [essay] N. Hentoff. 81:21-3, Aug '70.

LAST night thoughts of Bobby Dylan [poem] G. Malanga. 67:64, Jan '69.

LAST performance at the Living Theatre invective [poem] J. Malina. 33:49-51, Aug/Sept '64.

The LAST stand of the dispensables [essay] N. Hentoff. 70:59-62, Sept '69.

LAST stop at La Maquina [essay] L. Martin. 79:90, Je '70.

LATIN AMERICA--FOREIGN RELATIONS--U. S.
On Latin America, the Left, and the U. S. [interview] C. Mills. 19:110-22, Jan/Feb '61.

LAUGHTER [satire] M. Schwob. 13:112-4, May/Je '60.

LAUGHTER
see
HUMOR

LAVISH are the dead [story] K. Oe. 38:17-21+, Nov '65.

The LAW is an ass (male) [essay] N. Hentoff. 84:49-51+, Nov '70.

LAWRENCE, DAVID HERBERT - CRITICISM AND INTERPRETATION
Lady Chatterley's lover

On Lady Chatterley's lover.
M. Schorer. 1:150-78, '57.

The LEAN rats on the march;
after Heinrich Heine. [poem]
A. Hollo. 31:28-30, Oct/Nov
'63.

LEARNING
see
EDUCATION OF CHILDREN

LEARY, Timothy
The magical mystery trip
[essay] 56:57-61+, Jl '68.

LEARY, TIMOTHY,
(drawing of) 56:56, Jl '68.

LEE, Bill
[cartoon] 70:64-5, Sept '69;
71:30, Oct '69; 72:60, 66, Nov
'69; 73:63, 70, Dec '69; 74:60,
74, Jan '70; 75:52, 62, 68,
Feb '70; 78:67, May '70.
[illus] 73:cover, Dec '69.

LEE, Don L.
Contradiction in essence
[poem] 53:66, Apr '68.

LEE, James
Portfolio of photographs. 58:
35-41, Sept '68.

The LEG irons [poem] Ho-Chi-
Minh. 43:44, Oct '66.

LÉGER, Alexis Saint-Léger
see
PERSE, St. John [pseud]

LEGMAN, GERSHON
The last cause. J. Holmes.
44:28-32+, Dec '66.

LEIRIS, Michel
On the use of Catholic religious prints by the practitioners of Voodoo in Haiti [essay]
13:84-94, May/Je '60.

LEIRIS, MICHEL
(photograph of) 13:84, May/
Je '60.

LENNY Bruce: 1926-66 [essay]
J. Tallmer. 44:22-3, Dec '66.

LEO in Jerusalem--I [essay]
L. Skir. 64:19-23+, Mar '69.

LEON
[cartoon] 73:66, Dec '69;
74:69, Jan '70; 84:69, Nov '70;
85:54, Dec '70.

LEÓN-Paul Fargue: explorer.
[essay] H. Bouché 13:115-6,
May/Je '60.

LEÓN-PORTILLA, Miguel
A Nahuatl concept of art
[essay] 7:157-67, winter '59.

LEPER colony (for John Lind-
bery) [poem] P. Therox 47:28-
9, Je '67.

LEROY [poem] L. Jones. 50:
48, Dec '69.

LESLIE, ALFRED - CRITICISM
AND INTERPRETATION
Permanently
Poets and painters in collab-
oration. F. Porter. 20:121-6,
Sept/Oct '61.

LESSNESS [story] S. Beckett.
80:35-6, Jl '70.

LESTER, Julius
The Black writer and the new
censorship [essay] 77:19-21+,
Apr '70.
Blacks and Jews: an inter-
view with Julius Lester. N.
Hentoff. 65:20-5+, Apr '69.
Mandabi: confronting Africa
[review essay] 78:55-8+, May
'70.
The Martin Luther King I
remember [essay] 74:16-21+,

Jan '70.

Notes from the underground: Jimi Hendrix: goin' toward heaven [essay] 85:18-9+, Dec '70.

White woman--Black man [essay] 70:21-3+, Sept '69.
_____(part II) 71:29-32+, Oct '69.

Woman--the male fantasy [essay] 82:31-3+, Sept '70.

LESTER Young: originality beyond swing [essay] M. Williams. 39:71-3, Feb '66.

LETTER from Germany [essay] W. Höllerer. 15:135-8, Nov/Dec '60.

LETTER from Havana [essay] L. Martin. 83:24 Oct '70. .

LETTER from Kyoto [essay] G. Snyder. 3:132-4, '57.

LETTER from Paris [essay] J. Barry. 26:101-9, Sept/Oct '62.

LETTER from Paris [essay] R. Howard. 8:171-4, spring '59.

LETTER on Pollock. C. Greenberg. 5:160, summer '58.

LETTER to an ex-radical [essay] J. Newfield. 62:31-2+, Jan '69.

A LETTER to his magnificence the Vice-curator Baron on the subject of the rogues that cheat us of our wars [satire] B. Vian. 13:54-61, May/Je '60.

LETTER to René Daumal. J. Torma. 13:120-1, May/Je '60.

LETTERS from Rodez. A. Artaud. 11:60-84, Jan/Feb '60.

LETTICK, Dave

[cartoon] 76:65, May '70; 79:76, Je '70; 83:66, Oct '70.

LEVERTOV, Denise
The 5-day rain [poem] 9:35, summer '59.
Scenes from the life of the peppertrees [poem] 5:86-7, summer '58.

LEVERTOV, Denise, translator
see
PAZ, O.   Salamander.

LEVIN, Arnold
[illus] 39:28, Feb '66; 42:64, Aug '66.

LEVINSON, Michael S.
Trans [poem] 74:62, Jan '70.

LEWIS, JOHN - CRITICISM AND INTERPRETATION
John Lewis and the Modern Jazz Quartet. M. Williams. 23:112-25, Mar/Apr '62.

LEWIS, JOHN
(photograph of) 23:112, Mar/Apr '62.

LEWIS, Tim
[illus] 69:34, Aug '69; 74:36, Jan '70.

LI YÜ
Jou pu tuan; a seventeenth century erotic moral novel [excerpt] 29:58-74, Mar/Apr '63.
The noble bandit [story] 23:79-92, Mar/Apr '62.

The LIBERAL book [satire] M. O'Donoghue. 84:33-9, Nov '70.

LIBERALISM
Green Beret liberalism. J. Newfield. 57:62-5, Aug '68.
see also
NEW LEFT (Politics)

The LID [story] H. Gold. 64:
39-40+, Mar '69.

LIEHM, Antonin
An interview with Jaromil
Jires. 76:31-3, Mar '70.

The LIFE line [story] C.
Fuentes. 7:75-84, winter '59.

The LIGHT is not pure [poem]
P. Neruda. 44:20-1, Dec '66.

LIGHT on dark corners [book
excerpt] G. Jefferis and J.
Nichols. 52:73-7, Mar '68.

LIKE America, beautiful and
evil [review] D. Rader. 75:
16, Feb '70.

LIKE the last two people on
the face of the earth [essay]
J. Schultz. 82:23-7+, Sept '70.

LIMA, Frank
Hotel Park (East 110 St.)
[poem] 27:32-3, Nov/Dec '62.
Pudgy [poem] 27:30-2, Nov/
Dec '62.

LIND, Jakov
Hurrah for freedom [story]
33:34-7+, Aug/Sept '64.
Ressurection [story] 28:12-
36, Jan/Feb '63.

LINDSAY, JOHN VLIET
Lindsay in New York: Act
one. J. Tallmer. 41:15-21+,
Je '66.
Lindsay: mayor at work. J.
Tallmer. 42:17-23+, Aug '66.
Lindsay vs. Lindsay. J. Tall-
mer. 43:60-4+, Oct '66.

LINYATTA
Fitting [story] 66:23-4,
May '69.

LIPPMAN, Peter
[illus] 72:48-9, Nov '69; 84:

40, Nov '70.

LIPS [poem] P. Brown. 38:25,
Nov '65.

LIPTON, LAWRENCE - CRITI-
CISM AND INTERPRETATION
The holy barbarian
The holy barbarians. S.
Krim. 9:208-14, summer '59.

LISTENING to Sonny Rollins at
the Five-Spot [poem] P. Blackburn. 48:41, Aug '67.

LITERARY CRITICISM
Against interpretation. S.
Sontag. 34:76-80+, Dec '64.

LITERATURE
see
ESKIMO LITERATURE
FICTION
OBSCENE LITERATURE
WRITING

LITERATURE and freedom
[essay] J. Chalupecký. 68:51-
4+, Jl '69.

LITERATURE AND POLITICS
Literature and freedom. J.
Chalupecký. 68:51-4+, Jl '69.
The literature of the move-
ment. J. Newfield. 46:50-3+,
Apr '67.

LITTLE home scene [poem] J.
Crews. 28:85, Jan/Feb '63.

LITTLE, Malcolm
see
MALCOLM X

A LITTLE treatise on dying
[essay] J. Kott. 48:61-3, Aug
'67.

A LITTLE treatise on erotics
[essay] J. Kott. 43:54-5,
Oct '66.

LIVING THEATRE
In search of a new mythology. J. Lahr. 62:55-8+, Jan '69.

Notes from the underground: The Living Theatre. L. Skir. 62:22-3+, Jan '69.

Notes from the underground: theater and revolution. J. Beck. 54:14-5+, May '68.

Signalling through the flames: the Living Theatre in Europe. S. Gottlieb. 45:24-32+, Feb '67.

The LOCAL stigmatic [play] H. Williams. 50:33-43, Dec '67.

LOGAN, John
On the death of the artist's mother thirty-three years later [poem] 4:75-9, '57.

Tale of a later Leander [poem] 29:18-20, Mar/Apr '63.

A trip to four or five towns [poem] 12:86-9, Mar/Apr '60.

LoGRIPPO, Robert
[illus] 77:25, Apr '70.

LOIR RIVER, FRANCE
The sources of the Loir at Illiers. M. Proust. 19:55-62, Jl/Aug '61.

LOLA in L. A. : an interview with Jacques Demy. M. Delahaye. 65:29-31+, Apr '69.

LOLITA and Justine [review essay] E. Seldon. 6:56-9, autumn '58.

LOLITA and Mr. Girodias [essay] V. Nabokov. 45:37-41, Feb '67.

LOLITA, Nabokov, and I [essay] M. Girodias. 37:44-7+, Sept '65.

LONDON portfolio [photographs] P. Horn. 22:49-56, Jan/Feb '62.

The LONG walk at San Francisco State [essay] K. Boyle. 76:21-3+, Mar '70.

LONIDIER, Lynn
Shades of paintstore orange [illus] 41:38-9, Je '66.

LOOKING for money [autobiographical essay] I. Karp. 8: 42-55, spring '59.

LORCA, Federico García
see
GARCÍA LORCA, Federico

The LORDLY and isolate satyrs [poem] C. Olson. 4:5-8, '57.

LOS ANGELES, CALIFORNIA
The city of lost angels [essay] J. Rechy. 10:10-27, Nov/Dec '59.

A LOT of people (Un tas de gens) [poem] P. Reverdy. 11: 27, Jan/Feb '60.

LOUIS Armstrong: style beyond style [review essay] M. Williams. 24:111-20, May/Je '62

LOVE again (Encore l'amour) [poem] P. Reverdy. 11:28, Jan/Feb '60.

LOVE in the middle of the air [poem] L. Kandel. 41:47, Je '66.

LOVE is a spy's best friend: the confessions of DBX [pictorial satire] P. Neuberg and D. Young. 48:57-60, Aug '67.

LOVE poem. H. Heifetz. 52: 82, Mar '68.

LOVE song for a slut [poem] C. Moffett. 76:66, Mar '70.

LOVE story [poem] S. Ken-
worthy. 30:70-1, May/Je '63.

LOVER of Lorca [essay] A.
Voznesensky. 31:48-52, Oct/
Nov '63.

The LOVERS [story] M. Bula-
tovie. 27:60-74, Nov/Dec '62.

LOWELL, Robert
Commander Lowell (1887-
1950) [poem] 8:39-41, spring
'59.

"LOWER" California [essay]
L. Ferlinghetti. 24:61-71, May/
Je '62

LOWER case "n" [essay] J.
Potter. 36:62-3, Je '65.

LU, Ch'iu-Yin
Preface to the poems of
Han-shan. 6:69-72, autumn '58.

LYND, Staughton
Reply to L. Kolakowski
[essay] 47:89-90, Je '67.

LYND, STAUGHTON
(photograph of) 47:89, Je '67.

LYON, Fred
[photo] 2:cover, '57.

LYSERGIC acid [poem] A. Ginsberg. 18:80-4, May/Je '61.

LYTTLE, David
Lady Overboard [poem] 5:
105, summer '58.

- M -

M. a column that promotes
broken watches for high school
dropouts [satire] M. O'Donoghue.
36:66-7, Je '65.

The M. team [story] J. Brunot.
49:80-5, Oct '67.

McCLURE, Michael
The beard [play] 49:64-79,
Oct '67.
Cat's air [poem] 2:46, '57.
Drug notes [essay] 25:103-
17, Jl/Aug '62.
Freewheelin' Frank [narra-
tive; as told to Michael Mc-
Clure] 47:22-5+, Je '67.
_____part II. 48:
64-8, Aug '67.
The growl [play] 32:75-7+,
Apr/May '64.
Mystery song [poem] 69:29,
Aug '69.
Night words: the ravishing
[poem] 2:46, '57.
Note [poem] 2:48, '57.
Ode to Jackson Pollock
[poem] 6:124-6, autumn '58.
On seeing through Shelley's
eyes the Medusa [poem] 20:37-
9, Sept/Oct '61.
The robe [poem] 2:49, '57.
The rug [poem] 2:47, '57.
The [poem] 2:48, '57.

McCLURE, MICHAEL
(photograph of) 2:between
page 64 and 65, '57.

McCOY, Dan
[photo] 77:30, Apr '70.

McCOY, Esther
Felix Candela: shells in
architecture [essay] 7:127-33,
winter '59.

McCRARY, Jim
Wine [story] 81:31-3+, Aug
'70.

McDONALD, Country Joe
Clichy [song] 85:41, Dec '70.

MacGUINNESS, WILLIAM P.
MacGuinness. H. Williams.
37:19-25+, Sept '65.
(photograph of) 37:23, Sept
'65.

MACK, Stan
[cartoon] 55:42-3, Je '68.
[illus] 55:51, Je '68; 63:28,
Feb '69; 70:58, Sept '69; 73:
21-3, Dec '69.

McKAIN, David
Fifty-third Street [poem] 68:
64, Jl '69.

McKEE, Jon
[cartoon] 48:89, Aug '67;
49:83, Oct '67; 51:79, Feb '68;
53:63, Apr '68; 54:93, May '68.

McLEAN, Willson
[illus] 83:34, Oct '70.

McMULLEN, Jim
[illus] 49:22, Oct '67.

McRAE, CARMEN - CRITICISM
AND INTERPRETATION
Sarah Vaughan: some notes
on a singer before it's too late.
M. Williams. 42:74-7, Aug '66.

McREYNOLDS, David
Reply to L. Kolakowski
[essay] 47:92, Je '67.

McREYNOLDS, DAVID
(photograph of) 47:92, Je '67.

MAD love [poem] R. Handke.
75:29, Feb '70.

MADAME Edwarda [story] G.
Bataille. 34:63-7, Dec '64.

MADISON, Russ
The sacred tapes of Dr.
Chicago [story] 83:42-5, Oct
'70.

The MADMAN's house [poem]
J. Broughton. 2:109, '57.

MADONIA, Gail
In town [poem] 69:57, Aug
'69.

MAFFIA, Daniel
[illus] 77:56, Apr '70; 84:
52, Nov '70.

The MAGIC box [essay] J.
Tallmer. 19:117-22, Jl/Aug
'61.

The MAGICAL mystery trip
[essay] T. Leary. 56:57-61+,
Jl '68.

MAGNOLIA [story] M. Thomas.
18:89-63, May/Je '61.

MAILER, Norman
The killer [story] 32:26-7+,
Apr/May '64.
Truth and being; nothing and
time: a broken fragment from
a long novel. 26:68-74, Sept/
Oct '62.

MAILER, NORMAN - CRITI-
CISM AND INTERPRETATION
An open letter to Norman
Mailer. S. Krim. 45:89-96,
Feb '67.
Advertisements for myself
A hungry mental lion. S.
Krim. 11:178-85, Jan/Feb
'60.
The armies of the night
Behold the new journalism-
it's coming after you! N.
Hentoff. 56:49-51, Jl '68.
Wild 90
Notes from the underground:
Wild 90. L. Eliscu. 53:15+,
Apr '68.

MAISEL, Jay
[photo] 46:66, Apr '67.

La MAISON de rendez-vous
[novel excerpt] A. Robbe-
Grillet. 43:50-3+, Oct '66.

MAL
[cartoon] 48:49, Aug '67;
51:91, Feb '68; 56:74, Jl '68;
67:67, Je '69; 68:49, 74, Jl

'69; 70:70, Sept '70.

MALANGA, Gerald
Last night thoughts of Bobby
Dylan [poem] 67:64, Je '69.

MALAPARTE, Curzio
Mamma Marcia [novel ex-
cerpt] 42:46-9, Aug '66.

MALCOLM X
God's judgment of white
America [speech] 50:54-7+,
Dec '67.
(photograph of) 50:54, Dec
'67.

MALINA, Judith
Last performance at the
Living Theatre invective [poem]
33:49-51, Aug/Sept '64.

MALONE, John Williams
Except for the heat [story]
24:52-7, May/Je '62.

MAMA, Mama, look at sis!
[poem] T. Fiofori. 56:27, Jl
'68.

MAMA Marcia [novel excerpt]
C. Malaparte 42:46-9, Aug '66.

The MAN in the fake Chanel
suit [story] M. Mason. 47:
68-9+, Je '67.

MAN in the zoo: George Grosz'
Ecce Homo [essay] 40:30-9,
Apr '66.

MAN (philosophy)
Human universe. C. Olson.
5:88-102, summer '58.

The MAN who played himself
[story] L. Welch. 17:97-105,
Mar/Apr '61.

The MAN who rode away [poem]
L. Ferlinghetti. 27:90-2, Nov/
Dec '62.

The MAN with the axe [poem]
A. Jarry. 13:146, May/Je '60.

MANCEAUX, Michele
Jean Genêt and the Black
Panthers [interview] 82:35-7+,
Sept '70.

MANDABI: confronting Africa
[review essay] J. Lester. 78:
55-8+, May '70.

MANDALA [poem] A. Ginsberg.
18:84, May/Je '61.

MAN'S total communication system [essay] R. Fuller. 83:39-
4+, Oct '70.

MARCEL Schwob, double soul
[essay] 13:111, May/Je '60.

MARCORELLES, Louis
Solanas: film as a political
essay [essay] 68:31-3+, Jl '69.

MARDI Gras [story] J. Rechy.
5:60-70, summer '58.

MARIJUANA
Marijuana and sex. E.
Goode. 66:19-21+, May '61.

MARIJUANA and sex [essay]
E. Goode. 66:19-21+, May '69.

MARIJUANA witchhunt [essay]
G. Brennan. 55:55-6+, Je '68.

MARK, Mary Ellen
see
WOLFF, Tony and Mary Ellen
Mark

MARK Tobey [essay] D. Ashton.
11:29-36, Jan/Feb '60.

MARKOPOULOS, Gregory J.
Thirteen true confessions?
[reply to A. Vogel] 48:54-5,
Aug '67.

MAROWITZ, Charles
Artaud at Rodez [essay] 53:
64-7+, Apr '68.

MARQUIS de Sade
see
SADE, Donatien Alphonse François Marquis de

MARRIAGE; for Mr. and Mrs.
Mike Goldberg [poem] G. Corso.
9:160-3, summer '59.

MARSHALL, John
Help wanted! [satire] 78:
33, May '70.

MARTIN, Jerome
[cartoon] 31:53, Oct/Nov '63.
[illus] 32:44, Apr/May '64;
48:52-3, Aug '67.

MARTIN, Lionel
Last stop at La Maquina
[essay] 79:90, Je '70.
Letter from Havana [essay]
83:24, Oct '70.

The MARTIN Luther King I remember [essay] J. Lester. 74:
16-21+, Jan '70.

MASON, Michael
A good education: spon-
taneous demonstration I [story]
59:53-4+, Oct '68.
In the afternoons [story] 28:
101-6, Jan/Feb '63.
The man in the fake Chanel
suit [story] 47:68-9+, Je '67.

MASS MEDIA
see
COMMUNICATION

MASS MEDIA--U. S.
Students as media critics: a
new course. N. Hentoff. 72:
53-5, Nov '69.

MASSA'S in the cold cold
brown 4 April 1968 [poem] L.

Dupree. 55:53, Je '68.

MASSIN
see
CADOO, Emil J., Massin, and
Michel Rivgauche.

MATILDA waltzes but still
keeps her maidenhead [essay]
J. Williamson. 35:86-8, Mar
'65.

MATRU Desh [poem] G. Sharat
Chandra. 85:37, Dec '70.

MATTELSON, Marvin
[illus] 82:38, Sept '70; 83:
42-5, Oct '70.

MAUD, 1966 [poem] B. Patten.
44:55, Dec '66.

MAURIAC, FRANÇOIS
(photograph of) 23:cover,
Mar/Apr '62.

MAURICE, Bob
see
WADLEIGH, Michael and Bob
Maurice.

MAVERICK head kick [essay]
S. Krim. 48:19-20, Aug '67.

MAX, Peter
[illus] 49:49, Oct '67.

MAY, ROLLO - CRITICISM
AND INTERPRETATION
Existence
The possibility of existential
analysis. M. Green. 8:184-93,
spring '59.

MAYA [poem] G. Snyder. 34:
41, Dec '64.

MAYAKOVSKY, Vladimir
And you think you could?
[poem] 20:89, Sept/Oct '61.
Once more on Petersburg
[poem] 20:89, Sept/Oct '61.

The tragedy of Vladimir
Mayakovsky (The prologue)
[poem] 77:25, Apr '70.

MAYES, R. Inskip
One sentence [poem] 9:89,
summer '59.

MEAT hoist [poem] M. Rumaker.
55:73, Je '68.

MED Cruise [poem] R. O'Connell.   15:57-60, Nov/Dec '60.

MEDNICK, Murry
Paranoia [poem] 52:89,
Mar '68.
The revolution [poem] 71:
21, Oct '69.
Three voices found on the
deserted floor of a subway
train at five o'clock in the
morning. [poem] 48:100, Aug
'67.

MEDUSA in Gramercy Park
[poem] H. Gregory. 22:81-5,
Jan/Feb '62.

MEETING [poem] T. Roze-
wicz. 39:83, Feb '66.

The MEMORIAL [story] R. Elman. 35:44-50, Mar '65.

MEMORY gardens [poem] A.
Ginsberg.   80:27-9, Jl '70.

A MEMORY of King Bolden
[essay] D. Barker. 37:66-74,
Sept '65.

MENA
[cartoon] 73:57, Dec '69.

MENDELSON, Ed
[cartoon] 51:41, Feb '68.

MENDÈS-FRANCE, Pierre
Peace is a duty in the Near
East as in Vietnam [essay] 56:
47-8, Jl '68.

MENG-LUNG, Feng
Song (translated by Arthur
Waley) [poem] 10:47, Nov/
Dec '59.

MENKITI, Ifeanyi
The nigra mind [poem] 71:
40, Oct '69.

MEN'S crapper [poem] C.
Bukowski. 50:75, Dec '67.

The MENU [essay] R. Brautigan.   42:30-2+, Aug '66.

MENUHIN, YEHUDI - CRITI-
CISM AND INTERPRETATION
From the third eye... pop
freak and passing fancy.   A.
Aronowitz. 77:86-8, Apr '70.

MERCEDES (automobile)
The car with the pointed
helmet [with photos] J. F. Held.
59:62-5, Oct '68.

MERRILL, James
Landscape with torrent
[poem] 8:96, spring '59.

MERWIN, WILLIAM S
As the dark snow continues
to fall [poem] 35:50, Mar '65.
The complaint of my family
[poem] 35:50, Mar '65.
Return to the mountains
[story] 31:91-106, Oct/Nov '63.
We continue [poem] 27:75,
Nov/Dec '62.

MESCALIN
Miserable miracle. H.
Michaux. 1:37-67, '57.

MESSAGE [poem] J. Miles. 2:
51, '57.

A MESSAGE to my friends
[essay] R. Debray. 51:48-9+,
Feb '68.

MESSAGE to the civilized or

uncivilized world [satirical essay]
J. Mollet.   13:187-91, May/Je
'60.

METAL SCULPTURE
   Sculpture by Ron Boise: the
Kama Sutra theme.   A. Watts.
36:64-5, Je '65.

The MEX would arrive in
Gentry's Junction at 12:10 [story]
R. Coover. 47:62-5+, Je '67.

MEXICAN PAINTING
            see
PAINTING, Mexican

MEXICAN POETRY
            see
POETRY, Mexican

MEXICO
   The Eye of Mexico [special·
issue devoted to young Mexican
painters, poets, and prose
writers]   7: winter '59.
            see also
ART, MEXICAN
ART, NÁHUATL
ARCHITECTURE, MEXICAN
BAYA CALIFORNIA
CHAMULA INDIANS
CORRIDO (Mexican ballad)
JUAREZ, MEXICO

MEXICO - CULTURE AND
   TRADITIONS
Todos santos, día de muertos.
O. Paz.   7:22-37, winter '59.

MEXICO: the 1968 olympics
[poem] O. Paz. 64:16, Mar '69.

MEYEROWITZ, Michey
   [illus] 78:33, May '70.

MEYEROWITZ, Rick
   [cartoon] 54:63, 73, May '68;
59:84, Oct '68.
   [illus] 57:62, Aug '68; 65:44,
Apr '69; 68:18-19, Jl '69; 81:
47-51, Aug '70.

MICHAELS, Leonard
   A green thought [story] 65:
32-5, Apr '69.

MICHAUX, Henri
   Miserable miracle [essay] 1:
37-67, '57.

MICHELSON, Annette
   The camera as fountain pen
[essay] 48:56+, Aug '67.

MIDDLE CLASS AMERICANS
   Driving across the Prairie
[reminiscence] E. Dorn. 68:
35-7+, Jl '69.

MIKE Nichols: the downhill
racer [review] N. Hentoff. 83:
69-70, Oct '70.

MIKUWAIA
   [illus] 45:57, 61, 67, 70,
Feb '67.

MILES Davis: conception in
search of a sound [essay] M.
Williams.   34:88-91, Dec '64.

MILES, Josephine
   Message [poem] 2:51, '57.
   Orderly [poem] 2:51, '57.
   Project [poem] 2:50, '57.
   Reception [poem] 2:50, '57.

MILITARY SCHOOLS
            see
WEST POINT

MILLER, Charles
   Dieppe to Newhaven 1961
[autobiographical essay] 26:89-
97, Sept/Oct '62.

MILLER, Henry
   Big Sur and the good life
[essay] 2:36-45, '57.
   Defence of the freedom to
read [letter to Trygve Hirsch,
barrister-at-law, Oslo, Norway]
9:12-20, summer '59.

Man in the zoo: George Grosz' Ecce Homo [essay] 40: 30-9, Apr '66.

Nexus [novel excerpt] 10: 68-82, Nov/Dec '59.

Paris la nuit; a portfolio of photographs [text excerpt from Quiet days in Clichy] 24:12-22, May/Je '62.

Quiet days in Clichy [novel excerpt and scenes from the film] 85:39-47, Dec '70.

The world of sex [autobiographical essay] 17:21-31, Mar/Apr '61.

MILLER, HENRY
(photograph of) 81:37, Aug '70.

MILLER, Steve
[illus] 56:52, Jl '68.

MILLER'S "Tropic" on trial [essay] D. Bess. 23:12-37, Mar/Apr '62.

MILLS, C. Wright
On Latin America, the Left, and the U. S. [interviews] 16: 110-22, Jan/Feb '61.

MINEO, SAL - CRITICISM AND INTERPRETATION
Fortune and men's eyes
Notes from the underground: like America, beautiful and evil. D. Rader. 75:16, Feb '70.

MINER, John W.
see
COLLINS, Lee. Jazz:from Lee Collins' story.

MINI-COOPER S (automobile)
The red globules [essay] J. Held. 53:56-9, Apr '68.

The MINISTER of Information raps: an interview with Eldridge Cleaver. C. Brown. 59:44-6+, Oct '68.

MINUS
[cartoon] 73:72, Dec '69.

MIRÓ, Joan
[illus] 13:142, May/Je '60.

MISERABLE miracle [essay] H. Michaux. 1:37-67, '57.

MISHIMA, Yukio [pseud]
Rites of love and death [photographs from his film] 43:56-9, Oct '66.

MISS All-American [essay] J. Nathan. 47:19-21, Je '67.

MR. Buckley [essay] D. Phelps. 37:32-4+, Sept '65.

MISTER Freedom: a storyboard sequence. [synopsis and photographs] 77:51-5, Apr '70.

MISTER Freedom: an interview with William Klein. A. Segal. 77:49-50, Apr '70.

MR. president; for e. e. cummings, were he still alive. [poem] A. Hollo. 45:94, Feb '67.

MITCHELL, James O.
[photo] 6:65, autumn '58.

MITCHELL, James O. and Don Charles
Harlem, Summer 1964 [photo] 34:48-57, Dec '64.

MITCHELL, Joan
[painting] 12:between 79 and 80, Mar/Apr '60.

MITCHELL, JOAN - CRITICISM AND INTERPRETATION
The poems
Poets and painters in collaboration. F. Porter. 20:121-6, Sept/Oct '61.

MITCHELL, Julian
The grocer's assistant
[story] 72:49-52+, Nov '69.
[photo] 79:26, Je '70.

MODERN JAZZ QUARTET
John Lewis and the Modern
Jazz Quartet. M. Williams.
23:112-25, Mar/Apr '62.
(photograph of) 23:113,
Mar/Apr '62.

MOFFETT, Cleveland
Love song for a slut [poem]
76:66, Mar '70.

MOFFITT, Peggy
(photographs of) 50:65-9,
Dec '67.

MOLINARO, Ursule
Desire game [novel excerpt]
40:46-9, Apr '66.

MOLLET, Jean
Message to the civilized or
uncivilized world [satirical
essay] 13:187-91, May/Je '60.

MOLLY'S suggestion [story]
A. Kaye. 12:56-8, Mar/Apr
'60.

MONDRAGON, Sergio
And all this, for what?
[poem] 67:50, Je '69.

MONK, THELONIOUS - CRITI-
CISM AND INTERPRETATION
Thelonius Monk; modern jazz
in search of maturity. M. Williams. 7:178-89, winter '59.

MONK, THELONIOUS
(photograph of) 7:179,
winter '59.

MONROE, MARILYN
(photograph of) 81:38,
Aug '70.

MONSIEUR Juva's flint statues

[essay] J. Dubuffet. 13:73-8,
May/Je '60.

MONTES de OCA, Marco An-
tonio
Ode on the death of Ché
Guevara [poem] 71:26, Oct '69.
On the threshold of a plea
[poem] 7:105-10, winter '59.

MORAFF, Barbara
This poem has no title
[poem] 24:72, May/Je '62.
Tune [poem] 10:47, Nov/
Dec '59.

MORAL ATTITUDES
Waiting for Nuremberg. N.
Hentoff. 45:74-80, Feb '67.

The MORAL unneutrality of
science [excerpt from an address before the American Association of Science, Dec. 27,
1960] C. P. Snow. 17:1-2,
Mar/Apr '61.

MORE adult animals [portfolio
of cartoons] P. Wende. 44:
65-9, Dec '66.

MORGAN [story] J. Schultz.
67:57-66, Je '69.

MORGAN (automobile)
The classless cars. J.
Held. 54:57-61, May '68.

MORGAN, Edward
O pioneers! [poem] 38:26,
Nov '65.

MORIN, Edgar
The case of James Dean
[essay] 5:5-12, summer '58.

The MORNING glory [story] M.
Rumaker. 17:68-77, Mar/Apr
'61.

MORNING: phone rings [poem]
H. Anzai. 84:51, Nov '70.

93 MORRISSETT, Ann

MORRISSETT, Ann
An account of the events preceding the death of Bill Burroughs [essay] 29:103-8, Mar/
Apr '63.
Dialogue with Arrabal 15:
70-5, Nov/Dec '60.

MORRISSETTE, Bruce
New structure in the Novel:
Jealousy, by Alain Robbe-
Grillet [review essay] 10:103-
7+, Nov/Dec '59.

MORSE, Carl
A report to be found in the
files of the CIA in the year
3000 [poem] 24:35, May/Je '62.

MORTON, JELLY ROLL -
CRITICISM AND INTERPRE-
TATION
Jelly Roll Morton: three-
minute form. M. Williams.
12:114-20, Mar/Apr '60.

MOSCHELLA, Michelle
[illus] 73:16, Dec '69.

The MOST expensive restaurant
ever built [essay] B. H. Friedman. 10:108-16, Nov/Dec '59.

MOTELS
see
HOLIDAY Inn University

MOTION will be denied. [essay]
J. Schultz. 75:21-5+, Feb '70.

MOTION PICTURES
see
FILMS

The MOTOR show [play] E.
Ionesco. 32:64-6, Apr/May '64.

MOTORCYCLE GANGS
see
HELL'S ANGELS

MOUNTAIN flowers [poem] J.

Ashbery. 8:98, spring '59.

MOVING PICTURES
see
FILMS

MROZEK, Slawomir
Three Polish tales: From
the darkness; Children; Poetry.
[stories] 29:9-17, Mar/Apr '63.

MROZEK, SLAWOMIR - CRITI-
CISM AND INTERPRETATION
Tango
Slawomir Mrozek: the masks
of irony. J. Lahr. 67:53-5+,
Je '69.

MROZEK, SLAWOMIR
(photograph of) McCarten.
67:52, Je '69.

MUCKING with the real [re-
view essay] L. Carson 82:
77-9, Sept '70.

MUGGING the Constitution
[essay] N. Hentoff. 75:51-3,
Feb '70.

MULLIGAN, GERRY - CRITI-
CISM AND INTERPRETATION
Mulligan and Desmond at
work. M. Williams. 28:117-
26, Jan/Feb '63.

MUNZLINGER, Tony
[cartoon] 35:75, Mar '65;
36:78-9, 84, Je '65; 37:80-1,
Sept '65; 38:64, Nov '65; 39:
79, Feb '66; 42:53, Aug '66;
44:63, 75, 77, Dec '66; 45:93,
Feb '67; 47:45, 71, Je '67;
48:84, 100, 104-5, Aug '67;
49:84, Oct '67; 53:94, Apr '68;
55:84, 80, Je '68; 56:31, Jl
'68; 59:51, 56, Oct '68; 62:62,
Jan '67; 67:45, 61, Je '69; 69:
36, 68, Aug '69; 70:67, Sept
'69; 72:30-1, Nov '69; 79:78,
Je '70; 81:70, Aug '70; 82:32,
Sept '70.

MURAKAWA, Gennosuke
[illus] 43:24-5, 27, Oct '66.

The MURDER of Swinburne [excerpt from the novel Vanity of Duluoz] J. Kerouac. 51:61-3+, Feb '68.

MURRAY
[cartoon] 84:59, Nov '70.

MUSIALOWICZ, Henryk
[illus] 10:cover, 98-102, Nov/Dec '59.

MUSIC
see
JAZZ
MUSICAL COMEDY
ROCK MUSIC

MUSIC FESTIVALS
see
WOODSTOCK WEST

MUSIC, MEXICAN
see
CORRIDO (Mexican ballad)

MUSICAL COMEDY
The American musical: the slavery of escape. J. Lahr. 58: 22-5+, Sept '68.

MUSICIANS
see
COMPOSERS
JAZZ COMPOSERS
JAZZ MUSICIANS
JAZZ SINGERS
MENUHIN, YEHUDI
ROCK MUSICIANS
SHANKAR, RAVI
SINGERS
SUN RA

MUSRUM [story] E. Thacker and A. Earnshaw. 63:47-9+, Feb '69.

The MUTE [story] O. Walter. 21:94-100, Nov/Dec '61.

MY drawings [essay with drawings] W. Saroyan. 8:147-51, spring '59.

MY mother and I would like to know [story] W. Burroughs. 67: 35-7, Je '69.

MY mother's bedroom [autobiographical excerpt] G. Amor 7:121-6, winter '59.

MY nineteen-thirties [autobiographical essay] J. Wain. 9:76-89, summer '59; 14:71-87, Sept/Oct '60.

MY silent war [autobiographical excerpts] K. Philby. 53:17-31+, Apr '68; 54:16-31, May '68.

MYERS, David
Seven days from Zen camp [poem] 64:28-9, Mar '69.

MYERS, John Bernard
The impact of Surrealism on the New York School [essay] 12: 75-85, Mar/Apr '60.

MYERS, Lou
Group therapy [cartoon] 34: 26-7, Dec '64.
The landlord [story] 44:56-60, Dec '66.
Who would you...? [cartoon] 33:77-9, Aug/Sept '64.
The women of Düsseldorf [cartoon] 32:79-81, Apr/May '64.
[cartoon] 33:77-9, Aug/Sept '64; 43:79, 84, Oct '66; 51: 100, Feb '68.

MYERS, Paul E.
Anethema [poem] 49:52-3, Oct '67.

MYSTERY on stage [essay] J. Lahr. 73:53-7, Dec '69.

MYSTERY song [poem] M.
McClure.   69:29, Aug '69.

The MYSTERY that isn't: how
do you get those slum savages
to learn? [essay] N. Hentoff.
54:40-3, May '68.

MYSTICISM
see
INTERNATIONAL SOCIETY FOR
KRISHNA CONSCIOUSNESS

- N -

NABOKOV, Vladimir
Lolita and Mr. Girodias
[essay] 45:37-41, Feb '67.

NABOKOV, VLADIMIR
Lolita, Nabokov, and I. M.
Girodias.   37:44-7+, Sept '65.

NABOKOV, VLADIMIR - CRITI-
CISM AND INTERPRETATION
Lolita
Lolita and Justine.   E.
Seldon.   6:156-9, autumn, '58.

A NÁHUATL concept of art
[essay] M. León-Portilla. 7:
157-67, winter '59.

NAKAMURA, Masaya
[photo] 35:cover, Mar '65.

NAKED lunch [novel excerpt]
W. Burroughs.   16:18-31, Jan/
Feb '61.

NAMUTH, Hans
[photo] 3:cover, '57.

NARCOTIC ADDICTS
The addict in the street:
Hector Rodriguez. J. Larner.
35:11-15, Mar '65.
Deposition: testimony concerning a sickness.   W. Burroughs.   11:15-23, Jan/Feb '60.

NARCOTICS

see
COCAINE
HALLUCINOGENIC DRUGS
HEROIN
PEYOTE

NATHAN, John
Notes from the underground:
abortion [essay] 46:23-5, Apr
'67.
Notes from the underground:
Destruction in art [essay] 46:
21-3, Apr '67.
Notes from the underground:
International Society for Krishna
Consciousness [essay] 45:7-16,
Feb '67.
Notes from the underground:
Miss All-American [essay] 47:
19-21, Je '67.
Notes from the underground:
San Francisco censorship [es-
say] 45:16-20, Feb '67.

The NATIVES abroad [poem]
J. Stowers. 65:27, Apr '69.

NATIVITY 1956 [poem] J.
Broughton.   2:106, '57.

NEAL vs. Jimmy the fag
[story] J. Gelber.   34:58-61,
Dec '64.

NEGRO-WHITE RELATIONS
see
RACE RELATIONS

NEGROES
see
BLACK AUTHORS
BLACK IDENTITY
BLACK PANTHERS
BLACK POETRY
BLACK POWER

NEIDE, Peter
[photo] 64:18-23+, Mar '69.

NELSON, RALPH - CRITICISM
AND INTERPRETATION
Soldier blue

From the third eye... Hollywood's last stand.   T. Seligson.
85:78-9, Dec '70.

NERUDA, Pablo
Gentleman alone [poem]   22:
36-7, Jan/Feb '62.
Pastoral [poem]   22:21, Jan/
Feb '62.
A pinecone, a toy sheep...
[autobiographical essay]   22:22-
35, Jan/Feb '62.
Stationary point [poem]   22:
38, Jan/Feb '62.
Three poems [The truth; The
light is not pure; Soliloquy in
the waves]   44:20-1, Dec '66.

NERUDA, PABLO
The GLP arrives!   D. Newlove.   44:17-9+, Dec '66.
(photograph of)   F. Stein.
44:17-19, Dec '66.

NESSIM, Barbara
[illus]   66:22, May '69.

NEUBERG, Paul and Dan Young
Love is a spy's best friend:
the private confessions of DBX
[pictorical satire]   48:57-60,
Aug '67.

NEVELSON, Louise
[painting]   12:79, Mar/Apr
'60.

NEVELSON, Susan
[photo]   6:cover, autumn '58.

NEVER mind [poem]   M. Steingesser.   67:33, Je '69.

The NEW American cinema:
five replies to Amos Vogel.
48:54-6+, Aug '67.

A NEW comic style: Arrabal
[essay] G. Serreau.   15:61-9,
Nov/Dec '60.

The NEW eroticism [essay] D.

Davis.   58:48-55, Sept '68.

NEW LEFT
The idea of the New Left.
C. Oglesby.   63:51-4+, Feb
'69.
Letter to an ex-radical. J.
Newfield.   62:31-2+, Jan '69.
Notes from the underground:
the New Left. L. Skir.   63:
22-3+, Feb '69.
The prison of words: lan-
guage and the New Left.   N.
Hentoff.   65:61-3, Apr '69.

NEW LEFT (Politics)
Hayden-Marat/Dylan-Sade:
defining a generation.   J. New-
field.   52:23-5, Mar '68.
Reply to L. Kolakowski [S.
Lynd, T. Hayden, D. Mc-
Reynolds, J. Newfield] 47:91,
Je '67.
We shall overcome-when?
N. Hentoff.   39:58-62, Feb '66.
What is the left today? L.
Kolakowski.   47:30-2+, Je '67.
see also
LATIN AMERICA - FOREIGN
RELATIONS - U. S.

NEW LEFT (Politics) - LIT-
ERATURE
The literature of the move-
ment. J. Newfield.   46:50-3+,
Apr '67.

The NEW life; a day on a col-
lective farm. [novel] F.
Abramov.   30:1-64, May/Je
'63.

The NEW movement [essay] N.
Hentoff.   42:66-73, Aug '66.

NEW Orleans beginnings [and]
Jazz on the river [autobio-
graphical essay] B. Dodds. 1:
110-48, '57.

The NEW politics: is there life
before death? [essay] N.

Hentoff.   49:51-3+, Oct '67.

The NEW sheriff [poem] L.
Jones.   19:96, Jl/Aug '61.

NEW structure in the novel:
Jealousy, by Alain Robbe-Grillet
[review essay] B. Morrissette.
10:103-7+, Nov/Dec '59.

The NEW theater: a retreat
from realism [essay] J. Lahr.
60:54-7+, Nov '68.

NEW Year's every day [story]
K. Roehler.   15:96-119, Nov/
Dec '60.

NEW York Blues [poem] D.
Propper.   51:63, Feb '68.

NEW YORK (City)
   Where we all came into town.
B. Behan.   18:18-32, May/Je
'61.
                    see also
HARLEM

NEW YORK (City) - EDUCATION
   Educators as dropouts: New
York City's schools.   N. Hentoff.
43:19-23+, Oct '66.

NEW YORK (City) - PARKS AND
   PLAYGROUNDS
   Hoving, go go medievalist.
R. Gustaitis.   43:72-9, Oct '66.

NEW YORK (City) - SCHOOLS
                    see
NEW YORK (City) - EDUCATION

NEW YORK SCHOOL (Art)
   The impact of Surrealism on
the New York School [with photographs and prints] J. Myers.
12:75-85, Mar/Apr '60.

NEWARK, N. J. - RIOTS
   "They think you're an airplane and you're really a bird"
[interview] L. Jones.   50:51-3+,

Dec '67.

NEWFIELD, Jack
   Chicago, honkies, and
Camus [essay] 50:58-60, Dec
'67.
   The day of the locust [essay]
67:29-33+, Je '69.
   Green Beret liberalism
[essay] 57:62-5, Aug '68.
   Hayden-Marat/Dylan-Sade:
defining a generation [essay]
52:23-5, Mar '68.
   Hubert Humphrey: lesser
evilism in 1972 [essay] 60:42-
5, Nov '68.
   Letter to an ex-radical
[essay] 62:31-2+, Jan '69.
   The literature of the move-
ment [essay] 46:50-3+, Apr '67.
   Reply to L. Kolakowski
[essay] 47:91, Je '67.
   SDS: from Port Huron to
La Chinoise [essay] 72:15-7+,
Dec '69.

NEWFIELD, JACK
   (photograph of) 47:91, Je
'67.

NEWLOVE, Donald
   Article [review essay] 85:
23-9+, Dec '70.
   The black eye [story] 77:57-
9+, Apr '70.
   The dead man's float in the
moon [story] 53:33-5+, Apr
'68.
   The GLP arrives! [essay]
44:17-9+, Dec '66.
   Trumpet [story] 72:21-3+,
Nov '69.

NEWS from the unfortunate
isles [story] R. Gourmont. 13:
108-10, May/Je '60.

NEWS REPORTAGE
   Notes from the underground:
uncovering news uncoverage.
N. Hentoff. 76:16-8, May '70.

The NEWSPAPER as literature.
Literature as leadership [essay]
S. Krim.   48:31-2+, Aug '67.

NEWSPAPERS
            see
JOURNALISM
UNDERGROUND PRESS
VILLAGE VOICE

NEWSPAPERS, radical
   The Village Voice. J. Kirk
Sale.   73:25-7+, Dec '69.

NEWSPAPERS - U. S.
   The daily newspaper in 1980.
N. Hentoff.   40:62-3+, Apr '66.

NEWTON, HUEY P.
   No one can be all things to
all people.   K. Boyle 81:63-7,
Aug '70.
   (photograph of) 81:62, Aug
'70.

NEXUS [novel excerpt] H.
Miller.   10:68-82, Nov/Dec '59.

NIBLOCK, Phil
   [photo] 66:62, May '69.

NICHOLS, J. L.
            see
JEFFRIS, G. AND J. L. Nichols

NICHOLS, MIKE - CRITICISM
   AND INTERPRETATION
            Catch 22
   Mike Nichols: the downhill
racer.   N. Hentoff.   83:69-70,
Oct '70.

NIGHT [poem] G. Snyder. 9:
129, summer '59.

The NIGHT before thinking
[story] A. Yacoubi. 20:18-30,
Sept/Oct '61.

NIGHT in the subway [poem] J.
Clifford. 8:102, spring '59.

The NIGHT of the giraffe
[story] A. Andersch. 16:32-
55, Jan/Feb '61.

NIGHT words: the ravishing
[poem] M. McClure. 2:46, '57.

The NIGRA mind [poem] I.
Menkiti. 71:40, Oct '69.

NIMS, John Frederich, trans-
   lator
            see
GARCÍA LORCA, Federico.
The unfaithful wife.

NIXON, RICHARD
   Billy Graham and friend. D.
Rader. 74:31-5+, Jan '70.

NO more masterpieces [essay]
A. Artaud. 5:150-9, summer
'58.

NO one can be all things to all
people [essay] K. Boyle. 81:
63-7, Aug '70.

The NOBLE bandit [story] Li
Yü. 23:79-92, Mar/Apr '62.

NOBLE, Richard
   [photo] 69:cover, Aug '69.

"NOBODY operates like an IBM
machine;" for Frank O'Hara
[poem] P. Southgate. 45:109,
Feb '67.

A NOCTURNAL emission in the
house of George Orenstein
[story] L. Skir. 53:45-6+,
Apr '68.

NORDENSTRÖM, Hans
   [cartoon] 12:98-9, Mar/Apr
'60; 14:112-3, Sept/Oct '60;
15:50-1, Nov/Dec '60; 33:82,
Aug/Sept '64.

NORETORP-Noretsyh [poem] K.
Rexroth. 2:15-6, '57.

NORRIS, Hoke
"Cancer" in Chicago [essay]
25:41-66, Jl/Aug '62.

NORRIS, Susan
Nothing for the ladies [poem]
57:31, Aug '68.

NORSE, Harold
I heard Evtushenko [poem]
31:62-71, Oct/Nov '63.
I see America daily (an oral
collage) [poem] 37:30-1,
Sept '65.
Now France [poem] 23:110-1,
Mar/Apr '62.

NORTH Beach alba [poem] G.
Snyder. 2:114, '57.

NOTE [poem] M. McClure. 2:
48, '57.

NOTE on "Babii Yar" [essay]
22:60, Jan/Feb '62.

A NOTE on George Orwell [re-
view essay] A. Trocchi. 6:
150-5, autumn '58.

A NOTE on Story of O [essay]
S. Destré. 31:31-2, Oct/Nov
'63.

NOTES [poem] A. Trocchi. 30:
95-7, May/Je '63.

NOTES from the underground:
a guide to all good things in
life [review] A. Vogel. 75:19,
Feb '70.

NOTES from the underground:
abortion [essay] J. Nathan. 46:
23-5, Apr '67.

NOTES from the underground:
book bust in Brighton [essay]
76:18+, Mar '70.

NOTES from the underground:
Boston [essay] D. Rader. 59:
18-9+, Oct '68.

NOTES from the underground:
but whose Turkey? [essay] A.
Seymour. 85:74-7, Dec '70.

NOTES from the underground:
censorship [essay] L. Raphael.
67:20-1+, Je '69.

NOTES from the underground:
Chappaqua [review essay] L.
Shainberg. 50:22-5+, Dec '67.

NOTES from the underground:
destruction in art [essay] J.
Nathan. 46:21-3, Apr '67.

NOTES from the underground:
gay liberation: all the sad
young men [essay] D. Rader.
84:18-20+, Nov '70.

NOTES from the underground:
H. Rap Brown [essay] J.
James. 57:16-7+, Aug '68.

NOTES from the underground:
Haircut [essay] R. Schechner.
51:24-6, Feb '68.

NOTES from the underground:
have you seen it all, Dennis
Hopper? [essay] L. Carson.
81:16-8, Aug '70.

NOTES from the underground:
head kick [essay] S. Krim 48:
19-20, Aug '67.

NOTES from the underground:
high school underground [re-
view] N. Hentoff. 75:16-8,
Feb '70.

NOTES from the underground:
impressions of Cuba [essay]
M. Randall 49:20-1+, Oct '67.

NOTES from the underground:
International Society for Krishna
Consciousness [essay] J.
Nathan. 45:7-16, Feb '67.

NOTES from the underground:
"it could only happen in California" [review essay] D.
Rader.   80:72-4, Jl '70.

NOTES from the underground:
Jimi Hendrix: goin' toward
heaven [essay] J. Lester. 85:
18-9+, Dec '70.

NOTES from the underground:
like America, beautiful and evil
[review] D. Rader. 75:16,
Feb '70.

NOTES from the underground:
Miss All-American [essay]   J.
Nathan.   47:19-21, Je '67.

NOTES from the underground:
now you see it, now you don't
[essay] H. Greer.   79:16-8+,
Je '70.

NOTES from the underground:
Nude restaurant [review]   S.
Brecht.   53:98-100, Apr '68.

NOTES from the underground:
Relativity - a cosmic dream
[review] P. Tyler.   48:21+,
Aug '67.

NOTES from the underground:
revolution in the Rockies: Woodstock West [essay] J. Bishop.
80:71-2, Jl '70.

NOTES from the underground:
right on with the best generation [essay] D. Rader. 76:18,
Mar '70.

NOTES from the underground:
St. James Baths [essay] D.
Rader.   58:88-92, Sept '68.

NOTES from the underground:
San Francisco censorship [essay]
45:16-20, Feb '67.

NOTES from the underground:

seeing America first with Andy
Warhol [review essay] D.
Rader.   78:22+, May '70.

NOTES from the underground:
stained lass [satire] M. O'Donoghue 48:20-1, Aug '67.

NOTES from the underground:
sugar cane and the "free-world"
press [essay] R. Seaver. 77:
16+, Apr '70.

NOTES from the underground:
Sun Ra [review] S. Brecht.
54:88-90, May '68.

NOTES from the underground:
The Living Theatre [narrative]
L. Skir.   63:22-3+, Feb '69.

NOTES from the underground:
The New Left [essay] L. Skir.
63:22-3+, Feb '69.

NOTES from the underground:
the road is known [essay] L.
Skir.   82:16-20+, Sept '70.

NOTES from the underground:
theater and revolution [essay]
J. Beck.   54:14-5+, May '68.

NOTES from the underground:
uncovering news uncoverage
[essay] N. Hentoff. 76:16-8,
Mar '70.

NOTES from the underground:
West Point [essay] D. Rader.
58:17+, Sept '68.

NOTES from the underground:
Wild 90 [review] L. Eliscu
53:15+, Apr '68.

NOTES from the underground:
Women's Lib: save the last
dance for me [narrative] T.
Seligson.   80:18-21+, Jl '70.

NOTES on Eskimo literature

[essay] L. Kemp. 33:72-3, Aug/Sept '64.

NOTES on the off-Broadway theater [essay] J. Unterecker. 8:152-63, spring '59.

NOTES written on finally recording Howl [essay] A. Ginsberg. 10:132-5, Nov/Dec '59.

NOTHING for the ladies [poem] S. Norris. 57:31, Aug '68.

NOVA express [novel excerpt] W. Burroughs. 22:103-9, Jan/Feb '62; 29:109-16, Mar/Apr '63.

NOVEL
          see
FICTION (Technique)

NOVEL, philosophy of the
   Old "values" and the new novel (nature, humanism, tragedy) A. Robbe-Grillet. 9: 98-118, summer '59.

NOVEL, theory of the
   Beyond the novel. E. M. Cioran. 17:80-92, Mar/Apr '61.

NOVELS
          single works
   see name of author for full entry.
The armies of the night. Mailer, Norman. The bronc people. Eastlake, William. Doctor Zhivago. Pasternak, Boris. Jealousy. Robbe-Grillet, Alain. Lady Chatterley's lover. Lawrence, D. H. Last exit to Brooklyn. Selby, Hubert. The last of the just. Schwarz-Bart, André. Lolita. Nabokov, Vladimir. Naked lunch. Burroughs, William S. The story of O. Reage, Pauline.

NOVIA express
          see
NOVA express

NOW France [poem] H. Norse. 23:110-1, Mar/Apr '62.

NOW Lucifer is not dead [story] W. Eastlake. 60:22-4+, Nov '68.

NOW you see it, now you don't [essay] H. Greer. 79:16-8+, Je '70.

NUDISM
   Philosophy in the surf. A. Vogel. 41:41, Je '66.

NUDITY IN THE THEATER
   The theater's voluptuary itch. J. Lahr. 56:32-4+, Jl '68.

NUMBERS [novel excerpt] J. Rechy. 50:30-2+, Dec '67.

NUÑO
   [cartoon] 84:66, Nov '70.

The NUT house pickings [story] J. F. Ryan. 51:31-2+, Feb '68.

NUTTALL, Jeff
   Fag money [poem] 38:25-6, Nov '65.

The NYMPHETTES of Siegmaringen [autobiographical excerpt from Castle to castle] L.-F. Céline. 60:36-40+, Nov '68.

- O -

O pioneers! [poem] E. Morgan. 38:26, Nov '65.

O'BANNON
   [cartoon] 62:27, Jan '69.

OBSCENE LITERATURE
An anniversary unnoticed. R.
Seaver.   36:53-6, Je '65.

OBSCENITY
                  see
CENSORSHIP
TRIALS (Obscenity)

O'CONNELL, Richard
Med cruise [poem]   15:57-60,
Nov/Dec '60.

O'CONNOR, Philip
Steiner's tour [novel excerpt]
11:85-96, Jan/Feb '60.

OCTOBER in the railroad earth
[story] J. Kerouac. 2:119-36,
'57.

ODE on the death of Ché Guevara
[poem] M. Montes de Oca. 71:
26, Oct '69.

ODE to Jackson Pollock [poem]
M. McClure.   6:124-6, autumn
'58.

ODIER, Daniel
Journey through time--space:
an interview with William A.
Burroughs.   67:39-41+, Je '69.

O'DOHERTY, Brian
Stuart Davis: a memoir
[essay] 39:22-7, Feb '66.

O'DONOGHUE, Michael
The automation of caprice.
[play] 33:38-41, Aug/Sept '64.
Capriccio to Djuna [poem]
47:66-7, Je '67.
The kiss of death [poem] 73:
33-8, Dec '69.
The liberal book [satire] 84:
33-9, Nov '70.
M. a column that promotes
broken watches for high school
dropouts. [satire] 36:66-7, Je
'65.

Notes from the underground:
Stained lass [satire] 48:20-1,
Aug '67.
Paris in the twenties [satire]
37:48-53, Sept '65.
Someday what you really are
is going to catch up with you
[satire] 46:38-41, Apr '67.
'30's [poem] 81:24-5, Aug
'70.
The twilight maelstrom of
Cookie Lavagetto [play] 35:32-
7, Mar '65.

O'DONOGHUE, Michael and
Eric Bach
Fish waif [pictorial satire]
53:49-55, Apr '68.

O'DONOGHUE, Michael and Chaz
Evergreen drops in on a
dropout [pictorial satire] 43:33-
40, Oct '66.
Gridiron maidens [pictorial
satire] 48:33-40, Aug '67.
Spotlight on Miss Marigold
Flagg [pictorial satire] 42:33-
40, Aug '66.

O'DONOGHUE, Michael and Tom
Lafferty
Auto eroticism [pictorial
satire] 55:33-9, Je '68.
Binders keepers [pictorial
satire] 62:33-9, Jan '69.
Driven mod [pictorial satire]
51:53-9, Feb '68.

O'DONOGHUE, Michael and
Frank Springer
The adventures of Phoebe
Zeit-Geist [comic strip] 38:58-
61, Nov '65; 39:54-7, Feb '66;
49:50-3, Apr '66; 41:57-61, Je
'66; 42:58-62, Aug '66; 43:66-
73, Oct '66; 44:48-51, Dec '66;
45:48-52, Feb '67; 46:92-7, Apr
'67; 47:33-40, Je '67; 49:31-9,
Oct '67.

O'DONOGHUE, Michael and
others.

The crucifixion of the gold
dust twins & the resurrection
of Mr. Clean (or) I could have
sworn I saw a dove fly into
Virgin Mary's window! [pic-
torial] 64:33-7, Mar '69.

OE, Kenzaburo
Aghwee the sky monster
[story] 54:44-8+, May '68.
The catch [story] 45:53-72,
Feb '67.
Lavish are the dead [story]
38:17-21+, Nov '65.

OF one month's reading of
English newspapers [poem] G.
Corso.   22:48, Jan/Feb '62.

OFF-BROADWAY THEATER
Notes on the off-Broadway
theater. J. Unterecker. 8:
152-63, spring '59.

The OFFENDING party [story]
J. Schultz. 55:40-4+, Je '68.

OGLESBY, Carl
The idea of the New Left
[essay] 63:51-4+, Feb '69.

OH! Calcutta!
Two plays from Oh! Cal-
cutta! [Rock Garden; Who:
Whom] 69:49-53, Aug '69.

O'HARA, Frank
About Zhivago and his poems
[essay] 7:230-8, winter '59.
Franz Kline talking [dialogue]
6:58-64, autumn, '58.
In memory of my feelings
[poem] 6:18-23, autumn '58.
On Rachmaninoff's birthday
[poem] 3:61, '57.
Rhapsody [poem] 43:29,
Oct '66.
A step away from them
[poem] 3:60-1, '57.
Three airs [poems] 9:34,
summer '59.
Why I am not a painter [poem]

3:59, '57.

O'HARA, FRANK - CRITICISM
AND INTERPRETATION
Odes
Poets and painters in collab-
oration. F. Porter. 20:121-6,
Sept/Oct '61.

O'HARA, Frank and Bill Berkson
Hymn to St. Bridget's steeple
[poem] 24:107, May/Je '62.
Us looking up to St. Bridget
[poem] 24:107-10, May/Je '62.

O'HARA, Frank and Larry
Rivers
How to proceed in the arts;
a detailed study of the creative
act [essay] 19:97-101, Jl/Aug
'61.

OLD angel midnight-2 [story]
J. Kerouac. 33:68-71+, Aug/
Sept '64.

OLD movies [poems] E. Field.
34:17-25, Dec '64.

The OLD tune [play] R. Pinget.
17:47-60, Mar/Apr '61.

OLD "values" and the new novel
(nature, humanism, tragedy)
[essay] A. Robbe-Grillet 9:
98-118, summer '59.

The OLIVER band. [autobi-
ographical essay] B. Dodds.
4:80-100, '57.

OLIVER, JOE
The Oliver band. B. Dodds.
4:80-100, '57.

OLSEN
[cartoon] 85:33, Dec '70.

OLSON, Charles
The Company of men [poem]
8:119-20, spring '59.

Human universe [essay] 5:
88-102, summer '58.
The lordly and isolate satyrs
[poem] 4:5-8, '57.
Paterson (book five) [review]
9:220-1, summer '59.

OMNIBUS CRIME CONTROL
   AND SAFE STREETS ACT,
   1968
Mugging the Constitution. N.
Hentoff.   75:51-3, Feb '70.

ON a certain experience of
death [essay] E. M. Cioran.
6:108-23, autumn '58.

ON a lewd servant [poem]
Archilochos.   25:91, Jl/Aug '62.

ON a study of Camus [review]
W. Fowlie.   8:198-9, spring '59.

ON basic self-defense at public
meetings [essay] N. Hentoff. 68:
69-71, Jl '69.

ON becoming an historian [essay]
M. Duberman. 65:57-9+, Apr
'69.

ON bringing democracy to
America [essay] N. Hentoff.
69:46-7+, Aug '69.

ON chimpanzees [essay] C.
Rosset.   34:68-71, Dec '64.

ON dancing [poem] A. Young.
76:34-5, Mar '70.

ON Lady Chatterley's lover
[essay] M. Schorer. 1:150-78,
'57.

ON Latin America, the Left,
and the U. S. [interviews] C.
Mills.   19:110-22, Jan/Feb '61.

ON Rachmaninoff's birthday
[poem] F. O'Hara. 3:61, '57.

ON revolutionary professional-
ism [essay] N. Hentoff.   59:
55-7, Oct '68.

ON Rikers Island [essay] T.
Seligson.   77:45-7+, Apr '70.

ON seeing through Shelley's
eyes the Medusa [poem] M.
McClure.   20:37-9, Sept/Oct
'61.

ON the back stairs [story] W.
Gombrowicz.   35:26-31+, Mar
'65.

ON the death of the artist's
mother thirty-three years later
[poem] J. Logan. 4:75-9, '57.

ON the death of the pilot Francis Gary Powers [poem] G.
Dowden.   17:78-9, Mar/Apr
'61.

ON the male organ [poem]
Archilochos.   25:91, Jl/Aug
'62.

ON the road to Florida [story]
J. Kerouac.   74:43-7+, Jan
'70.

ON the threshold of a plea
[poem] M. De Oca. 7:105-10,
winter '59.

ON the use of Catholic religious
prints by the practitioners of
Voodoo in Haiti [essay] M.
Leiris.   13:84-94, May/Je '60.

ON their own feet [story] J.
Jahn.   20:72-88, Sept/Oct '61.

ON translating Sade [essay] A.
Wainhouse.   42:50-6+, Aug '66.

ONCE more on Petersburg
[poem] V. Mayakovsky.   20:
89, Sept/Oct '61.

ONDINE'S Mare [excerpt from
the novel a] A. Warhol. 58:
26-31+, Sept '68.

ONE China or two? [essay]
Étiemble. 8:24-34, spring '59.

101 ways to make love. [satire]
T. Kupferberg. 63:36-41, Feb
'68.

ONE hundred dollar misunder-
standing [novel excerpt] R.
Gover. 26:12-9, Sept/Oct '62.

ONE of the truly good men.
[review] D. Woolf. 8:194-6,
spring '59.

ONE sentence [poem] R. Mayes.
9:89, summer '59.

ONE thousand fearful words for
Fidel Castro [poem] L. Ferlinghetti. 18:59-63, May/Je
'61.

The ONE thousand ryo pledge
[story] A. Tanino, trans. 64:
25-7+, Mar '69.

The ONLY man in Paris without
a woman [story] L. Garrett.
68:23-5+, Jl '69.

An OPEN letter to Norman
Mailer [essay] S. Krim. 45:
89-96, Feb '67.

An OPEN letter to Pope Paul
VI on the pill [essay] E. Arsan.
69:21-3+, Aug '69.

THE OPEN THEATRE
   The open theatre: beyond the
absurd. J. Lahr. 66:63-8,
May '69.

OPERAS
           see
SCHULLER, GÜNTHER - CRITI-
   CISM AND INTERPRETATION

The visitation

OPINION: U. S. District Court,
Southern District of New York,
civil 147-87. Grove Press, Inc.
and Readers' Subscription, Inc.,
plaintiffs--against--Robert K.
Christenberry, individually and
as Postmaster of the City of
New York, defendant. F.
Bryan. 9:37-68, summer '59.

OPPENHEIMER, Joel
   Un bel di [story] 28:86-94,
Jan/Feb '63.
   Poem for the one-hundred
fiftieth anniversary of the Battle
of New Orleans. 39:63, Feb
'66.
   A quiet Sunday at home
[story] 73:19-20, Dec '69.
   Six-day and ball-bearing
[poem] 70:31, Sept '69.
   The three and a half minute
mile [poem] 47:61, Je '67.

OPUS pataphysicum [satirical
essay] I. Sandomir. 13:169-
80, May/Je '60.

ORCHESTRAS
        see
JAZZ ORCHESTRAS

ORCHIDS [poem] J. Ashbery.
8:100, spring '59.

ORDERLY [poem] J. Miles.
2:51, '57.

The ORIGINAL irreplaceable
vision [interviews] R. Walford.
76:47-9+, Mar '70.

ORLOVSKY, PETER
   (photograph of)
        see
GINSBERG, ALLEN AND
   PETER ORLOVSKY,
   (photograph of)

ORNETTE Coleman [review

essay] A. Spellman. 47:78-
80, Je '67.

ORNETTE Coleman: the meaning
of innovation [review essay] M.
Williams. 15:123-33, Nov/Dec
'60.

The ORPHAN [autobiographical
excerpt] D. Charhadi. 26:23-
34, Sept/Oct '62.

ORTON, Joe
Until she screams [play] 78:
51-3, May '70.

ORTON, JOE - CRITICISM AND
INTERPRETATION
Artist of the outrageous. J.
Lahr. 75:31-4+, Feb '70.

ORWELL, GEORGE - CRITICISM
AND INTERPRETATION
A note on George Orwell. A.
Trocchi. 6:150-5, autumn '58.

OSHIMA, Nagisa
An interview with Nagisa
Oshima. P. Bonitzer, M. Dela-
haye, and S. Pierre. 80:31-3+,
Jl '70.

OUR dance [poem] J. Gross.
9:36, summer '59.

OUR lady of the flowers [novel
excerpt] J. Genêt, 18:33-58,
May/Je '61.

OUR man in Madras [play] G.
Hofmann. 63:55-61, Feb '69.

OUR times [notations] F.
Fénéon. 13:104-5, May/Je '60.

OUT of it [poem] P. Whalen.
2:118, '57.

OUT of the ash [poem] Brother
Antoninus. 2:20, '57.

OUTSKIRTS of the city [excerpt

from the novel Novia express]
W. Burroughs. 25:73-8, Jl/
Aug '62.

OVID, meet a metamorphodite
[poem] J. Williams. 17:45-6,
Mar/Apr '61.

OZICK, Cynthia
We ignoble savages [autobi-
ographical essay] 10:48-52+,
Nov/Dec '59.

- P -

PAINTERS
see
CUEVAS, José Luis
DAVIS, Stuart
DUBUFFET, Jean
ERNST, Max
FRANKENTHALER, Helen
GOLDBERG, Michael
GROSZ, George
GUSTON, Philip
HARTIGAN, Grace
JOHNS, Jasper
KLINE, Franz
LESLIE, Alfred
MIRÓ, Joan
MITCHELL, Joan
NEVELSON, Louise
POLLOCK, Jackson
RAUSCHENBERG, Robert
SORIANO, Juan
TOBEY, Mark

PAINTING
see
ART
NEW YORK SCHOOL (Art)
SAN FRANCISCO SCHOOL (Art)
SURREALISM (Art)

PAINTING, AMERICAN
An Eastern view of the San
Francisco school. D. Ashton.
2:148-59, '57.

PAINTING, MEXICAN
Interview with Juan Soriano.
E. Ponialowska. 7:141-52,

winter '59.

PALCEWSKI, John
    Elegy, as if I meant it
[poem] 46:36-7, Apr '67.
    Peripatetic [poem] 66:25,
May '69.

PALESTINE - GUERILLAS
              see
    AMAR, Abu

PALESTINE LIBERATION
    MOVEMENT
    Al Fatah speaks: a conver-
sation with "Abu Amar" [inter-
view] A. Schliefer. 56:44-6+,
Jl '68.

PAPA had a bird (a creation
myth) [poem] J. Broughton.
24:91-2, May/Je '62.

PAPADOPOLOUS, Peter
    [photo] 69:54, Aug '69; 85:
30, Dec '70.

PAPALEO, Joseph
    The shyster's wedding [story]
80:49-51+, Jl '70.

PAPATAKIS, NICO - CRITICISM
    AND INTERPRETATION
    From the third eye... tiger
in a think tank. P. Tyler. 83:
70-4, Oct '70.

PAPO got his gun! [poem] V.
Cruz. 48:73-80, Aug '67.

A PARABLE about Russian emigres [poem] Z. Herbert. 39:
46, Feb '66.

A PARABLE of rebellion [re-
view] D. Rader. 78:9, May '70.

PARACHUTES, my love, could
carry us higher [poem] B.
Guest. 3:114, '57.

PARANOIA [poem] M. Mednick.

52:89, Mar '68.

PARANOIA in Crete [poem] G.
Corso. 8:58, spring '59.

PARÉ
    [cartoon] 53:82, 84, Apr
'68; 54:67, 84, May '68; 55:
75, 93, Je '68; 56:68, 83, Jl
'68; 57:93, Aug '68; 58:61,
Sept '68; 59:60, Oct '68; 60:
63, Nov '68; 63:27, Feb '69;
66:79, May '69; 67:37, 62, 71,
Je '69; 68:20, 76-7, 84, Jl
'69; 73:40, Dec '69.

PARIS
    Letter from Paris. J. Barry.
26:101-9, Sept/Oct '62.
    Paris la nuit; a portfolio of
photographs [text by Henry
Miller] Brassaï. 24:12-22,
May/Je '62.
    Satori in Paris. J. Kerouac.
39:17-21+, Feb '66; 40:56-9,
Apr '66; 41:50-3, Je '66.

PARIS - LITERARY SCENE
    Letter from Paris. R.
Howard. 8:171-4, spring '59.

PARIS in the twenties [satire]
M. O'Donoghue. 37:48-53,
Sept '65.

PARIS VC [poem] S. Canada.
51:114, Feb '68.

PARISE, Goffredo
    Wife in the saddle [story]
56:28-31+, Jl '68.

The PARK at Montsouris: a
savage elegy [poem] J. García
Térres. 7:87-9, winter '59.

PARKER, CHARLIE - CRITI-
    CISM AND INTERPRETATION
    Charlie Parker: the burden
of innovation. M. Williams.
14:141-52, Sept/Oct '60.

PARTICIPATORY television
[essay] N. Hentoff. 71:53-5,
Oct '69.

PARTS shared [story] J.
Shuffler. 57:18-21+, Aug '68.

PAS de deux [portfolio of pho-
tographs] R. Kirstel. 70:33-9,
Sept '69.

PASCAL, David
   [cartoon] 50:82, 107, Dec
'67; 56:70, Jl '68; 57:70, Aug
'68; 58:25, Sept '68; 60:77,
Nov '68; 63:68, Feb '68; 64:72,
Mar '69; 67:77, Je '69; 71:60,
Oct '69.

PASOLINI, PAOLO - CRITICISM
   AND INTERPRETATION
              Teorama
Rimbaud's desert as seen by
Pasolini. W. Fowlie. 74:27-
9+, Jan '70.

PASS [poem] R. Jackson. 74:
56, Jan '70.

PASSAGE to more than India
[essay] G. Snyder. 52:41-3+,
Mar '68.

PASSALACQUA, David
   [illus] 48:42, Aug '67.

PASTERNAK, Boris
   Icefloe [poem] 8:37, spring
'59.

PASTERNAK, BORIS - CRITI-
   CISM AND INTERPRETATION
          Doctor Zhivago
About Zhivago and his poems.
F. O'Hara. 7:230-8, winter '59.

PASTORAL [poem] P. Neruda.
22:21, Jan/Feb '62.

PATALAS, Enno
   The film in a divided Germany
[review essay] 21:110-8, Nov/

Dec '61.

'PATAPHYSICS
   What is 'pataphysics.
[special issue] 13: May/Je '60.

PATERNITY [poem] E. Bur-
rows. 3:92, '57.

PATERSON (book five) [review]
C. Olson. 9:220-1, summer
'59.

PATTEN, Brian
   Maud, 1966 [poem] 44:55,
Dec '66.

PAUL VI, Pope
   An open letter to Paul VI on
the pill. E. Arsan. 69:21-
3+, Aug '69.

PAVAN for a dead prince
[poem] S. Delaney. 30:16-23,
May/Je '63.

PAZ, Octavio
   The blue bouquet [story] 18:
99-101, May/Je '61.
   The dialectic of solitude
[essay] 20:100-13, Sept/Oct '61.
   Mexico: the 1968 Olympics
[poem] 64:16, Mar '69.
   Salamander; translated by
Denise Levertov [poem] 36:24-
7, Je '65.
   Todos Santos, día de
muertos. [essay] 7:22-37,
winter '59.
   Two poems: The river; The
broken water jar. 7:38-44,
winter '59.

PAZ, OCTAVIO
   (photograph of) 64:17, Mar
'69.

PEACE DEMONSTRATIONS
   Them and us: are peace
protests self-therapy? N.
Hentoff. 48:46-9+, Aug '67.
       see also

VIETNAMESE WAR, 1957 -
PROTESTS, DEMONSTRA-
TIONS, ETC.

PEACE is a duty in the Near
East as in Vietnam [essay] P.
Mendès-France. 56:47-8, Jl
'68.

PEDRO Páramo [novel excerpt]
J. Rulfo. 7:45-58, winter '59.

PEKAR, Harvey
The achievement of Lee
Konitz [essay] 43:30-2, Oct '66.

PENDEL, Dale
People travel to Paris [poem]
48:68, Aug '67.

A PENITENTIAL psalm [poem]
Brother Antoninus. 2:18, '57.

PENN, Arthur
Bonnie and Clyde [interview]
55:61-3, Je '68.

PEOPLE travel to Paris [poem]
D. Pendel. 48:68, Aug '67.

PERFORMANCE GROUP
Putting Shakespeare in a new
environment. J. Lahr. 76:63-
8, Mar '70.

PERIPATETIC [poem] J.
Palcewski. 66:25, May '69.

PERSE, ST. -JOHN [pseud] -
CRITICISM AND INTERPRE-
TATION
Amers
St. -John Perse's new poem.
K. Koch. 7:216-9, winter '59.

PETERSEN, Will
Stone garden [essay] 4:127-
37, '57.

PETERSON, OSCAR - CRITICISM
AND INTERPRETATION
Jottings on pianists. M.

Williams. 29:120-7, Mar/Apr
'63.

PEYOTE
Drug notes. M. McClure.
25:103-17, Jl/Aug '62.

PHELPS, Donald
Mr. Buckley [essay] 37:32-
4+, Sept '65.

PHILBY, Kim
My silent war [autobio-
graphical excerpts] 53:17-31+,
Apr '68; 54:16-31, May '68.

PHILIP Guston [essay] D.
Ashton. 14:88-91, Sept/Oct
'60.

PHILOSOPHY - SATIRE
see
'PATAPHYSICS

PHILOSOPHY in the surf
[essay] A. Vogel. 41:41, Je
'66.

PHOEBE Zeit-Geist
see
The ADVENTURES of Phoebe
Zeit-Geist

The PHOTOGRAPH of the
colonel [story] E. Ionesco.
3:117-31, '57.

PHOTOGRAPHERS
see
AVEDON, RICHARD

PIA, Pascal
Marcel Schwob, double soul
[essay] 13:111, May/Je '60.

PIA, PASCAL
(photograph of) 13:96, May/
Je '60.

PIAF, EDITH
(photographs of) Hommage
à Piaf [song and photographs]

E. Cadoo, Massin, and M. Rivgauche. 38:28-33, Nov '65.

PICHA
[cartoon]   49:91, Oct '67; 51:110-11, Feb '68; 70:84, Sept '69; 71:59, Oct '69; 76:74, 80, Mar '70; 77:69, Apr '70; 79:47, Je '70; 81:77, Aug '70.

PICNIC on the battlefield [play] F. Arrabal.   15:76-90, Nov/ Dec '60.

PIERRE, Sylvie
see
BONITZER, Pascal; Michel Delahaye, and Sylvie Pierre.

PIEYRE DE MANDIARGUES, André
Childishness [story] 6:5-17, autumn '58.
The diamond [story] 22:61-80, Jan/Feb '62.
The tide [story] 46:32-3+, Apr '67.

PIGS, Prague, Chicago, other Democrats, and the sleeper in the park [essay] J. Schultz. 60:26-35+, Nov '68.

PILLAR of salt [story] L. Corey.   83:53, Oct '70.

A PINECONE, a toy sheep... [autobiographical essay] P. Neruda.   22:22-35, Jan/Feb '62.

PINGET, Robert
The old tune; English version by Samuel Beckett [play] 17: 47-60, Mar/Apr '61.

PINK champagne [story] J. Skvorecky.   64:57-9+, Mar '69.

PINKTOES [novel excerpt] C. Himes.   35:16-8+, Mar '65.

PINTER, Harold

Landscape [play] 68:55-61, Jl '69.
Writing for the theatre [essay] 33:80-2, Aug/Sept '64.

PINTER, HAROLD - CRITI-CISM AND INTERPRETATION
Pinter the spaceman.   J. Lahr.   55:49-52+, Je '68.

The PIPE [story] M. Rumaker. 9:134-59, summer '59.

PLANISPHERE of the Pata-physical world [map] 13:158-9, May/Je '60.

PLAY [play] S. Beckett.   34: 42-7, Dec '64.

PLAYING with Alice [review essay] J. Lahr.   82:59-64, Sept '70.

PLAYS
see
DRAMAS

PLAYWRIGHTING
see
DRAMA--TECHNIQUE

PLAYWRIGHTS
see
DRAMATISTS

PLEASE do not feed the sena-tors [poem] J. Broughton. 2: 108, '57.

PLEASURE, need and taboo [essay] L. Ullerstam. 40:40-5, Apr '66.

PLYMELL, Charles
In San Francisco [poem] 64: 41-3, Mar '69.

POEM. A. Russo.   71:51, Oct '69.

POEM. T. Kooser.   72:62, Nov '69.

A POEM beginning with a line
by Pindar. R. Duncan. 11:
134-42, Jan/Feb '60.

A POEM for early risers. J.
Wieners. 9:164-5, summer '59.

POEM for perverts. L. Kandel.
35:20-1, Mar '65.

A POEM for the affluent society. H. Enzensberger. 21:
93, Nov/Dec '61.

POEM for the left hand. E.
Field. 5:71, summer '58.

POEM for the one-hundred
fiftieth anniversary of the Battle
of New Orleans. J. Oppen-
heimer. 39:63, Feb '66.

POEMS recorded by Richard
Wilbur [review] S. Kunitz. 8:
201-2, spring '59.

POETRY [story] S. Mrozek.
29:15-7, Mar/Apr '63.

POETRY, AMERICAN
            see
BEAT POETRY

POETRY, JAPANESE
            see
KANGIN SHU

POETRY, MEXICAN
   Anthology of Mexican poetry.
J. Schuyler. 7:221, winter '59.

POETRY, MODERN
   Fake it new. A. Hollo.
26:110-4, Sept/Oct '62.

POETRY, RUSSIAN
   Interview with Andrei Voznesensky. E. Sutherland. 28:
37-42, Jan/Feb '63.

POETS
            see

ASHBERY, John
CORSO, Gregory
CUMMINGS, e. e.
ELIOT, T. S.
EVTUSHENKO, Evgeny
GARCÍA LORCA, Federico
GINSBERG, Allen
HAN-SHAN
KOCH, Kenneth
NERUDA, Pablo
O'HARA, Frank
PERSE, St. -John
POUND, Ezra
SAROYAN, Aram
SCHUYLER, James
TORMA, Julien
WILBUR, Richard
WILLIAMS, William Carlos
YEATS, William Butler

POETS, AMERICAN
   San Francisco letter. K.
Rexroth. 2:5-14, '57.

POETS and painters in collaboration [review] F. Porter. 20:
121-6, Sept/Oct '61.

POETS hitchhiking on the high-
way [poem] G. Corso. 3:79,
'57.

The POET'S new audience [car-
toon] A. Sens. 20:90-3,
Sept/Oct '61.

POINTS of distinction between
sedative and consciousness-expanding drugs [essay] W. Burroughs. 34:72-4, Dec '64.

POLANSKI, ROMAN - CRITI-
   CISM AND INTERPRETATION
   The vampire killers
   An interview with Roman
Polanski. M. Delahaye and J.
Narboni. 66:27-9+, May '69.

The POLE who died on time
[essay] R. Hochhuth. 55:30-
2+, Je '68.

POLICE - U. S.
Report from Times Square.
J. Beck.   24:121-5, May/Je '62.

POLITICAL ATTITUDES - U. S.
Counterpolitics: the decade
ahead.   N. Hentoff.   63:25-7,
Feb '69.

POLITICAL COMMENTATORS
see
BUCKLEY, WILLIAM F.

POLITICAL FILMS
Solanes: film as a political
essay.   L. Marcorelles.   68:
31-3+, Jl '69.

POLITICIANS
see
HUMPHREY, HUBERT
JOHNSON, LYNDON BAINES
LINDSAY, JOHN VLIET
NIXON, RICHARD

POLITICS
see
STUDENTS--POLITICS

POLITICS - U. S.
Counterpolitics: the decade
ahead.   N. Hentoff.   63:25-7,
Feb '69.
The new politics: is there
life before death? N. Hentoff.
49:51-3+, Oct '67.
see also
DISSENTERS
LATIN AMERICA - FOREIGN
RELATIONS - U. S.
LIBERALISM
NEW LEFT (Politics)

POLLOCK, JACKSON
Jackson, Pollock.   C. Greenberg.   3:95-6, '57.
Letter on Pollock.   C.
Greenberg.   5:160, summer '58.
(photograph of) 3:cover, between 96 and 97, '57.

PONIATOWSKA, Elena

Interview with Juan Soriano.
7:141-52, winter '59.

POOR - U. S.
We shall overcome--when?
N. Hentoff.   39:58-62, Feb '66.

POOR dog [poem] P. Blackburn.   51:85, Feb '68.

POOR PEOPLES UNIFICATION
The new movement.   N.
Hentoff.   42:66-73, Aug '66.

POP freak and passing fancy
[review essay] A. Aronowitz.
77:86-8, Apr '70.

PORKY [story] P. Johnson. 6:
24-39, autumn '58.

PORNOGRAPHY
The erotic society.   M.
Girodias.   39:64-9, Feb '66.
see also
EROTIC ART

PORTER, Fairfield
Poets and painters in collab-
oration [review] 20:121-6,
Sept/Oct '61.

PORTRAIT [poem] A. Trocchi.
30:97-8, May/Je '63.

PORTRAIT of a house detective
[poem] H. Enzensberger. 36:
72, Je '65.

PORTRAIT of a woman at her
bath [poem] W. C. Williams.
17:64, Mar/Apr '61.

PORTRAIT of an artist with
twenty-six horses [story] W.
Eastlake.   5:74-85, summer
'58.

A PORTRAIT of the Irish as
James Joyce [review essay] H.
Gregory.   11:186-93, Jan/Feb
'60.

POSNER, David
Ballad [poem] 32:43, Apr/
May '64.

The POSSESSED [poem] M.
Dúran. 7:85, winter '59.

The POSSIBILITY of existential
analysis [review essay] M.
Green. 8:184-93, spring '59.

POSTER [poem] L. Kandel.
41:46, Je '66.

POSTER ART
                see
ART, RUSSIAN

POTTER, Jeffrey
Lower case "n" [essay] 36:
62-3, Je '65.

POUND, EZRA
A conversation between Ezra
Pound and Allen Ginsberg. M.
Reck. 55:26-9+, Je '68.
(photograph of) 81:37, Aug
'70.

POUZET
[cartoon] 34:61, Dec '64.

POVERTY, U. S. A. [portfolio
of photographs] G. de Vincent.
35:60-5, Mar '65.

The POWER and the glory
[poem] M. Dúran. 7:86, winter
'59.

POWER failure [poem] T. L.
Jackrell. 17:93, Mar/Apr '61.

The POWER of non-politics or
the death of the square left
[essay] R. Gleason. 49:40-5+,
Oct '67.

POZAS ARCINIEGA, Ricardo
Juan Pérez Jolote, part I
[narrative] 7:91-104, winter '59.

PRESENT past, past present
[excerpts from his memoir] E.
Ionesco. 85:53-5+, Dec '70.

PRESTIGIOUS (a review for all
book seasons) [poem] B.
Roueché. 51:83, Feb '68.

The PREVALENCE of rock; or,
rock lives! [essay] E. Salzman. 47:42-5+, Je '67.

PRÉVERT, Jacques
Blood orange [poem] 14:70,
Sept/Oct '60.
Chant song [poem] 13:62-3,
May/Je '60.
...It droppeth as the gentle
rain (a ballet) [story] 13:64-6,
May/Je '60.

PRÉVERT, JACQUES
(photograph of) 13:62, May/
Je '60.

PRICE, Bill
Jimmy's home [story] 77:
23-4, Apr '70.

PRICE, James
The Andalusian smile: re-
flections on Luis Buñuel [essay]
40:24-9+, Apr '66.
A film is a film: some notes
on Jean Luc Godard [essay] 38:
46-53, Nov '65.

PRICK lore [poem] E. Field.
56:55, Jl '68.

The PRINCE of Homburg [poem]
B. Brecht. 12:53, Mar/Apr
'60.

The PRISON of words: language
and the New Left [essay] N.
Hentoff. 65:61-3, Apr '69.

PRISON poems. Ho-Chi-Minh.
43:44-5, Oct '66.

PRISONERS, Condemned

The menu. R. Brautigan.
42:30-2+, Aug '66.

PRISONS
see
RIKERS ISLAND PRISON
SAN QUENTIN PRISON

PRIVACY, RIGHT OF
The secrect companions. N.
Hentoff.   82:55-7, Sept '70.
Sounds of silence.   N.
Hentoff.   80:53-5, Jl '70.

PROJECT [poem] J. Miles.
2:50, '57.

PROPAGANDA
Theater and propaganda. J.
Lahr.   52:33-7, Mar '68.

PROPPER, Dan
New York blues [poem] 51:
63, Feb '68.

PROTEST DEMONSTRATIONS
see
PEACE DEMONSTRATIONS
VIETNAMESE WAR, 1957 -
PROTESTS, DEMONSTRA-
TIONS, ETC.

PROUST, Marcel
The sources of the Loir at
Illiers [essay] 19:55-62, Jl/
Aug '61.

PSYCHEDELIC burlesque!
[photographic essay] M. Mark
and T. Wolff.   56:35-43, Jl '68.

PSYCHOANALYSIS: an elegy
[poem] J. Spicer.   2:56-7, '57.

The PUBLIC bath [poem] G.
Snyder.   29:75-6, Mar/Apr '63.

PUBLIC independent education
[essay] N. Hentoff.   83:55-7,
Oct '70.

PUBLIC MEETINGS - DISRUP-

TIONS
On basic self-defense at
public meetings. N. Hentoff.
68:69-71, Jl '69.

PUBLISHERS
see
GIRODIAS, MAURICE

PUBLISHING - DISCRIMINA-
TION
The Black writer and the
new censorship. J. Lester.
77:19-21+, Apr '70.

PUDGY [poem] F. Lima. 27:
30-2, Nov/Dec '62.

PURDY, James
Cutting edge [story] 1:99-
109, '57.
Scrap of paper [story] 48:
22-5+, Aug '67.

A PURPLE dog, a flying
squirrel, and the art of television [review] M. Williams.
20:114-20, Sept/Oct '61.

PUT-down [story] T. Southern.
9:70-5, summer '59.

PUTTING Shakespeare in a new
environment [review essay] J.
Lahr.   76:63-8, Mar '70.

PUZZLE for Wilhelm Reich
[poem] P. Gray. 37:87, Sept
'65.

- Q -

QUADRANGLE [story] D.
Woolf.   27:93-4, Nov/Dec '62.

A QUARREL over strategy!
[reply to A. Vogel] D. Talbot.
48:54, Aug '67.

A QUARTER ahead [story] J.
Rechy.   19:14-30, Jl/Aug '61.

QUAY, Stephen
[illus] 67:56, Je '69; 68:34,
Jl '69.

The QUEEN is dead [story] H.
Selby. 34:13-7+, Dec '64.

QUENEAU, Raymond
A fish's life [novel excerpt]
13:36-45, May/Je '60.

QUENEAU, RAYMOND
(photograph of) 13:36, May/
Je '60.

QUIET days in Clichy [novel excerpt and scenes from the film]
H. Miller. 85:39-47, Dec '70.

QUIET days in Clichy [song] J.
McDonald. 85:41, Dec '70.

A QUIET Sunday at home [story]
J. Oppenheimer. 73:19-20,
Dec '69.

QUOTATIONS from chairman
LBJ [satire] J. Shepherd and
C. Wren. 51:27-9, Feb '68.

- R -

RACE PREJUDICE
White woman - Black man.
J. Lester. 70:21-3+, Sept '69.
_____ part II. 71:
29-32+, Oct '69.

RACE RELATIONS
God's judgment of white
America. Malcolm X. 50:54-
7+, Dec '67.
Lower case "n". J. Potter.
36:62-3, Je '65.

RACISM
see
SEX AND RACE

RADER, Dotson
Billy Graham and friend.
[essay] 74:31-5+, Jan '70.

Blood and fire [story] 84:
53-5, Nov '70.
Catalogue of small defeats
[review] 83:24-6, Oct '70.
David Cartwright [story] 66:
31-2+, May '69.
From the third eye... a
parable of rebellion [review]
78:91, May '70.
Government-inspected meat
[story] 72:29-33+, Nov '69.
Notes from the underground:
Boston [essay] 59:18-9+, Oct
'68.
Notes from the underground:
gay liberation: all the sad young
men [essay] 84:18-20+, Nov '70.
Notes from the underground:
"It could only happen in Cali-
fornia" [review essay] 80:72-
4, Jl '70.
Notes from the underground:
like America, beautiful and evil
[review] 75:16, Feb '70.
Notes from the underground:
right on with the best generation
[essay] 76:18, Mar '70.
Notes from the underground:
St. James Baths [essay] 58:88-
92, Sept '68.
Notes from the underground:
seeing America first with Andy
Warhol [review essay] 78:22+,
May '70.
Notes from the underground:
West Point [essay] 58:17+,
Sept '68.
Rosalie [narrative] 63:63-5+,
Feb '69.
The ultimate all-American
technetronic queen [story] 78:
29-32+, May '70.
Up against the wall! [essay]
57:22-5+, Aug '68.
Vision of the gun [essay] 75:
61-3+, Feb '70.
What do you think of your
blue-eyed artist, now, Mr.
Death? [essay] 80:38-41+, Jl
'70.

The RAILROAD Earth (conclu-

sion) [story] J. Kerouac. 11:
37-59, Jan/Feb '60.

RANDALL, Margaret
A family [poem] 46:84-6,
Apr '67.
Notes from the underground:
impressions of Cuba [essay]
49:20-1+, Oct '67.

RAPHAEL, Lennox
Che!
Notes from the underground:
censorship [essay] 67:20-1+,
Je '69.

RAPOPORT, Louis H.
Flower power: an interview
with a hippie. H. Brown and
J. Seitz. 49:54-7+, Oct '67.
The strike: student power
in Berkeley [essay] 46:80-2,
Apr '67.

The RASPBERRY patch [story]
B. Roueché. 58:58-61, Sept '68.

RAUCH
[cartoon] 76:49, 77, Mar '70;
77:70, 76, 84, Apr '70; 78:49,
May '70; 80:57, Jl '70; 85:64,
Dec '70.

RAUSCHENBERG, Robert
[painting] 12:between 79 and
80, Mar/Apr '60.

The RAVEN [poem] A. Yesenin-
Volpin. 20:69-71, Sept/Oct '61.

RAWORTH, Tom
Sliding two mirrors together
[poem] 38:26, Nov '65.

RAYFIELD, Fred
How the war ended in Vietnam [satire] 49:25-7+, Oct '67.

READERS' SUBSCRIPTION, INC.
Opinion: U. S. District
Court...New York...[for the
plaintiffs] Grove Press, Inc. and

Readers' Subscription, Inc....
F. Bryan. 9:37-68, summer
'59.

REAGE, Pauline [pseud]
Story of O: the lovers of
Roissy [novel excerpt] 31:33-
44, Oct/Nov '63.

REAGE, PAULINE [pseud] -
CRITICISM AND INTERPRE-
TATION
Story of O
A note on Story of O. S.
Destré. 31:31-2, Oct/Nov '63.

A REAL Parisian affair [story]
A. Allais. 13:98-102, May/Je
'60.

REALISM IN LITERATURE
From realism to reality. A.
Robbe-Grillet. 39:50-3+, Feb
'66.

REAVIS, Charles S.
Studley Hungwell III [poem]
68:37, Jl '69.

RECEPTION [poem] J. Miles.
2:50, '57.

RECHY, John
By the motel pool [excerpt
from his novel Numbers] 50:
30-2+, Dec '67.
The city of lost angels
[essay] 10:10-27, Nov/Dec '59.
El Paso del Norte [essay]
6:127-40, autumn '58.
It begins in the wind [ex-
cerpt from his novel City of
night] 24:23-34, May/Je '62.
Mardi Gras [story] 5:60-70,
summer '58.
A quarter ahead [story] 19:
14-30, Jl/Aug '61.
Three kinds of angels [ex-
cerpt from his novel City of
night] 26:38-48, Sept/Oct '62.

RECK, Michael

A conversation between Ezra Pound and Allen Ginsberg [essay] 55:26-9+, Je '68.

RECOLLECTIONS of childhood [essay] J. Cuevas. 29:40-56, Mar/Apr '63.

RECORDING with Big Joe [review essay] 25:118-27, Jl/Aug '62.

RECORDINGS of William Butler Yeats [review] D. Greene. 8: 200-1, spring '59.

RED CHINA
                    see
CHINA (People's Republic)

RED-dirt Marihuana [novel excerpt] T. Southern. 11:116-29, Jan/Feb '60.

The RED globules [essay] J. Held. 53:56-9, Apr '68.

RED man, white man, man on the moon [essay] F. Turner. 80:22-6+, Jl '70.

RED Skelton [review essay] M. Williams. 46:68-71, Apr '67.

REDL, Harry
    [photo] 2:between 64 and 65, '57.

REDRESS and revolution [essay] W. Douglas. 77:41-3+, Apr '70.

REDSTONE [poem] R. Hoff. 15: 46, Nov/Dec '60.

REFLECTIONS on the guillotine [essay] A. Camus. 3:5-55, '57; 12:special supplement, Mar/Apr '60.

REHEARSAL diary [essay] M. Williams. 31:115-27, Oct/Nov '63.

The RELATIONSHIP of religious ritual to orgasm frequency among the tribal women of Fungoolistan [satire] L. Dupree. 49:62-3, Oct '67.

RELIGIONS
                    see
VOODOOISM

RELIGIOUS LEADERS
                    see
GRAHAM, BILLY

REMY de Gourmont; man of masks [essay] N. Arnaud. 13: 106-7, Nay/Je '60.

RENÉ Daumal, experimental mystic [essay] L. Etienne. 13: 122-3, May/Je '60.

REPORT from Times Square [essay] J. Beck. 24:121-5, Mat/Je '62.

A REPORT to be found in the files of the CIA in the year 3000 [poem] C. Morse. 24:35, May/Je '62.

REPORT to the corps of prov-editors on some concrete historical problems concerning pataphysical activity posed by the fiftieth anniversary of the death of Jarry [satirical essay] N. Kamenev. 13:181-5, May/ Je '60.

REPRESSION and rebellion [essay] T. Hayden. 77:26-9, Apr '70.

REQUIEM for a princess--M. M. [poem] A. Hollo. 27:16-7, Nov/Dec '62.

RESNAIS, ALAIN - CRITICISM
    AND INTERPRETATION
        Hiroshima, mon armour
    An analysis of Alain Resnais'

film Hiroshima mon Amour. A.
Hodeir. 12:102-13, Mar/Apr
'60.

RESTAURANTS
see
FOUR SEASONS RESTAURANT

RESURRECTION [story] J. Lind.
28:12-36, Jan/Feb '63.

RETURN to the mountains [story]
W. Merwin. 31:91-106, Oct/
Nov '63.

REVELLI, George
Commander Amanda Night-
ingale [novel excerpt] 62:25-9+,
Jan '69.

REVERDY, Pierre
Clear winter (Clair hiver)
[poem] 11:26, Jan/Feb '60.
Endless journeys (Voyages
sans fin) [poem] 11:26, Jan/
Feb '60.
The Invasion (L'Invasion)
[poem] 11:24, Jan/Feb '60.
A lot of people (Un tas de
gens) [poem] 11:27, Jan/Feb
'60.
Love again (Encore l'amour)
[poem] 11:28, Jan/Feb '60.
That memory (Ce Souvenir)
[poem] 11:25, Jan/Feb '60.

REVIVAL [story] M. Thomas.
26:80-4, Sept/Oct '62.

The REVOLUTION [poem] M.
Mednick. 71:21, Oct '69.

REVOLUTION in the Rockies:
Woodstock West [essay] J.
Bishop 80:71-2, Jl '70.

REVOLUTIONISTS
The end of the underground.
J. Lahr. 65:45-8+, Apr '69.
On revolutionary profession-
alism. N. Hentoff. 59:55-7,
Oct '68.

The original irreplaceable
vision [interviews] R. Walford.
76:47-9+, Mar '70.
see also
AMAR, ABU
BROWN, H. RAP
CLEAVER, ELDRIDGE
DEBRAY, REGIS
GUEVARA, CHE
HAYDEN, TOM
HIPPIES
HOFFMAN, ABBIE
NEWTON, HUEY P.
STUDENTS FOR A DEMO-
CRATIC SOCIETY
WEATHERMEN
YIPPIES

REVOLUTIONS
see
FILM AND REVOLUTION...

REXROTH, Kenneth
Noretorp-noretsyh [poem]
2:15-6, '57.
San Francisco letter [essay]
2:5-14, '57.

REXROTH, KENNETH
(photograph of) 2:between
64 and 65, '57.

REYNOLDS, Frank
Freewheelin' Frank [narra-
tive] 47:22-5+, Je '67.
_____part II. 48:
64-8, Aug '67.

REYNOLDS, FRANK
(photograph of) 47:22, Je
'67; 48:64, Aug '67.

RHAPSODY [poem] F. O'Hara.
43:29, Oct '66.

RHENISH winter: a montage
after Apollinaire [poem] C.
Tomlinson. 23:38-40, Mar/Apr
'62.

RHODESIA
Black blood: a South African

diary. A. Higgins. 34:28-32+,
Dec '64.

RICE, Stan
   The dogchain gang [poem]
84:25, Nov '70.

RICHIE, Donald
   Bobo, the priest [story] 46:
67+, Apr '67.

RICKERT, Richard
   What is Zen [poem] 67:72,
Je '69.

RIEMENS, Henry
   [photo] 10:56-67, Nov/Dec
'59.

RIGHT on with the best generation [essay] D. Rader. 76:18,
Mar '70.

RIKERS ISLAND PRISON
   On Rikers Island. T. Seligson. 77:45-7+, Apr '70.

RIMBAUD'S desert as seen by
Pasolini [review essay] W.
Fowlie. 74:27-9+, Jan '70.

RINCIARI, Ken
   [cartoon] 65:73, Apr '69;
67:24, Je '69.
   [illus] 67:72, Je '69; 69:57,
Aug '69; 71:51, Oct '69.

RIOTS
           see
NEWARK, N. J. - RIOTS

RITES of love and death [photo-
graphs from his film] Y.
Mishima. 43:56-9, Oct '66.

The RIVER [poem] O. Paz. 7:
38-40, winter '59.

RIVERS, Larry
           see
O'HARA, Frank and Larry
   Rivers

RIVGAUCHE, Michel
           see
CADOO, Emil J., Massin, and
Michel Rivgauche.

The ROAD is known [essay] L.
Skir. 82:16-20+, Sept '70.

The ROAD-runner [poem] P.
Whalen. 2:115, '57.

ROBBE-Grillet, Alain
   A fresh start for fiction
[essay] 3:97-104, '57.
   From realism to reality
[essay] 39:50-3+, Feb '66.
   La maison de rendez-vous
[novel excerpt] 43:50-3+, Oct
'66.
   Old "values" and the new
novel (nature, humanism,
tragedy) [essay] 9:98-118, summer '59.
   Three reflected visions
[story] 3:105-13, '57.
   A voyeur in the labyrinth:
an interview with Alain Robbe-
Grillet. P. Démeron. 43:46-
9+, Oct '66.

ROBBE-GRILLET, ALAIN -
CRITICISM AND INTERPRE-
TATION
   Alain Robbe-Grillet. R.
Barthes. 5:113-26, summer
'58.
           Jealousy
   New structure in the novel:
Jealousy. B. Morrissetts. 10:
103-7+, Nov/Dec '59.

The ROBE [poem] M. McClure.
2:49, '57.

ROBERTE ce soir [novel ex-
cerpt] P. Klossowski. 27:76-
86, Nov/Dec '62.

ROBINS, Ted
   [cartoon] 57:80, Aug '68;
58:75, Sept '68.

ROBINSON Crusoe [poem] J.
Ashbery. 8:99, spring '59.

ROCCO, PAT - CRITICISM AND
    INTERPRETATION
        Mondo Rocco
"It could only happen in
California" D. Rader. 80:72-
4, Jl '70.

ROCHA, GLAUBER
    Brazil's Cinema Nôvo: an
interview with Glauber Rocha.
M. Delahaye. 73:29-32+, Dec
'69.

ROCHA, GLAUBER - CRITICISM
    AND INTERPRETATION
        Black god, white devil
Rocha's film as carnival.
F. Grafe. 73:30+, Dec '69.

ROCHA'S film as carnival
[essay] F. Grafe. 73:30+,
Dec '69.

ROCHE, Paul
    After Eliot: some notes
toward a reassessment [essay]
39:84-92, Feb '66.
    The catharsis of anguish;
days following the assassination
of President Kennedy [poem]
32:21-5, Apr/May '64.
    Spring-song of the petroleum
board meeting (an after luncheon
fancy for voices and music)
[poem] 30:24-9, May/Je '63.

ROCK garden [play excerpt from
Oh! Calcutta!] 69:49-51, Aug '69.

ROCK MUSIC
    '50s teenagers and '50s rock
(by Frank Zappa, as told to
Richard Blackburn) 81:43-6,
Aug '70.
    The prevalence of rock; or,
rock lives! E. Salzman. 47:
42-5+, Je '67.
    Something's happening and you
don't know what it is, do you

Mr. Jones? N. Hentoff. 41:
54-6, Je '66.

ROCK MUSICIANS
        see
DYLAN, BOB
HENDRIX, JIMI

RODRIGUES
    [cartoon] 62:79, Jan '69; 64:
82, Mar '69; 67:75, 88, Je '69;
69:71, Aug '69; 79:67, Je '70.

RODRIGUEZ, HECTOR
    The addict in the street:
Hector Rodriguez. J. Larner.
35:11-5, Mar '65.

ROEHLER, Klaus
    New Year's every day [story]
15:96-119, Nov/Dec '60.

ROLLINS, SONNY - CRITICISM
    AND INTERPRETATION
    Sonny Rollins: spontaneous
orchestration. M. Williams.
22:114-22, Jan/Feb '62.

ROLLINS, SONNY
    (photograph of) 22:115, Jan/
Feb '62.

ROLLS-ROYCE (automobile)
    The classless cars. J. Held.
54:57-61, May '68.

ROOKS, CONRAD - CRITICISM
    AND INTERPRETATION
        Chappaqua
Notes from the underground:
Chappaqua. L. Shainberg. 50:
22-5+, Dec '67.

ROOM 24 [poem] P. Gleason.
9:133, summer '59.

ROSALIE [narrative] D. Rader.
63:63-5+, Feb '69.

ROSENCRANTZ & Guildenstern
are dead [play] T. Stoppard.
52:47-72, Mar '68.

ROSENTHAL, Irving
Sheeper [novel excerpt] 46:
49+, Apr '67.

ROSS, Larry
[cartoon] 55:63, 83, Je '68.

ROSSET, Clement
On chimpanzees [essay] 34:
68-71, Dec '64.

ROSSET, Loly
[photo] 33:cover, Aug/Sept
'64.

ROSTEN, Norman
Ballad for anyone listening
[poem] 38:69, Nov '65.

ROTH, George Andrew
I was arrested with Debray
[essay] 51:44-7+, Feb '68.

ROTH, Sanford H.
[photo] 5: cover, summer
'58.

ROTHENBERG, Jerome, trans-
    lator
                see
CELAN, P. A death fugue.
ENZENSBERGER, H. Foam.

ROUECHÉ, Berton
The gun [story] 42:63-4,
Aug '66.
Prestigious (a review for all
book seasons) [poem] 51:83,
Feb '68.
The raspberry patch [story]
58:58-61, Sept '68.
A walk on the beach [story]
82:29+, Sept '70.

ROWE, William
[illus] 64:42, Mar '69.

The ROYAL toilet [poem] A.
Jarry. 13:147, May/Je '60.

ROZEWICZ, Tadeusz
Meeting [poem] 39:83, Feb '66.

RUBIN, Jerry
A Yippie manifesto [essay]
66:41-3+, May '69.
(photograph of) 66:40, May
'69; 81:40, Aug '70.

RUBINGTON, Norman
[illus] 37:50, 52, 53, Sept
'65.

RUCKUS poem D. Henderson.
55:57-9, Je '68.

RUDD, Mark
"We don't want to be edu-
cated for the CIA!" [interview]
P. Spike. 57:51-5+, Aug '68.

RUDD, MARK
(photograph of) 57:50, Aug
'68.

The RUG [poem] M. McClure.
2:47, '57.

RUKEYSER, Muriel
Bunk Johnson blowing [poem]
51:77, Feb '68.

RULFO, Juan
Pedro Páramo [novel ex-
cerpt] 7:45-58, winter '59.

RUMAKER, Michael
Camden, N. J. [poem] 80:
37, Jl '70.
Carson McCullers 2/19/17-
9/29/67 [poem] 50:97, Dec '67.
The desert [story] 2:65-105,
'57.
Eiko + Jim [story] 23:94-
109, Mar/Apr '62.
Exit 3 [story] 5:127-49, sum-
mer '58.
For Charles Olson [poem]
76:27, Mar '70.
Gringos [story] 38:54-7+,
Nov '65.
Meat hoist [poem] 55:73,
Je '68.
The morning glory [story]
17:68-77, Mar/Apr '61.

The pipe [story] 9:134-59, summer '59.

To a motocyclist killed on Route 9W [poem] 67:27, Je '69.

To a 19-year-old marine killed near Danang [poem] 43: 88, Oct '66.

The truck [story] 46:58-63, Apr '67.

You [poem] 35:71, Mar '65.

RUSHING, Jimmy
Jimmy Rushing's story as told to Frank Driggs. 40:64-9, Apr '66.

RUSHING, JIMMY
(photograph of) 40:66, Apr '66.

RUSSELL, PEE WEE - CRITI-
CISM AND INTERPRETATION
Whatever happened to the clarinet? M. Williams. 32: 81-2, Apr/May '64.

RUSSIA - POLITICS AND GOVERNMENT
see
KERENSKY, ALEXANDER

RUSSIAN revolutionary posters, 1917-1929 [reproductions and notes] D. Congrat-Butler. 46: 74-9, Apr '67.

RUSSO, A. P.
Poem 71:51, Oct '69.

RYAN, John Fergus
Holiday Inn University [essay] 83:29-33+, Oct '70.

The nut house pickings [story] 51:31-2+, Feb '68.

Stay in school so you'll get a good job, have lots of money, and be able to buy the nice things around you [satire] 85: 56-9, Dec '70.

RYAN, Pat M.
Two songs of Christian

America [poems] 55:51, Je '68.

RYŌANJI GARDEN
Stone garden.   W. Petersen. 4:127-37, '57.

- S -

SDS
see
STUDENTS FOR A DEMO-
CRATIC SOCIETY

SABINES, Jaime
Two poems: Bach's music moves curtains; Smashed. 7: 139-40, winter '59.

SABRINA
see
DOROSHOW, Jack (Flawless Sabrina)

The SACRED tapes of Dr. Chicago [story] R. Madison. 83:42-5, Oct '70.

SADE, Donatien Alphonse, François, Marquis de
Justine [novel excerpt] 36: 57-60+, Je '65.

SADE, DONATIEN ALPHONSE FRANÇOIS, MARQUIS DE - CRITICISM AND INTERPRE-
TATION
An anniversary unnoticed. R. Seaver. 36:53-6, Je '65.

On translating Sade. A. Wainhouse. 42:50-6+, Aug '66.

SAFE flights [poem] B. Guest. 3:116, '57.

SAGESSE [poem] H. D. 5:27-36, summer '58.

SAGGESE, Robert
A bird in the word [poem] 53:62, Apr '68.

SAILLET, Maurice
    Close to Antonin Artaud
[essay] 13:79-83, May/Je '60.

SAILLET, MAURICE
    (photograph of) 13:79, May/
Je '60.

ST. BRIDGET'S CHURCH, New
    York City
    [photo] P. Horn. 24:108,
110, May/Je '62.

ST. JAMES BATHS
    Notes from the underground:
St. James Baths. D. Rader.
58:88-92, Sept '68.

ST. -John Perse's new poem
[review] K. Koch. 7:216-9,
winter '59.

SALAMANDER; translated by
Denis Levertov [poem] O. Paz.
36:24-7, Je '65.

SALAS, Floyd
    The king's X [story] 48:42-
5+, Aug '67.

SALE, J. Kirk
    The Village Voice (You've
come a long way, Baby, but
you got stuck there) [essay] 73:
25-7+, Dec '69.

SALTZMAN, Tony
    [cartoon] 48:63, Aug '67.

SALUTE! [poem] L. Ferlinghetti. 54:39, May '68.

SALZMAN, Eric
    The prevalence of rock; or,
rock lives! [essay] 47:42-5+,
Je '67.

The SAME old jazz [poem] P.
Whalen. 14:92-4, Sept/Oct '60.

The SAME old soup [story] L.
Bianciardi. 55:16-21+, Je '68.

SAMETH, Martin
    [photo] 7:cover, winter '59.

SANDLER, Irving
    American construction sculp-
ture [essay] 8:136-46, spring
'59.

SANDOMIR, I. L.
    Epanorthosis on the moral
climanem [satirical verse] 13:
186, May/Je '60.
    Opus pataphysicum [satirical
essay] 13:169-80, May/Je '60.

SAN FRANCISCO - LITERARY
    SCENE
San Francisco letter. K.
Rexroth. 2:5-14, '57.

SAN Francisco jazz scene
[essay] R. Gleason. 2:59-64,
'57.

SAN Francisco letter [essay]
K. Rexroth. 2:5-14, '57.

SAN Francisco poem. G.
Fowler. 48:50-1, Aug '67.

SAN FRANCISCO MIME
    THEATER
    Theater and propaganda. J.
Lahr. 52:33-7, Mar '68.

SAN FRANCISCO PRESIDIO
    STOCKADE
            see
COURTS MARTIAL AND
    COURTS OF INQUIRY

SAN FRANCISCO SCHOOL (Art)
    An eastern view of the San
Francisco school. D. Ashton.
2:148-59, '57.

SAN FRANCISCO STATE
    COLLEGE
            see
CALIFORNIA. STATE
    COLLEGE, SAN FRAN-
    CISCO

SÁNCHEZ Salazar, Gustavo A.
        see
    Sánchez Salazar.

SANDERS, Ed
    Festival of life [story] 76:
37-8+, Mar '70.

A SANITY test for self and
society [essay] N. Hentoff. 60:
51-3+, Nov '68.

SAN QUENTIN PRISON
    The menu. R. Brautigan.
42:30-2, Aug '66.

SANTOCE, Charles
    [illus] 49:58, Oct '67.

SAPPHO [poem] W. C. Williams.
3:57, '57.

SARAH Vaughan: some notes
on a singer before its too late
[essay] M. Williams. 42:74-
7, Aug '66.

SARGENT, Elizabeth
    We poets [poem] 58:82,
Sept '68.

SAROYAN, ARAM - CRITICISM
    AND INTERPRETATION
        Aram Saroyan
    Saroyan: the "new" old
poetry. M. Steingesser. 81:
76-7, Aug '70.

SAROYAN, William
    My drawings [essay with
drawings] 8:147-51, spring '59.

SARTAIN, Gailard
    [illus] 57:18, Aug '68.

SARTRE, Jean-Paul
    After Budapest [interview]
1:5-23, '57.
    The socialism that came in
from the cold [essay] 84:27-32+,
Nov '70.
    The theater [interview] 11:

143-52, Jan/Feb '60.

SARTRE, JEAN-PAUL
    (photograph of) 11:147, 151,
Jan/Feb '60.

SATHER gate illumination
[poem] A. Ginsberg. 11:96-9,
Jan/Feb '60.

SATIRE
    Jules Feiffer: satire as sub-
version. J. Lahr. 63:33-4+,
Feb '69.

SATORI in Paris: 1 [essay] J.
Kerouac. 39:17-21+, Feb '66.
_____: 2 [essay]
J. Kerouac. 40:56-9, Apr '66.
_____: 3 [essay]
J. Kerouac. 41:50-3+, Je '66.

SATURDAY [novel excerpt] J.
Williamson. 28:73-9, Jan/Feb
'63.

SAWYER, Kenneth
    The importance of a wall:
galleries [essay] 8:122-35,
spring '59.

SAXON, Charles D.
    [cartoon] 24:93, May/Je '62;
25:79, Jl/Aug '62; 26:67, Sept/
Oct '62.

SCENES from the life of the
peppertrees [poem] D. Levertov. 5:85-6, summer '58.

SCHAUMANN, Peter
    [illus] 66:30, May '69; 69:20,
Aug '69; 72:51, Nov '69; 74:22-
3, Jan '70; 77:66-7, Apr '70;
80:23, Jl '70; 82:28, Sept '70.

SCHECHNER, Richard
    Notes from the underground:
Haircut [essay] 51:24-6, Feb
'68.

SCHECHNER, RICHARD -

CRITICISM AND INTERPRE-
TATION
Theater and propaganda. J.
Lahr. 52:33-7, Mar '68.
Macbeth (modern version)
Putting Shakespeare in a new
environment. J. Lahr. 76:63-
8, Mar '70.

SCHICKEL, Richard
A film is not a painting [re-
ply to A. Vogel] 48:56, Aug '67.

SCHIFFRIN, LALO
Rehearsal diary [essay] M.
Williams. 31:115-27, Oct/Nov
'63.

SCHLEIFER, Abdullah
Al Fatah speaks: a conversation with "Abu Amar" [inter-
view] 56:44-6+, Jl '68.
The fall of Jerusalem [essay]
50:26-9+, Dec '67.

SCHLESINGER, Steven
[photo] 67:26, Je '69

SCHLITTEN, Don
[photo] 44:52, Dec '66; 46:
72-3, Apr '67.

SCHNEIDER, Alan
From the third eye...Behind
the iron (theater) curtain [essay]
79:91-4, Je '70.

SCHOOLS AND SOCIO-ECO-
NOMIC PROBLEMS
see
NEW YORK (City) - EDUCATION

SCHOOLS, COMMUNITY CON-
TROL OF
see
COMMUNITY CONTROL OF
SCHOOLS

SCHOOLS, jails, and the god-
dam system [essay] J. Bishop.
81:53-5+, Aug '70.

SCHORER, Mark
On Lady Chatterley's lover
[essay] 1:150-78, '57.

SCHREITER, Rick
[illus] 62:30, Jan '69; 63:
24, Feb '69.

SCHULENBERG, Robert
[illus] 55:70, Je '68; 57:26,
Aug '68; 68:22, Jl '69; 71:18,
Oct '69; 75:30, Feb '70; 76:62,
Mar '70.

SCHULLER, GUNTHER
Rehearsal diary. M. Wil-
liams. 31:115-27, Oct/Nov '63.

SCHULLER, GUNTHER - CRIT-
ICISM AND INTERPRETA-
TION
Third stream problems. M.
Williams. 30:113-25, May/Je
'63.
The visitation
Kafka Jones, the singing
fool! N. Hentoff. 50:61-4,
Dec '67.

SCHULTZ, John
Border crossing [essay] 30:
99-112, May/Je '63.
Custom [novel excerpt] 24:
85-90, May/Je '62.
Goodbye [story] 19:72-82,
Jl/Aug '61.
Jesse had a wife [story] 52:
79-82, Mar '68.
Like the last two people on
the face of the earth [essay]
82:23-7+, Sept '70.
Morgan [story] 67:57-66,
Je '69.
Motion will be denied [essay]
75:21-5+, Feb '70.
The offending party [story]
55:40-4+, Je '68.
Pigs, Prague, Chicago, other
Democrats, and the sleeper in
the park [essay] 60:26-35+,
Nov '68.
The struggle for the laugh in

SCHULTZ, John   126

the courtroom [essay] 79:21-5+,
Je '70.

SCHUYLER, James
   Anthology of Mexican poetry
[review] 7:221, winter '59.

SCHUYLER, JAMES - CRITI-
   CISM AND INTERPRETATION
            Salute
Poets and painters in collab-
oration. F. Porter. 20:121-6,
Sept/Oct '61.

SCHWARZ-BART, ANDRÉ -
   CRITICISM AND INTERPRE-
   TATION
      The last of the just
The six million deaths of
Ernie Levy. J. Tallmer. 17:
115-20, Mar/Apr '61.

SCHWERIN, Ron
   [photo] 64:52, Mar '69.

SCHWOB, Marcel
   Laughter [satire] 13:112-14,
May/Je '60.

SCHWOB, MARCEL
   Marcel Schwob, double soul.
P. Pia. 13:111, May/Je '60.
   (photograph of) 13:96, May/
Je '60.

SCIENCE
         see
WAR AND SCIENCE

SCIENCE: an administrative
question [satire] J. Borzic. 13:
160-8, May/Je '60.

The SCIENCE fiction of Bertolt
Brecht [essay] E. Bentley. 41:
28-32+, Je '66.

SCRAP of paper [story] J. Purdy.
48:22-5+, Aug '67.

The SCROLL-work on the cas-
ket [prose-poem] J. Spicer. 2:

54-5, '57.

SCULPTORS, AMERICAN
         see
BOISE, Ron

SCULPTORS, FRENCH
         see
JUVA

SCULPTURE
         see
CONSTRUCTIVISM
KONARAK (temple)
METAL SCULPTURE
SCULPTORS

SCULPTURE, AMERICAN
   American construction sculpture. I. Sandler. 8:136-46,
spring '59.

SCULPTURE by Ron Boise: the
Kama Sutra theme [essay] A.
Watts. 36:64-5, Je '65.

SCULPTURE, METAL
         see
METAL SCULPTURE

SEALE, Bobby
   The double standard of justice [essay] 79:48-9, Je '70.

SEALE, BOBBY
   (drawing of) 75:20, Feb '70.

The SEAS of China [poem] B.
Vian. 82:41, Sept '70.

SEATTLE burlesque [story] J.
Kerouac. 4:106-12, '57.

SEAVER, Richard
   An anniversary unnoticed
[essay] 36:53-6, Je '65.
   Notes from the underground:
sugar cane and the "free-
world" press [essay] 77:16+,
Apr '70.

The SECOND son [story] R.

Coover. 31:72-88, Oct/Nov '63.

The SECRET companions [essay]
N. Hentoff. 82:55-7, Sept '70.

SEDATIVE DRUGS
Points between sedative and
consciousness-expanding drugs.
W. Burroughs. 34:72-4, Dec
'64.

SEEING America first with Andy
Warhol [review essay] D. Rader.
78:22+, May '70.

SEGAL, Abraham
Mister Freedom: an inter-
view with William Klein. 77:
49-50, Apr '70.

SEIDEL, Frederick
The walk there [poem] 26:
20-2, Sept/Oct '62.

SEITZ, Jane
see
BROWN, Helen and Jane Seitz

SELBY, Hubert
Fat Phil's day [story] 48:
52-3, Aug '67.
Happy birthday [story] 69:
35-7+, Aug '69.
The queen is dead [story] 34:
13-7+, Dec '64.
Solving the ice-cream cone
problem [essay] 57:56-8, Aug
'68.

SELBY, HUBERT - CRITICISM
AND INTERPRETATION
Last exit to Brooklyn
Hubert Selby: symbolic intent
and ideological resistance (or
cocksucking and revolution) S.
Yurick. 71:49-51+, Oct '69.

SELDON, E. S.
The cannibal feast [review]
22:110-3, Jan/Feb '62.
Lolita and Justine [review
essay] 6:156-9, autumn '58.

SELF determination in life
[cartoons] Siné. 11:130-3,
Jan/Feb '60.

SELIG, Sylvie
[illus] 44:25, Dec '66.

SELIGSON, Tom
From the third eye... Hollywood's last stand [review essay]
85:78-9, Dec '70.
Notes from the underground:
Women's Lib: save the last
dance for me [narrative] 80:18-
21+, Jl '70.
On Rikers Island [essay] 77:
45-7+, Apr '70.

SELIGSON, Tom, compiler.
Poems by Black children.
79:27-9, Je '70.

SELTZER, Isadore
[illus] 50:30, Dec '67; 57:56,
Aug '68; 78:28, May '70.

SELVON, Samuel
Knock on wood [story] 9:25-
33, summer '59.

SEMBENE, OUSMANE - CRITI-
CISM AND INTERPRETATION
Mandabi
Mandabi: confronting Africa.
J. Lester. 78:55-8+, May '70.

SEMPÉ
[cartoon] 36:45, Je '65; 40:
86-7, Apr '66; 44:78-9, Dec
'66; 45:45, Feb '67; 46:26, 48,
Apr '67; 48:45, 103, Aug '67;
55:80, Je '68; 59:69, Oct '68;
67:48, Je '69.

SENS, A. G.
After the war is over [car-
toons] 19:83-5, Jl/Aug '61.
The artist's studio [cartoon]
25:102, Jl/Aug '62.
The clean woman [cartoon]
36:61, Je '65.
The ladder of success [car-

toon] 22:86-7, Jan/Feb '62.
　The poet's new audience [cartoon] 20:90-3, Sept/Oct '61.
　A situation [cartoon] 33:66-7, Aug/Sept '64.
　[cartoons] 26:98, Sept/Oct
'62; 27:107, Nov/Dec '62; 28:
100, Jan/Feb '63; 29:119, Mar/
Apr '63; 30:45-6, May/Je '63;
31:107, Oct/Nov '63; 34:75,
Dec '64; 35:51, Mar '65; 42:45,
Aug '66; 43:65, Oct '66; 45:
107, Feb '67; 47:80, Je '67;
48:69, Aug '67; 51:73, Feb '68;
53:76, Apr '68; 58:82, Sept '68;
60:65, Nov '68; 62:57, 73, Jan
'69; 63:86, Feb '69; 65:65, Apr
'69; 70:74, Sept '69; 72:40,
Nov '69; 75:67, Feb '70; 77:72,
Apr '70; 79:81, Je '70.

SERREAU, Genevieve
　A new comic style: Arrabal
[essay] 15:61-9, Nov/Dec '60.

SEVEN days from Zen camp
[poem] D. Myers. 64:28-9,
Mar '69.

The SEVEN deadly sins [review]
J. Tallmer. 9:200-7, summer
'59.

SEVEN of velvet [poem] L.
Kandel.　75:49, Feb '70.

SEX
　What sex really is; or, name
it and you can have it.　P.
Tyler.　58:18-21+, Sept '68.

SEX and politics: an interview
with Vilgot Sjöman. J. Lahr.
56:22-6+, Jl '68.

SEX AND RACE
　Getting to the nitty-gritty:
sex, race, and racism.　N.
Hentoff.　36:68-74, Je '65.

SEX IN ART
　　　　　　see

EROTIC ART

SEX IN FILMS
　Do they or don't they?　Why
it matters so much.　P. Tyler.
78:25-7+, May '70.

SEX IN LITERATURE
　The erotic society.　M.
Girodias.　39:64-9, Feb '66.

SEX IN THE THEATER
　Do they or don't they?　Why
it matters so much.　P. Tyler.
78:25-7+, May '70.

SEXUAL BEHAVIOR
　The endless humiliation.　A.
Adamov.　8:64-95, spring '59.
　Marijuana and sex.　E.
Goode.　66:19-21+, May '69.
　Pleasure, need and taboo.
L. Ullerstam.　40:40-5, Apr
'66.

SEYMOUR, Alan
　Notes from the underground:
but whose Turkey? [essay] 85:
74-7, Dec '70.

SHADES of paintstore orange.
[illus] L. Lonidier.　41:38-9,
Je '66.

SHAINBERG, Lawrence
　Notes from the underground:
Chappaqua [review essay] 50:
22-5+, Dec '67.

SHAKESPEARE, WILLIAM -
　CRITICISM AND INTERPRE-
　TATION
　　　　King Lear
　King Lear or Endgame.　J.
Kott.　33:52-65. Aug/Sept '64.
　Macbeth (modern version)
　Putting Shakespeare in a new
environment.　J. Lahr.　76:63-
8, Mar '70.
　　　　Othello
　The two paradoxes of Othello.
J. Knott.　40:15-21+, Apr '66.

SHANKAR, RAVI - CRITICISM
AND INTERPRETATION
From the third eye... Pop
freak and passing fancy. A.
Aronowitz. 77:86-8, Apr '70.

SHAPIRO, Karl
Aubade [poem] 50:63, Dec
'67.
The Bourgeois Poet [poems]
32:50-5, Apr/May '64.

SHARAT Chandrá, G. S.
Matru desh [poem] 85:37,
Dec '70.

SHARKEY, John J.
US — A [poem] 60:45, Nov
'68.

SHATTUCK, Roger
Superliminal Note [essay]
13:24-33, May/Je '60.

SHAYBO [story] P. Boyle. 45:
21-3+, Feb '67.

SHE [poem] E. Field. 34:18-
9, Dec '64.

SHE [poem] V. Huidobro. 20:
99, Sept/Oct '61.

SHE [poem] R. Wilbur. 17:61-
2, Mar/Apr '61.

SHE went to stay [poem] R.
Creeley. 6:39, autumn '58.

SHEEPER [novel excerpt] I.
Rosenthal. 46:49+, Apr '67.

SHELL FORMS (Architecture)
Felix Canela: shells in
architecture. E. McCoy. 7:
127-33, winter '59.

SHEPARD, SAM - CRITICISM
AND INTERPRETATION
Operation sidewinder
Spectacles of disintegration.
J. Lahr. 79:31-3+, Je '70.

SHEPHERD, Jack and Christo-
pher S. Wren
Quotations from Chairman
LBJ [satire] 51:27-9, Feb '68.

SHINOYAMA, Kishin
Twins [a portfolio of photo-
graphs] 72:42-7, Nov '69.
Portfolio of photographs. 66:
50-7, May '69.
[photo] 64:cover, Mar '69;
66:cover, May '69; 72:cover,
Nov '69.

SHOULD I assume America is
already dead? [essay] S. Krim.
68:19-21+, Jl '69.

SCHUFFLER, Jack C.
The itchy tooth [story] 53:
60-3, Apr '68.
Parts shared [story] 57:18-
21+, Aug '68.

SHUSEKI, Hayashi
see
HUBBELL, Lindley Williams

The SHYSTER'S wedding [story]
J. Papaleo. 80:49-51+, Jl '70.

SIESTA in Xbalba and return to
the states [poem] A. Ginsberg.
4:29-47, '57.

SIGNALLING through the
flames: the Living Theatre in
Europe [essay] S. Gottlieb. 45:
24-32+, Feb '67.

SIGN and ground [story] A.
Higgins. 30:85-92, May/Je '63.

SIKORSKI, WLADISLAW (Gen-
eral)
The Pole who died on time.
R. Hochhuth. 55:30-2+, Je '68.

The SILENT theater of Richard
Avedon [essay] J. Lahr. 81:
34+, Aug '70.

SILKE, James R.
[photo] 63:cover, Feb '69.

SILVER, HORACE - CRITICISM
AND INTERPRETATION
The craftsmanship of Horace
Silver. M. Williams. 18:102-
8, May/Je '61.

SILVER, HORACE
(photograph of) 18:103, May/
Je '61.

SIMON, NEIL - CRITICISM AND
INTERPRETATION
Last of the red hot lovers
Broadway comedy: images
of impotence. J. Lahr. 78:39-
40+, May '70.

SIMPSON, Joseph W.
Thoughts on Allen Ginsberg's
visit to Birmingham [poem] 83:
37, Oct '70.

SINCLAIR, Bill
[cartoon] 55:47, Je '68.
[illus] 56:28, Jl '68; 60:41,
Nov '68.

SINÉ [pseud]
CIA [illus] 66:33-5, May '69.
Closing the Olympics [car-
toons] 15:94-5, Nov/Dec '60.
For Darwin's centenary [car-
toon] 12:54-5, Mar/Apr '60.
The good life [cartoons] 14:
66-9, Sept/Oct '60.
Self determination in life
[cartoons] 11:130-3, Jan/Feb
'60.
These weapons will still re-
main [cartoon] 10:42-6, Nov/
Dec '59.
W. C. [cartoons] 24:72-84,
May/Je '62.
[cartoons] 13:145, May/Je
'60; 39:cover, Feb '66; 46:91,
Apr '67.

SINET, Maurice
see

SINÉ [pseud]

SINGERS
see
FOLK SINGERS
JAZZ SINGERS
PIAF, EDITH
ROCK, MUSICIANS

SINGH, Khrushwant
Black jasmine [story] 37:54-
8, Sept '65.

SIRVENTIS [poem] P. Blackburn. 10:83-6, Nov/Dec '59.

SITTING reading Rilke [poem]
P. Brown. 20:63, Sept/Oct '61.

A SITUATION [cartoon] A.
Sens. 33:66-7, Aug/Sept '64.

SIX-day and ball-bearing [poem]
J. Oppenheimer. 70:31, Sept
'69.

The SIX million deaths of Ernie
Levy [review] J. Tallmer. 17:
115-20, Mar/Apr '61.

SJÖMAN, Vilgot
Sex and politics: an interview. J. Lahr. 56:22-6+, Jl
'68.

SJÖMAN, VILGOT - CRITICISM
AND INTERPRETATION
I am curious (blue)
Taboos and film: an inter-
view with Vilgot Sjoman. K.
Carroll. 82:49-53, Sept '70.
I am curious (yellow)
I was curious [diary excerpt]
56:18-21+, Jl '68.

SJÖMAN, VILGOT
(photograph of) 56:22, Jl '68.

SKELTON, RED - CRITICISM
AND INTERPRETATION
Clownish TV-II: Red Skelton.
M. Williams. 46:68-71, Apr '67.

SKIR, Leo
Angelina-in-the-wilderness or, the last freedom [story] 59:58-61, Oct '68.
Elise Cowen; a brief memoir of the fifties.   48:70-2+, Aug '67.
Leo in Jerusalem-I [essay] 64:19-23+, Mar '69.
A nocturnal emission in the house of George Orenstein [story] 53:45-6+, Apr '68.
Notes from the underground: The Living Theatre [narrative] 63:22-3+, Feb '69.
Notes from the underground: the New Left [essay] 62:22-3+, Feb '69.
Notes from the underground: the road is known [essay] 82: 16-20+, Sept '70.
This is a picture [story] 71: 23-7+, Oct '69.

SKVORECKY, Josef
Pink champagne [story] 64: 57-9+, Mar '69.
The uncelebrated jumping frog of Calaveras County [story] 82:39-41, Sept '70.

SLACKMAN, Charles B.
[illus] 71:52, Oct '69; 78: 38, May '70; 80:52, Jl '70; 81: 20, Aug '70; 82:22, Sept '70.

SLANG
The excluded words. W. Young. 32:28-32+, Apr/May '64.

SLATER, Philip E.
Kill anything that moves [excerpt from The pursuit of loneliness] 79:55-7+, Je '70.

SLAWOMIR Mrozek: the mask of irony [essay] J. Lahr. 67: 53-5+, Je '69.

SLIDING two mirrors together [poem] T. Raworth. 38:26, Nov '65.

SLIME [story]   E. Ionesco. 41:22-7+, Je '66.

SMALL poem.   P. Brown. 10: 55, Nov/Dec '59.

SMALL tantric sermon [poem] P. Whalen.   2:117-8, '57.

SMASHED [poem] J. Sabines. 7:140, winter '59.

SMITH, Herbert
Poem.   54:43, May '68.

SMITH, PERRY
(photograph of) 81:39, Aug '70.

SMITH, Richard
[illus] 83:52, Oct '70.

SMITH, William Jay
The vision [poem]   17:66, Mar/Apr '61.

The SNAKE [story] A. Lall. 22:93-8, Jan/Feb '62.

SNOW, Charles Percy
The moral unneutrality of science [excerpt from an address before the American Association of Science,   Dec. 27, 1960] 17:1-2, Mar/Apr '61.

SNYDER, Gary
A berry feast [poem] 2:110-4, '57.
Cartagena [poem] 9:130, summer '59.
Letter from Kyoto [essay] 3:132-4, '57.
Maya [poem] 34:41, Dec '64.
Night [poem] 9:129, summer '59.
North Beach alba [poem] 2: 114, '57.
Passage to more than India [essay] 52:41-3+, Mar '68.
The public bath [poem] 29: 75-6, Mar/Apr '63.

SNYDER, Gary, translator
see
HAN-SHAN. Cold Mountain
poems.

SO why not [poem] J. Grady.
3:81, '57.

SOCIAL CONDITIONS
see
SOCIAL PROBLEMS
U. S. - SOCIAL CONDITIONS

SOCIAL PROBLEMS
Why are there no alterna-
tives? P. Goodman. 16:1-5,
Jan/Feb '61.

The SOCIALISM that came in
from the cold [essay] J-P.
Sartre. 84:27-32+, Nov '70.

SOLAL, MARTIAL - CRITICISM
AND INTERPRETATION
Jottings on pianists. M.
Williams. 29:123-7, Mar/Apr
'63.

SOLANAS, FERNANDO - CRITI-
CISM AND INTERPRETATION
La hora de los hornos
Solanas: film as a political
essay. L. Marcorelles. 68:
31-3+, Jl '69.

A SOLID house [play] E. Garro.
7:62-74, winter '59.

SOLILOQUY in the waves [poem]
P. Neruda. 44:21, Dec '66.

SOLITUDE
The dialectic of solitude. O.
Paz. 20:100-13, Sept/Oct '61.

SOLVING the ice-cream cone
problem [essay] H. Selby. 57:
56-8, Aug '68.

SOME comments in appreciation
of Ellington [essay] M. Williams.
17:106-14, Mar/Apr '61.

SOME 16th century Japanese
love songs; from the Kanginshū
(translated by Bruce Watson)
[poems] 27:108-9, Nov/Dec '62.

SOMEDAY what you really are
is going to catch up with you
[satire] M. O'Donoghue. 46:
38-41, Apr '67.

SOMETHING big is happening
to me [story] W. Eastlake. 25:
8-21, Jl/Aug '62.

SOMETHING'S happening and
you don't know what it is, do
you Mr. Jones? [essay] N.
Hentoff. 41:54-6, Je '66.

SOMSKY, John
[illus] 60:46, Nov '68.

SONG [poem] F. Meng-Lung.
10:47, Nov/Dec '59.

SONG for a cool departure
[poem] P. Blackburn. 4:143-4,
'57.

The SONG of the bird in the
loins [poem] J. Spicer. 2:58,
'57.

SONGMY MASSACRE
see
VIETNAMESE WAR, 1957 -
ATROCITIES

SONNY Rollins: spontaneous
orchestration [review essay]
M. Williams. 22:114-22, Jan/
Feb '62.

SONTAG, Susan
Against interpretation [essay]
34:76-80+, Dec '64.

SORIANO, Juan
Interview with Juan Soriano.
E. Poniatowska. 7:141-52,
winter '59.

SORIANO, JUAN
(photograph of) 7:142, winter
'59.

SOUNDS of silence [essay] N.
Hentoff.   80:53-5, Jl '70.

SOUP, cosmos and tears [poem]
C. Bukowski. 79:37, Je '70.

The SOURCES of the Loir at
Illiers [essay] M. Proust. 19:
55-62, Jl/Aug '61.

SOUTH AFRICA
Black blood: a South African
diary. A. Higgins. 34:28-32+,
Dec '64.

The SOUTH coast [poem]
Brother Antoninus. 2:17, '57.

SOUTHERN, Terry
The blood of a wig [story]
49:22-4+, Oct '67.
Put-down [story] 9:70-5,
summer '59.
Red-dirt Marihuana [novel
excerpt] 11:116-29, Jan/Feb '60.

SOUTHGATE, Patsy
Artie [story] 9:120-8, sum-
mer, '59.
Fall in New England [poem]
52:95, Mar '68.
Freddy [play] 25:27-39, Jl/
Aug '62.
"Nobody operates like an
IBM machine;" for Frank O'Hara
[poem] 45:109, Feb '67.
A very important lady [story]
3:62-76, '57.

SPADE, SAM
The death of Sam Spade. J.
Goldberg. 28:107-16, Jan/Dec
'63.

The SPECIALIST [cartoon] R.
Brandreth. 56:46, Jl '68.

SPECTACLES of disintegration

[review essay] J. Lahr. 79:
31-3+, Je '70.

SPECULATIONS about Jakob
[novel excerpt] U. Johnson.
21:31-4, Nov/Dec '61.

SPELLMAN, A. B.
Genesis of the new music-I:
Coltrane [review essay] 45:81-
3, Feb '67.
Genesis of the new music-II:
Cecil Taylor [review essay] 46:
72-3+, Apr '67.
Genesis of the new music-
III: Ornette Coleman [review
essay] 47:78-80, Je '67.

SPICER, Jack
Berkeley in time of plague
[poem] 2:52, '57.
The dancing ape... [poem] 2:
52, '57.
Hibernation--after Morris
Graves [poem] 2:55, '57.
Psychoanalysis: an elegy
[poem] 2:56-7, '57.
The scroll-work on the cas-
ket [prose-poem] 2:54-5, '57.
The song of the bird in the
loins [poem] 2:58, '57.
Troy poem. 2:53, '57.

The SPIDER and the fly [story]
S. Lambert.   54:32-5+, May
'68.

The SPIDER-child of Madras
[story] P. Gascar. 9:91-5,
summer '59.

SPIES
                  see
PHILBY, Kim

SPIKE, Paul
Box 456 [story] 58:32-4,
Sept '68.
"We don't want to be edu-
cated for the CIA": an interview
with Mark Rudd.   57:50-5+,
Aug '68.

SPILT beer [autobiographical essay] A. Andersch. 21:47-53, Nov/Dec '66.

SPINA, Paul
[illus] 63:50, Feb '69; 73:27, Dec '69.

SPORT CARS
see
FERRARI
MINI-COOPER S

SPORTS, Nature of
The theater of sports. J. Lahr. 72:39-41+, Nov '69.

SPOTLIGHT on Miss Marigold Flagg [pictorial satire] M. O'Donoghue and Chaz. 42:33-40, Aug '66.

SPRING for Alison [story] F. Conroy. 12:90-101, Mar/Apr '60.

SPRING '61 [poem] L. Kandel. 32:78, Apr/May '64.

SPRING-song of the petroleum board meeting (an after luncheon fancy for voices and music) [poem] P. Roche. 30:24-9, May/Je '63.

SPRING thoughts for Freddie [memoir] D. di Prima. 55:65-9+, Je '68.

SPRINGER, Frank
[illus] 47:cover, Je '67.
see also
O'DONOGHUE, Michael and Frank Springer.

SPURT of blood [play] A. Artaud. 28:62-6, Jan/Feb '63.

The SQUARE-shooter and the saint; a story about Jerusalem. R. Coover. 25:92-101, Jl/Aug '62.

STAINED lass [satire] M. O'Donoghue. 48:20-1, Aug '67.

STAMATY
[cartoon] 71:56, Oct '69.

STANDING on a streetcorner; a little play. G. Corso. 23:63-78, Mar/Apr '62.

STANFORD, Herbert W.
Erecting a sacrilegious cross on a Saturday on Washburn Campus [poem] 16:109, Jan/Feb '61.

STATIONARY point [poem] P. Neruda. 22:38, Jan/Feb '62.

A STATUE of Goldsmith [essay] P. Goodman. 8:175-82, spring '59.

STAY in school so you'll get a good job, have lots of money, and be able to buy the nice things around you [satire] J. Ryan. 85:56-9, Dec '70.

STEINER, GEORGE - CRITI-CISM AND INTERPRETATION
The erotic society. M. Girodias. 39:64-9,- Feb '66.

STEINER'S tour [novel excerpt] P. O'Connor. 11:85-96, Jan/Feb '60.

STEINGESSER, Martin
Babyhip [poem] 64:66, Mar '69.
Never mind [poem] 67:33, Je '69.
Saroyan: the "new" old poetry [review] 81:76-7, Aug '70.
Watch out [poem] 57:53, Aug '68.

STEIR, Pat
[illus] 60:38, Nov '68; 68:66, Jl '69.

A STEP away from them [poem]
F. O'Hara. 3:60-1, '57.

STERN, BERT - CRITICISM
    AND INTERPRETATION
    "Jazz on a summer's day"
J. Tallmer. 14:126-33, Sept/
Oct '60.

STEVENS, Shane
    Way uptown in another world
[story] 27:44-9, Nov/Dec '62.

STEWART, Rex
    Duke Ellington: one of a kind
[essay] 44:52-4+, Dec '66.

STILL life [poem] M. Dúran.
7:86, winter '59.

STILL poem 9.   P. Lamantia.
11:100, Jan/Feb '60.

STITT, SONNY - CRITICISM
    AND INTERPRETATION
    Stitt in the studio. M. Wil-
liams. 27:119-28, Nov/Dec '62.

STITT, SONNY
    (photograph of) 27:120, Nov/
Dec '62.

STONE garden [essay] W.
Petersen. 4:127-37, '57.

STOPPARD, Tom
    Rosencrantz & Guildenstern
are dead [play] 52:47-72, Mar
'68.
    The story [story] 56:52-5,
Jl '68.

The STORY [story] T. Stoppard.
56:52-5, Jl '68.

STORY of O, the lovers of
Roissy [novel excerpt] P. Reage.
31:33-44, Oct/Nov '63.

The STORY of Tania: Ché's
woman in Bolivia [essay] L.
Gonzales and G. Sánchez Salazar.

60:18-21+, Nov '68.

STOWERS, J. Anthony
    Dakar [poem] 47:54, Je '67.
    Three poems [Zanj; Jomo;
The natives abroad] 65:26-7,
Apr '69.

STRAVINSKY, IGOR - CRITI-
    CISM AND INTERPRETATION
    Agon
    Three sides of Agon. E.
Denby. 7:168-76, winter '59.

The STREET scene: playing for
keeps [essay] J. Lahr. 59:48-
51+, Oct '68.

STRETCH to health [poem] T.
L. Jackrell. 17:94-5, Mar/Apr
'61.

The STRIKE: student power in
Berkeley [essay] L. Rapoport.
46:80-2, Apr '67.

STROMBERG, Robert
    A talk with Louis-Ferdinand
Céline [essay] 19:102-7, Jl/
Aug '61.

The STRUCTURE of rime
[poem] R. Duncan. 2:23-9, '57.

The STRUGGLE for the laugh in
the courtroom [essay] J.
Schultz. 79:21-5+, Je '70.

STUART Davis: a memoir
[essay] B. O'Doherty. 39:22-7,
Feb '66.

STUCKEL, Eugene
    To the soldier who shot
Lorca [poem] 74:35, Jan '70.

STUDENTS - POLITICS
    The last hurrah? N. Hentoff.
81:21-3, Aug '70.

STUDENTS as media critics: a
new course [essay] N. Hentoff.

72:53-5, Nov '69.

STUDENTS FOR A DEMOCRATIC
  SOCIETY
    SDS: from Port Huron to
La Chinoise. J. Newfield. 72:
15-7+, Dec '69.

STUDLEY Hungwell III [poem]
C. Reavis. 68:37, Jl '69.

SUGAR cane and the "free-
world" press [essay] R. Seaver.
77:16+, Apr '70.

SUMNER, Bill
    [illus] 78:cover, May '70.

SUN RA - CRITICISM AND IN-
  TERPRETATION
    Notes from the underground:
Sun Ra. S. Brecht. 54:88-90,
May '68.

SUNDAY sermon and acrostic
[poem] J. Beck 33:48, Aug/
Sept '64.

SUPERLIMINAL note [essay]
R. Shattuck. 13:24-33, May/Je
'60.

SURGAL, Jon
    High yellow put-down minuet
[poem] 59:47, Oct '68.

SURREALISM (Art)
    The impact of Surrealism on
the New York School [with photographs and prints] J. Myers.
12:75-85, Mar/Apr '60.

SUTHERLAND, Elizabeth
    Interview with Andrei Voz-
nesenksy. 28:37-42, Jan/Feb
'63.

SUZUKI, Daisetz T.
    Aspects of Japanese culture
[essay] 6:40-56, autumn '58.

SWAN, Jon

Football [play] 59:36-43,
Oct '68.

SWANSON, Karl W.
    [illus] 68: 46, Jl '69; 71:48,
Oct '69.

SWEET confessions [play] G.
Arnaud. 3:135-59, '57.

SWEET Gwendolyn + the
countess [poem] E. Field. 45:
97, Feb '67.

SWINEHERD [story] A. West.
8:16-21+, 50, spring '59.

The SWINGS [play] E. De
Grazia. 26:50-66, Sept/Oct
'62.

SWOPE, Martha
    [photo] 19:cover, Jl/Aug
'61; 52:47-72, Mar '68.

A SYLLABIC poem. P. Hoff-
man. 38:85, Nov '65.

TV: tell me a story [essay]
M. Williams. 47:70-2, Je '67.

TABOOS and film: an interview
with Vilgot Sjoman. K. Carroll. 82:49-53, Sept '70.

TAGGART, William and William
  Haines
    Fort Lauderdale beer bust
[book excerpt] 52:29-30+, Mar
'68.

TAIWAN
                    see
CHINA (Republic of)

TAKE, 25: III: 59 [poem] P.
Whalen. 9:131, summer '59.

TALBOT, Daniel
    A quarrel over strategy!
[reply to A. Vogel] 48:54, Aug
'67.

TALE of a later Leander [poem]
J. Logan. 29:18-20, Mar/Apr
'63.

A TALK with Louis-Ferdinand
Céline [essay] R. Stromberg
19:102-7, Jl/Aug '61.

TALKING with myself (with
limited apologies to Edmund
Wilson) [essay] M. Williams.
33:83-5, Aug/Sept '64.

TALLMAN, Warren
Kerouac's sound [essay] 11:
153-69, Jan/Feb '60.

TALLMER, Jerry
Applejack [review] 24:95-
106, May/Je '62.
Bye bye blackbird [essay]
10:117-31, Nov/Dec '59.
Down the Demerera [essay]
15:120-2, Nov/Dec '60.
Hold that tiger [review] 18:
109-13, May/Je '61.
"Jazz on a summer's day"
[review essay] 14:126-33, Sept/
Oct '60.
Lenny Bruce: 1926-1966
[essay] 44:22-3, Dec '66.
Lindsay in New York: Act
one [essay] 41:15-21+, Je '66.
Lindsay: mayor at work
[essay] 42:17-23+, Aug '66.
Lindsay vs. Lindsay [essay]
43:60-4+, Oct '66.
The magic box [essay] 19:
117-22, Jl/Aug '61.
The seven deadly sins [re-
view] 9:200-7, summer '59.
The six million deaths of
Ernie Levy [review] 17:115-20,
Mar/Apr '61.

TANGIERS
Glory hole (Nickel views of
the infidel in Tangiers) A.
Chester. 35:52-9, Mar '65.

TANIA [pseud]
The story of Tania: Che's

woman in Bolivia. L. Gonzalez
and G. Sánchez Salazar. 60:18-
21+, Nov '68.
(photograph of) 60:18, Nov
'68.

TANINO, Aki
Bride of a Samurai [story]
43:24-8+, Oct '66.
The tattooed wife [story] 56:
14-7+, Jl '68.

TANINO, Aki, translator
The one thousand ryo pledge
[story] 64:25-7+, Mar '69.

TARZAN. The Government.
Refrigerators. [story] B.
Anderson. 41:42-5, Je '66.

The TATTOOED wife [story]
A. Tanino. 56:14-7+, Jl '68.

TAYLOR, CECIL - CRITICISM
AND INTERPRETATION
Genesis of the new music-
II: Cecil Taylor. A. Spellman.
46:72-3+, Apr '67.

TAYLOR, CECIL
(photograph of) 46:72-3,
Apr '67.

TAYLOR, Simon Watson
An apodeictic outline [satire]
13:150-7, May/Je '60.

EL TEATRO CAMPESINO
Theater and propaganda. J.
Lahr. 52:33-7, Mar '68.

TELEVISION
The magic box. J. Tallmer.
19:117-22, Jl/Aug '61.
Participatory television. N.
Hentoff. 71:53-5, Oct '69.
TV: tell me a story. M.
Williams. 47:70-2, Je '67.
see also
CARTOON SHOWS (Television)
SKELTON, RED
VAN DYKE, DICK

TEN days in July [essay] K. Howard. 59:33-5+, Oct '68.

TERKEL, STUDS - CRITICISM AND INTERPRETATION
Hard times
Feeling the chill in the 70s. N. Hentoff. 77:16, Apr '70.

TERRELL, Robert
Discarding the dream [essay] 78:35-7+, May '70.

TEXT for nothing I [story] S. Beckett. 9:21-4, summer '59.

THACKER, Eric and Anthony Earnshaw
Musrum [story] 63:47-9+, Feb '69.

THAT memory (Ce Souvenir) [poem] P. Reverdy. 11:25, Jan/Feb '60.

THE [poem] M. McClure. 2:48, '57.

The THEATER [interview] J. Sartre. 11:143-52, Jan/Feb '60.

THEATER and propaganda [essay] J. Lahr. 52:33-7, Mar '68.

THEATER and revolution [essay] J. Beck. 54:14-5+, May '68.

The THEATER of sports [essay] J. Lahr. 72:39-41+, Nov '69.

THEATER
The new theater: a retreat from realism. J. Lahr. 60:54-7+, Nov '68.
The street scene: playing for keeps. J. Lahr. 59:48-51+, Oct '68.
The theater [interview] J. Sartre. 11:143-52, Jan/Feb '60.

The theatre of sports. J. Lahr. 72:39-41+, Nov '69.
There is no avant-garde theater. E. Ionesco. 4:101-5, '57.

see also
BLACK THEATER
DRAMA
HAPPENINGS
LIVING THEATRE
NUDITY IN THE THEATER
OFF-BROADWAY THEATER
THE OPEN THEATRE
PERFORMANCE GROUP
SAN FRANCISCO MIME THEATER
SEX IN THE THEATER
EL TEATRO CAMPESINO
THEATER OF CRUELTY
THEATER OF THE ABSURD

THEATER - CHINA (People's Republic)
A hundred flowers of the same kind. K. Karol. 45:42-5, Feb '67.

THEATER - EASTERN EUROPE
From the third eye... behind the iron (theater) curtain. A. Schneider. 79:91-4, Je '70.

THEATER, Nature of
The theatre of sports. J. Lahr. 72:39-41+, Nov '69.

THEATER OF CRUELTY
No more masterpieces. A. Artaud. 5:150-9, summer '58.

THEATER OF THE ABSURD
An interview with Eugene Ionesco. F. de Towarnicki. 85:49-51+, Dec '70.

THEATER - POLITICAL AS-PECTS
Notes from the underground: theater and revolution. J. Beck. 54:14-5+, May '68.
Theater and propaganda. J. Lahr. 52:33-7, Mar '68.

THEATER - U. S.
Decades of dream-walking.
J. Lahr. 74:37-9+, Jan '70.
Jules Feiffer: satire as sub-
version. J. Lahr. 63:33-4+,
Feb '69.
Mystery on stage. J. Lahr.
73:53-7, Dec '69.
Spectacles of disintegration.
J. Lahr. 79:31-3+, Je '70.

The THEATER'S voluptuary itch
[essay] J. Lahr. 56:32-4+,
Jl '68.

The THEATRE of sports [essay]
J. Lahr. 72:39-41+, Nov '69.

THEATRICAL DIRECTORS
see
BERGHOF, HERBERT
BROOK, PETER
GREGORY, ANDRÉ
MINEO, SAL
SCHECHNER, RICHARD
VARGAS, ENRIQUE

THELONIUS Monk: modern
jazz in search of maturity
[essay] M. Williams. 7:178-
89, winter '59.

THEM and us: are peace protests self-therapy? [essay] N.
Hentoff. 48:46-9+, Aug '67.

THERE is no avant-garde
theater [essay] E. Ionesco. 4:
101-5, '57.

THEROX, Paul
Leper colony (for John Lind-
berg) [poem] 47:28-9, Je '67.

THESE weapons will still re-
main [cartoon] Siné. 10:42-6,
Nov/Dec '59.

THEY just fade away [novel ex-
cerpt] W. Burroughs 32:62-3+,
Apr/May '64.

"THEY think you're an airplane
and you're really a bird" [in-
terview with LeRoi Jones] 50:
51-3+, Dec '67.

The THIRD book about Achim
[novel excerpt] U. Johnson. 29:
77-84, Mar/Apr '63.

THIRD stream problems [re-
view essay] M. Williams. 30:
113-25, May/Je '63.

13 confessions [essay] A.
Vogel. 47:50-3+, Je '67.

THIRTEEN true confessions?
[reply to A. Vogel] G. Markopoulos 48:54-5, Aug '67.

'30s [poem] M. O'Donoghue.
81:24-5, Aug '70.

THIS is a picture [story] L.
Skir. 71:23-7+, Oct '69.

THIS place, rumord to have
been Sodom... [poem] R.
Duncan. 2:21-2, '57.

THIS poem has no title [poem]
B. Moraff. 24:72, May/Je '62.

THIS was my meal [poem] G.
Corso. 3:78, '57.

THOMAS, John
The water wheel [story] 28:
96-9, Jan/Feb '63.

THOMAS, Mack Sheldon
Folksong [story] 22:39-47,
Jan/Feb '62.
I'm not complaining [story]
30:64-9, May/Je '63.
Magnolia [story] 18:86-93,
May/Je '61.
Revival [story] 26:80-4,
Sept/Oct '62.

THORNS of the flower children
[essay] A. Hoffman. 73:21-3,

Dec '69.

THOUGHTFUL [poem] P.
Brown.   18:32, May/Je '61.

THOUGHTS on Allen Ginberg's
visit to Birmingham [poem] J.
Simpson.   83:37, Oct '70.

The THREE and a half minute
mile [poem] J. Oppenheimer.
47:61, Je '67.

THREE airs [poems] F. O'Hara.
9:34, summer '59.

The THREE-cornered pear/
America [poem] A. Voznesensky.
28:44-51, Jan/Feb '63.

THREE episodes from jammin'
the Greek scene [poems] J.
Williams. 17:43-6, Mar/Apr
'61.

THREE heroes and a clown
[story] W. Eastlake. 10:87-98,
Nov/Dec '59.

THREE kinds of angels [ex-
cerpt from the novel City of
night] J. Rechy.   26:38-48,
Sept/Oct '62.

The THREE Ladies [poem] R.
Creeley.   5:25, summer '58.

THREE letters.   A. Artaud.
28:52-61, Jan/Feb '63.

THREE reflected visions [story]
A. Robbe-Grillet.   3:105-13,
'57.

THREE sides of Agon [review
essay] E. Denby. 7:168-76,
winter '59.

THREE versions of the oriental
squat: a triptych [narrative] R.
Walford. 51:64-70, Feb '68.

THREE voices found on the deserted floor of a subway train
at five o'clock in the morning
[poem] M. Mednick. 48:100,
Aug '67.

THRENODY [poem] W. Broughton.   31:45-7, Oct/Nov '63.

THURBER, JAMES - CRITI-
  CISM AND INTERPRETATION
   The years with Ross
Thurber's Ross: a minority re-
port. B. Friedman. 9:216-9,
summer '59.

THURBER'S Ross: a minority
report. [review] B. Friedman.
9:216-9, summer '59.

The TIDE [story] A. Pieyre de
Mandiargues. 46:32-3+, Apr
'67.

TIPTON, David
   From a Brooklyn apartment
[poem] 72:51, Nov '69.

TO a mother, buried [poem]
L. Ginsberg.   12:74, Mar/Apr
'60.

TO a motocyclist killed on
Route 9W [poem] M. Rumaker.
67:27, Je '69.

TO a 19-year-old marine killed
near Danang [poem] M.
Rumaker. 43:88, Oct '66.

TO all the gardeners: [poem]
G. Grass. 32:69, Apr/May '64.

TO the soldier who shot Lorca
[poem] E. Stuckel.   74:35,
Jan '70.

TOBEY, Mark
   [color plates] 11:29-36, Jan/
Feb '60.

TOBEY, MARK - CRITICISM

AND INTERPRETATION
Mark Tobey. D. Ashton.
11:29-36, Jan/Feb '60.

TODOS Santos, dia de Muertos
[essay] O. Paz. 7:22-37,
winter '59.

TOM Riley [story] S. Delaney.
16:102-8, Jan/Feb '61.

The TOMB [story] G. Haresnape. 42:42-4+, Aug '66.

TOMLINSON, Charles
The impalpabilities [poem]
14:95, Sept/Oct '60.
Rhenish winter: a montage
after Apollinaire [poem] 23:
38-40, Mar/Apr '62.

TOMLINSON, Roger
[illus] 64:38, Mar '69.

TOPOR, Roland
[illus] 80:34, Jl '70.

TORCH ballad for John Spicer:
d. 8/17/65 [poem] P. Blackburn. 43:81, Oct '66.

TORMA, Julien
Letter to René Daumal. 13:
120-1, May/Je '60.

TORMA, JULIEN - CRITICISM
AND INTERPRETATION
Julien Torma, author by
neglect. L. Barnier. 13:118-
9, May/Je '60.

TORMA, JULIEN
(photograph of) 13:96, May/
Je '60.

TORRE, Lou de la
[photo] 76:20-3, Mar '70.

TOWARNICKI, Frédéric de
An interview with Eugene
Ionesco. 85:49-51+, Dec '70.

The TOY drum [novel excerpt]
G. Grass. 21:36-44, Nov/Dec
'61.

TRADITION and the machine
[essay] T. Fitzsimmons and
R. Fukuda. 38:86-94, Nov '65.

TRAFFIC complaint [poem] J.
Grady. 3:81, '57.

The TRAGEDY of Vladimir
Mayakovsky (the prologue)
[poem] V. Mayakovsky. 77:25,
Apr '70.

TRANS [poem] M. Levinson.
74:62, Jan '70.

The TRANSSIBERIAN express
[poem] B. Cendrars. 33:20-31,
Aug/Sept '64.

TRAVEL with Flora [cartoons]
P. Flora. 26:75-9, Sept/Oct
'62.

TREZ
[cartoon] 72:54, Nov '69;
75:33, Feb '70.

TRIALS (conspiracy)
The double standard of justice.
B. Seale. 79:48-9, Je '70.
Motion will be denied. J.
Schultz. 75:21-5+, Feb '70.
The struggle for the laugh in
the courtroom. J. Schultz. 79:
21-5+, Je '70.

TRIALS (conspiracy) - Chicago
Like the last two people on
the face of the earth. J.
Schultz. 82:23-7+, Sept '70.
Repression and rebellion.
T. Hayden. 77:26-9, Apr '70.

TRIALS (military)
see
COURTS MARTIAL AND
COURTS OF INQUIRY

TRIALS (obscenity)
Howl
Horn on "Howl" L. Fer-
linghetti. 4:145-58, '57.
Lady Chatterley's lover
Opinion: U. S. District
Court... New York... [for the
plaintiffs] Grove Press, Inc.
and Readers' Subscription, Inc.
... F. Bryan.   9:37-68, sum-
mer '59.
Naked lunch
The Boston trail of "Naked
Lunch" [court excerpt] 36:40-
9, Je '65.
Tropic of cancer
Boston courtroom scene
[transcript excerpt] 28:81-4,
Jan/Feb '63.
"Cancer" in Chicago.   H.
Norris.   25:41-66, Jl/Aug '62.
Miller's "Tropic" on trial.
D. Bess.   23:12-37, Mar/Apr
'62.

A TRIP to four or five towns
[poem] J. Logan.   12:86-9,
Mar/Apr '60.

TROCCHI, Alexander
Cain's book [novel excerpt]
4:48-74, '57; 8:109-118, spring
'59; 12:16-23, Mar/Apr '60;
19:44-54, Jl/Aug '61.
Four poems: Wind from the
Bosphorus; He tasted history
with a yellow tooth; Notes; Portrait.   30:93-8, May/Je '63.
A note on George Orwell
[review essay] 6:150-5, autumn
'58.

TROPICAL butterflies [poem]
J. Ashbery.   8:98-9, spring '59.

The TROUBLED makers [story]
C. Foster.   4:9-28, '57.

TROUT fishing in America
[novel excerpt] R. Brautigan.
31:12-27, Oct/Nov '63.
_____ 2 [novel ex-

cerpt] R. Brautigan.   33:42-7,
Aug/Sept '64.

TROY poem [poem] J. Spicer.
2:53, '57.

The TRUCK [story] M. Rumaker.
46:58-63, Apr '67.

TRUMPET [story] D. Newlove.
72:21-3+, Nov '69.

The TRUTH [poem] P. Neruda.
44:20, Dec '66.

TRUTH and being; nothing and
time: a broken fragment from a
novel.   N. Mailer.   26:68-74,
Sept/Oct '62.

TUNE [poem] B. Moraff.   10:
47, Nov/Dec '59.

The TUNNEL [story] F. Dürrenmatt.   17:32-42, Mar/Apr
'61.

TURKEY - SOCIAL CONDI-
TIONS
Notes from the underground:
but whose Turkey?   A. Seymour.
85:74-7, Dec '70.

TURN on Guatemala! [story] R.
Elman.   59:20-2+, Oct '68.

TURNER, Frederick W.
Red man, white man, man on
the moon [essay] 80:22-6+, Jl
'70.

TURNING the camera into the
audience [essay] N. Hentoff. 53:
47-8+, Apr '68.

TUTUOLA, Amos
The animal that died but his
eyes still alive [novel excerpt]
5:107-12, summer '58.

The TWELVE [poem] A. Blok.
19:31-43, Jl/Aug '61.

21 points to The Physicists
[essay] F. Dürrenmatt. 34:34-
5, Dec '64.

TWILIGHT [poem] Ho-Chi-Minh.
43:44, Oct '66.

The TWILIGHT maelstrom of
Cookie LaVagetto [play] M.
O'Donoghue. 35:32-7, Mar '65.

TWINS [a portfolio of photo-
graphs] K. Shinoyama. 72:42-
7, Nov '69.

The TWO paradoxes of Othello
[essay] J. Kott. 40:15-21+,
Apr '66.

TWO poems; after Constantine
Cavafy. E. Field. 18:94,
May/Je '61.

TWO songs of Christian
America [poems] P. Ryan. 55:
51, Je '68.

TWO steps toward humanity
[reviews] A. Vogel. 77:88-9,
Apr '70.

TYLER, Parker
    Do they or don't they? Why
it matters so much [essay] 78:
25-7+, May '70.
    Dragtime and drugtime; or,
film à la Warhol [review essay]
46:27-31+, Apr '67.
    Fashion or passion: the NAC
and the avant-garde [reply to
A. Vogel] 48:55, Aug '67.
    From the third eye... Papa-
takis: tiger in a think tank
[essay] 83:70-4, Oct '70.
    Notes from the underground:
Relativity--a cosmic dream [re-
view] 48:21+, Aug '67.
    The tyranny of Warrendale
[review essay] 69:31-3+, Aug
'69.
    What sex really is; or, name
it and you can have it [essay]

58:18-21+, Sept '68.

TYNAN, Kenneth
    The Empress' new clothes
[essay] 73:43-7+, Dec '69.

The TYRANNY of Warrendale
[essay] P. Tyler. 69:31-3+,
Aug '69.

- U -

US--A [poem] J. Sharkey. 60:
45, Nov '68.

UBU Cocu (Act I) [play] A.
Jarry. 13:139-45, May/Je '60.

UEDA, Akinari
    The ghoul-priest [story] 60:
58-62, Nov '68.

ULLERSTAM, Lars
    Pleasure, need and taboo
[essay] 40:40-5, Apr '66.

The ULTIMATE all-American
technetronic queen [story] D.
Rader. 78:29-32+, May '70.

An UNAVOIDABLE delay [story]
D. Athill. 12:61-73, Mar/Apr
'60.

The UNCELEBRATED jumping
frog of Calaveras County [story]
J. Skvorecky. 82:39-41, Sept
'70.

UNCOVERING news uncoverage
[essay] N. Hentoff. 76:16-8,
Mar '70.

UNDERGROUND
          see
REVOLUTIONISTS

UNDERGROUND PRESS
    Notes from the underground:
high school underground. N.
Hentoff. 75:16-8, Feb '70.

The UNFAITHFUL wife [poem]
F. García Lorca. 30:43-4,
May/Je '63.

UNGERER, Tomi
Black power, white power
[illus] 50:47, Dec '67.
Girls [illus] 47:55-60, Je
'67.
[cartoon] 33:85, Aug/Sept
'64; 35:19, Mar '65; 42:57, 81,
Aug '66; 49:89, Oct '67.
[illus] 27:cover, Nov/Dec
'62; 45:cover, Feb '67; 79:50-
3, Je '70.

UNINVENTING the Negro. [essay]
N. Hentoff. 38:34-6+, Nov '65.

The UNIVERSITIES: a crisis of
legitimacy [essay] N. Hentoff.
62:47-9, Jan '69.

UNIVERSITY OF CALIFORNIA
AT BERKELEY
see
CALIFORNIA UNIVERSITY.
Berkeley.

UNIVERSITY OF DENVER
see
WOODSTOCK WEST

U. S. BUREAU OF CUSTOMS
Border crossing. J. Schultz.
30:99-112, May/Je '63.

U. S. --FOREIGN RELATIONS--
LATIN AMERICA
see
LATIN AMERICA--FOREIGN
RELATIONS--U. S.

U. S. - SOCIAL AND MORAL
CONDITIONS
Captain America's restau-
rant. N. Hentoff. 74:59-61,
Jan '70.
Decades of dream-walking.
J. Lahr. 74:37-9+, Jan '70.
Jules Feiffer: satire as sub-
version. J. Lahr. 63:33-4+,

Feb '69.
Kill anything that moves. P.
Slater. 79:55-7+, Je '70.
A sanity test for self and
society. N. Hentoff. 60:51-3+,
Nov '68.
Schools, jails, and the god-
dam system. J. Bishop. 81:
53-5+, Aug '70.
Spectacles of disintegration.
J. Lahr. 79:31-3+, Je '70.
see also
MIDDLE CLASS AMERICANS

The UNIVERSITIES: crisis of
legitimacy [essay] N. Hentoff.
62:47-9, Jan '69.

UNSUCCESSFUL raid [poem] G.
Grass. 36:93, Je '65.

UNTERECKER, John
Notes on the off-Broadway
theater [essay] 8:152-63,
spring '59.

UNTIL she screams [play] J.
Orton. 78:51-3, May '70.

UP again [poem] H. Knox. 73:
27, Dec '69.

UP against the wall! [essay]
D. Radar. 57:22-5+, Aug '68.

The UPBEAT beatnik [essay]
A. Buchwald. 14:153-4, Sept/
Oct '60.

US looking up to St. Bridget
[poem] B. Berkson and F.
O'Hara. 24:107-10, May/Je '62.

- V -

VAL
[cartoon] 65:82, Apr '69;
66:90, May '69; 77:81, Apr '70.

VALLEJO, César
Human poems. 55:23-5,
Je '68.

VALLEJO, CÉSAR
(photograph of) 55:22, Je '68.

VAN BUSKIRK, Alden
Three poems 33:74-6, Aug/
Sept '64.

VAN DYKE, DICK - CRITICISM
AND INTERPRETATION
Clownish TV-1: Dick Van
Dyke. M. Williams. 45:101-4,
Feb '67.

VAN DYKE, Willard
Early works: an interview
with Zelimir Zilnik. 75:43-5,
Feb '70.

VAN ITALLIE, JEAN CLAUDE -
CRITICISM AND INTERPRE-
TATION
The serpent
The Open Theatre: beyond
the absurd. J. Lahr. 66:63-8,
May '69.

VAN WOERKOM
[cartoon] 63:64, Feb '69.

VAQUERO [poem] E. Dorn. 5:
103, summer '58.

VARGAS, ENRIQUE
The street scene: playing
for keeps. J. Lahr. 59:48-
51+, Oct '68.
(photograph of) 59:48, Oct
'68.

VARIATIONS on the taste of
dried apricots [poem] G. Frumkin. 19:95, Jl/Aug '61.

VASCO
[cartoon] 82:68, 71, Sept
'70; 83:57, Oct '70; 84:55,
Nov '70.

VAUGHAN, SARAH - CRITICISM
AND INTERPRETATION
Sarah Vaughan: some notes
on a singer before it's too late.

M. Williams. 42:74-7, Aug
'66.

VELTRI, John
[photo] 82:58, Sept '70.

VERTOV, Dziga
We: a manifesto by film
worker Dziga Vertov. 83:50-1,
Oct '70.

A VERY important lady [story]
P. Southgate. 3:62-76, '57.

VIAN, Boris
I don't want to die [poem]
36:50-1, Je '65.
A letter to his magnificence
the Vice-curator Baron on the
subject of the rogues that cheat
us of our wars [satire] 13:54-
61, May/Je '60.
The seas of China [poem]
82:41, Sept '70.
The voyage to Khonostrov
[story] 49:58-61+, Oct '67.

VIAN, BORIS
(photograph of) 13:54, May/
Je '60.

A VICTIM of duty [story] E.
Ionesco. 29:21-6, Mar/Apr
'63.

The VICTORY--a fable [story]
A. Chester. 18:95-8, May/Je
'61.

VIETNAM déjà vu: a film review of Godard's La Chinoise.
L. Eliscu. 56:66-8, Jl '68.

VIETNAMESE WAR, 1957 -
ATROCITIES
The commonplace of Song
My. N. Hentoff. 76:59-61,
Mar '70.

VIETNAMESE WAR, 1957 -
PROTESTS, DEMONSTRA-
TIONS, ETC.

Report from Times Square. J. Beck. 24:121-5, May/Je '62.

VIETNAMESE WAR, 1957 -
PUBLIC OPINION
Waiting for Nurenberg. N. Hentoff. 45:74-80, Feb '67.

VIEW from an airliner [poem] E. Burrows. 3:93-4, '57.

VIEW of a woman at her bath [poem] W. C. Williams. 3:58, '57.

VIGNES, Michelle
[photo] 81:62, Aug '70.

The VILLAGE Voice (You've come a long way, Baby, but you got stuck there) [essay] J. Sale. 73:25-7+, Dec '69.

The VISION [poem] W. Smith. 17:66, Mar/Apr '61.

VISION of the gun [essay] D. Rader. 75:61-3+, Feb '70.

VIVA Vargas! Excerpts from the diary of a revolutionary. [story] W. Allen. 69:25-7, Aug '69.

VOGEL, Amos
The angry young film makers [essay] 6:163-83, autumn, '58.
The day Rap Brown became a press agent for Paramount [essay] 67:43-5+, Je '69.
From the third eye... Two steps toward humanity [reviews] 77:88-9, Apr '70.
Notes from the underground: a guide to all good things in life [review] 75:19, Feb '70.
Philosophy in the surf [essay] 41:41, Je '66.
13 confusions [essay] 47:50-3+, Je '67.

VOLKSWAGEN (automobile)

Drive, we'll do the rest. J. Held. 55:70-3, Je '68.

VOODOOISM
On the use of Catholic religious prints by the practitioners of Voodoo in Haiti. M. Leiris. 13:84-94, May/Je '60.

The VOYAGE to Khonostrov [story] B. Vian. 49:58-61+, Oct '67.

A VOYEUR in the labyrinth: an interview with Alain Robbe-Grillet. P. Démeron. 43:46-9+, Oct '66.

VOZNESENSKY, Andrei
Interview with Andrei Voznesensky. E. Sutherland. 28:37-42, Jan/Feb '63.
Lover of Lorca. [essay] 31:48-52, Oct/Nov '63.
The three-cornered pear/ America; English version by Anselm Hollo [poem] 28:44-51, Jan/Feb '63.

VOZNESENSKY, ANDREI
(photograph of) 28:43, Jan/Feb '63.

- W -

WADLEIGH, MICHAEL AND BOB MAURICE - CRITICISM AND INTERPRETATION
Woodstock
"Woodstock:" an interview with Michael Wadleigh and Bob Maurice. K. Carroll. 81:27-9+, Aug '70.

WAGNER, John
[illus] 62:50-1, Jan '69; 63:62, Feb '69; 65:16, Apr '69; 67:51, Je '69; 68:64, Jl '69.

WAIN, John
My nineteen-thirties [autobiographical essay] 9:76089,

summer '59; 14:71-87, Sept/
Oct '60.

WAINHOUSE, Austryn
    On translating Sade [essay]
42:50-6+, Aug '66.

WAITING for Nurenberg [essay]
N. Hentoff.   45:74-80, Feb '67.

WAKING [poem] P. Brown. 20:
63, Sept/Oct '61.

WALCOTT, Derek
    A far cry from Africa (re-
membering the Mau-Mau re-
bellion) [poem] 8:36, spring '59.

WALDMAN, Lester
    Formentera [photographs]
45:33-6, Feb '67.
    [photo] 42:cover, Aug '66;
44:cover, 70-1, Dec '66.

WALEY, Arthur, translator
                    see
MENG-LUNG, Feng. Song

WALFORD, Roy L.
    An expedition in search of
little fish [story] 65:17-9+,
Apr '69.
    The original irreplaceable
vision [interviews] 76:47-9+,
Mar '70.
    Three versions of the ori-
ental squat: a triptych [narrative]
51:64-70, Feb '68.

A WALK on the beach [story]
B. Roueché.   82:29+, Sept '70.

The WALK there [poem] F.
Seidel. 26:20-2, Sept/Oct '62.

WALLACE, GEORGE
    (photograph of) 81:39, Aug
'70.

WALLACH, Richard
    [photo] 83:54, Oct '70.

WALTER, Otto
    The mute [story] 21:94-100,
Nov/Dec '61.

The WANDERINGS of the tribe
[poem] A. Chumacero.   7:59-
61, winter '59.

WAR [poem] V. Havel. 48:88,
Aug '67.

The WAR machine [story] B.
Garner. 52:45-6+, Mar '68.

WAR
    A letter to his magnificence
the Vice-curator Baron on the
subject of the rogues that cheat
us of our wars [satire] B. Vain.
13:54-61, May/Je '60.

WAR AND SCIENCE
    The moral unneutrality of
science [excerpt from an address before the American Association of Science, Dec. 27,
1960] C. P. Snow. 17:1-2,
Mar/Apr '61.

WAREING, William
    Frontiersman [photo] 20:
cover, Sept/Oct '61.

WARHOL, Andy
    Ondine's Mare [excerpt from
his novel a] 58:26-31+, Sept
'68.

WARHOL, ANDY - CRITICISM
    AND INTERPRETATION
    Dragtime and drugtime; or,
film à la Warhol.   P. Tyler.
46:27-31+, Apr '67.
              Nude restaurant
    Notes from the underground:
Nude restaurant.   S. Brecht.
53:98-100, Apr '68.
                  Trash
    Notes from the underground:
seeing America first. D. Rader.
78:22+, May '70.

A WARRANT is out for the arrest of Henry Miller [poem] A. Hollo. 28:80, Jan/Feb '63.

WATCH out [poem] M. Steingesser. 57:53, Aug '68.

The WATER ration [poem] Ho-Chi-Minh. 43:44, Oct '66.

The WATER wheel [story] J. Thomas. 28:96-9, Jan/Feb '63.

WATSON, Burton, translator
                         see
KANGIN SHŪ

WATTS, Alan
    Sculpture by Ron Boise: the Kama Sutra theme [essay] 36:64-5, Je '65.

A WAY of life: an interview with John Cassavetes. A. Labarthe. 64:45-7, Mar '69.

WAY uptown in another world [story] S. Stevens. 27:44-9, Nov/Dec '62.

WE: a manifesto by film worker Dziga Vertov. 83:50-1, Oct '70.

We continue [poem] W. Merwin. 27:75, Nov/Dec '62.

"WE don't want to be educated for the CIA!" An interview with Mark Rudd. P. Spike. 57:50-5+, Aug '68.

WE ignoble savages [autobiographical essay] C. Ozick. 10:48-52+, Nov/Dec '59.

WE poets [poem] E. Sargent. 58:82, Sept '68.

WE shall overcome--when? [essay] N. Hentoff. 39:58-62, Feb '66.

"WE want to be humane, but we're only human" [review essay] J. Lahr. 53:36-40+, Apr '68.

WEAR you off my mind [poem] T. Fiofori. 56:27, Jl '68.

WEATHERMEN
    Vision of the gun. D. Rader. 75:61-3+, Feb '70.

WEBB, Charles Graham
    Ball/ta-moore [poem] 57:21, Aug '68.

WEBER, David O.
    American pastime [story] 84:23-5+, Nov '70.

WEDDING march [story] M. Bieler. 40:54-5, Apr '66.

WEILL, KURT - CRITICISM AND INTERPRETATION
    The seven deadly sins
    The seven deadly sins [review] J. Tallmer. 9:200-7, summer '59.

WEISMAN, Ann
    [illus] 52:26, Mar '68; 64:56, Mar '69; 75:64, Feb '70; 80:48, Jl '70; 82:27, Sept '70; 84:51, Nov '70.

WEISS, Chicago
    [illus] 55:40-4+, Je '68; 56:32, Jl '68; 58:22, 42, 44-7, Sept '68; 66:36, May '69.

WELCH, Lew
    The man who played himself [story] 17:97-105, Mar/Apr '61.

WELLS, Robert
    The big sale [poem] 82:27, Sept '70.

WENDE, Philip
    Adult animals [cartoons] 41:33-7, Je '66.

The adventures of Tom &
Dick Smith [comic strip] 45:
84-8, Feb '67.
More adult animals [car-
toons] 44:65-9, Dec '66.
[cartoon] 60:61, Nov '68.

WESSUM
[cartoon] 78:31, 80, May
'70; 79:68, Je '70; 81:65, 69,
Aug '70; 83:64, Oct '70.

WEST, Anthony C.
Swineherd [story] 8:16-21+,
spring '59.

WEST POINT
Notes from the underground:
West Point. D. Rader. 58:17+,
Sept '68.

WHALEN, Philip
Fond farewell to the Chicago
Review [poem] 9:131, summer
'59.
For a picture by Mike
Nathan [poem] 34:74, Dec '64.
For C [poem] 5:58-9, sum-
mer '58.
Historical disquisitions
[poem] 24:58-60, May/Je '62.
Homage to Lucretius [poem]
2:116, '57.
Homage to Robert Creeley
[poem] 2:115, '57.
Out of it [poem] 2:118, '57.
The road-runner [poem] 2:
115, '57.
The same old jazz [poem]
14:92-4, Sept/Oct '60.
Small tantric sermon [poem]
2:117-8, '58.
Take, 25:III:59 [poem] 9:
131, summer '59.

WHALEN, PHILIP
(photograph of) 2:between
p. 64 and 65, '57.

WHAT do you think of your
blue-eyed artist now, Mr. Death?
[essay] D. Rader. 80:38-41+,

Jl '70.

WHAT happened? [story] A.
Clarke. 85:21-2+, Dec '70.

WHAT is 'Pataphysics [spe-
cial issue] 13: May/Je '60.

WHAT is the left today?
[essay] L. Kolakowski. 47:30-
2+, Je '67.

WHAT is Zen [poem] R.
Rickert. 67:72, Je '69.

WHAT sex really is; or, name
it and you can have it [essay]
P. Tyler. 58:18-21+, Sept '68.

WHATEVER happened to the
clarinet? [essay] M. Williams.
32:82-3, Apr/May '64.

WHEN I was five I saw a dying
Indian [autobiographical sketch]
G. Corso. 48:28-30+, Aug '67.

WHERE it all began: the land-
ing in Cuba [book excerpt] C.
Guevara. 51:39-41+, Feb '68.

WHERE now? Who now? [es-
say] M. Blanchot. 7:222-9,
winter '59.

WHERE we all came into town
[essay] B. Behan. 18:18-32,
May/Je '61.

WHITE, Charles
[illus] 78:50, May '70; 81:
24-5, Aug '70.

WHITE man still speak with
forked tongue [review essay]
R. Wolf. 78:91-3, May '70.

WHITE woman--Black man
[essay] J. Lester. 70:21-3+,
Sept '69.
_____(part II) 71:29-
32+, Oct '69.

WHITESIDES, Kim
[illus] 59:58, Oct '68; 65:33,
Apr '69; 70:44-5, Sept '69; 78:
34-5, May '70; 81:42, Aug '70;
85:34-5, Dec '70.

WHO are the angels? [poem]
D. Cunliffe. 38:25, Nov '65.

WHO else can make so much
out of passing out?: the sur-
prising survival of an anti-play
[review essay] N. Hentoff. 11:
170-7, Jan/Feb '60.

WHO: whom [play excerpt from
Oh! Calcutta!] 69:51-3, Aug
'69.

WHO would you...? [cartoon]
L. Myers. 33:77-9, Aug/Sept
'64.

The WHORE [novel excerpt] D.
Charhadi. 30:30-42, May/Je '63.

WHO'S afraid of Leonard Woolf?
[autobiographical essay] D.
Woolf. 31:111-4, Oct/Nov '63.

WHO'S who in Ché's diary [bi-
ographical notes] 57:36-7, Aug
'68.

WHY [poem] F. Berry. 73:55,
Dec '69.

WHY are there no alternatives
[essay] P. Goodman. 16:1-5,
Jan/Feb '61.

WHY I am not a painter [poem]
F. O'Hara. 3:59, '57.

WHY President Kennedy was
killed [essay] P. Flammonde.
62:41-2+, Jan '69.

The WIDE skirt [excerpt from
the novel, The toy drum] G.
Grass. 21:36-44, Nov/Dec '61.

WIDOWER'S monologue [poem]
A. Chumacero.   7:59-61,
winter '59.

WIENERS, John
A poem for early risers. 9:
164-5, summer '59.
Two poems: Dope; The eagle
bar. 42:41, Aug '66.

WIFE in the saddle [story] G.
Parise. 56:28-31+, Jl '68.

WILBUR, Richard
She [poem] 17:61-2, Mar/
Apr '61.

WILBUR, RICHARD - CRITI-
CISM AND INTERPRETATION
Poems recorded by Richard
Wilbur. S. Kunitz. 8:201-2,
spring '59.

WILCOX, David
[illus] 79:54, Je '70.

WILLIAMS, Heathcote
The local stigmatic [play]
50:33-43, Dec '67.
MacGuinness [essay] 37:19-
25+, Sept '65.

WILLIAMS, JOE LEE - CRITI-
CISM AND INTERPRETATION
Recording with Big Joe. M.
Williams.   25:118-27, Jl/Aug
'62.

WILLIAMS, JOE LEE
(photograph of) 25:119, Jl/
Aug '62.

WILLIAMS, Jonathan
Hearts of stone [poem] 17:
43-4, Mar/Apr '61.
The honey lamb [poem] 17:
44-5, Mar/Apr '61.
Ovid, meet a metamorphodite
[poem] 17:45-6, Mar/Apr '61.
Three episodes from jammin'
the Greek scene [poems] 17:
43-6, Mar/Apr '61.

WILLIAMS, Martin

Billie Holiday: actress without an act [review essay] 26: 115-25, Sept/Oct '62.

Bix Beiderbecke and the white man's burden [review essay] 19:108-13, Jl/Aug '61.

Charlie Parker: the burden of innovation [review essay] 14: 141-52, Sept/Oct '60.

Clownish TV-1: Dick Van Dyke [review essay] 45:101-4, Feb '67.

Clownish TV-II: Red Skelton [review essay] 46:71, Apr '67.

Coleman Hawkins: some notes on a phoenix [essay] 36: 75-8, Je '65.

Count Basie: style beyond swing [essay] 38:62-5, Nov '65.

The craftsmanship of Horace Silver [review essay] 18:102-8, May/Je '61.

Funk for sale [review] 10: 136-40, Nov/Dec '59.

Instant jazz [essay] 8:164-70, spring '59.

The jazz avant garde: who's in charge here? [essay] 41: 64-8, Je '66.

Jelly Roll Morton: three-minute form [review essay] 12: 114-20, Mar/Apr '60.

John Lewis and the Modern Jazz Quartet [review essay] 23: 112-25, Mar/Apr '62.

Jottings on pianists [essay] 29:120-7, Mar/Apr '63.

Lester Young: originality beyond swing [essay] 39:71-3, Feb '66.

Louis Armstrong: style beyond style [review essay] 24: 111-20, May/Je '62.

Miles Davis: conception in search of a sound [essay] 34: 88-91, Dec '64.

Mulligan and Desmond at work [essay] 28:117-26, Jan/Feb '63.

Ornette Coleman: the meaning of innovation [review essay] 15:

123-33, Nov/Dec '60.

A purple dog, a flying squirrel, and the art of television [review] 20:114-20, Sept/Oct '61.

Recording with Big Joe [review essay] 25:118-27, Jl/Aug '62.

Rehearsal diary [essay] 31: 115-27, Oct/Nov '63.

Sarah Vaughan: some notes on a singer before it's too late [essay] 42:74-7, Aug '66.

Some comments in appreciation of Ellington [essay] 17: 106-14, Mar/Apr '61.

Sonny Rollins: spontaneous orchestration [review essay] 22:114-22, Jan/Feb '62.

Stitt in the studio [review essay] 27:119-28, Nov/Dec '62.

TV: tell me a story [essay] 47:70-2, Je '67.

Talking with myself (with limited apologies to Edmund Wilson) [essay] 33:83-5, Aug/Sept '64.

Thelonius Monk: modern jazz in search of maturity [essay] 7:178-89, winter '59.

Third stream problems [review essay] 30:113-25, May/Je '63.

Whatever happened to the clarinet? [essay] 32:82-3, Apr/May '64.

WILLIAMS, Tennessee

Young men waking at daybreak [poem] 50:29, Dec '67.

WILLIAMS, William Carlos

e. e. Cummings [review] 7: 214-6, winter '59.

The high bridge above the Tagus River at Toledo [poem] 3:56, '57.

Portrait of a woman at her bath [poem] 17:64, Mar/Apr '61.

Sappho [poem] 3:57, '57.

View of a woman at her bath

[poem] 3:58, '57.

WILLIAMS, WILLIAM CARLOS -
CRITICISM AND INTERPRE-
TATION
Patterson (book five) [review]
C. Olson. 9:220-1, summer '59.

WILLIAMSON, John
Aughatane [story] 16: 84-
101, Jan/Feb '61.
Matilda waltzes but still keeps
her maidenhead [essay] 35:86-8,
Mar '65.
Saturday [novel excerpt] 28:
73-9, Jan/Feb '63.

WIND from the Bosphorus [poem]
A. Trocchi. 30:93-4, May/Je
'63.

WINE [story] J. McCrary. 81:
31-3+, Aug '70.

WINTER offensive [story] A.
Higgins. 18:64-79, May/Je '61.

WOLF, Roger C.
From the third eye... white
man still speak with forked
tongue [review essay] 78:91-3,
May '70.

WOLFF, Tony and Mary Ellen
Mark
Psychedelic burlesque! [pho-
tographic essay] 56:35-43, Jl
'68.

WOLINSKI
[cartoon] 53:34, Apr '68;
54:74, May '68; 56:51, Jl '68;
66:66, May '69.

WOLTZ
[cartoon] 75:79, Feb '70.

WOMAN
Woman--the male fantasy. J.
Lester. 82:31-3+, Sept '70.

The WOMEN of Düsseldorf [car-

toon] L. Myers. 32:79-81,
Apr/May '64.

WOMEN'S Lib: save the last
dance for me [narrative] T.
Seligson. 80:18-21+, Jl '70.

WOMEN'S LIBERATION
Notes from the underground:
Women's Lib: save the last
dance for me. T. Seligson. 80:
18-21+, Jl '70.
see also
WOMEN'S RIGHTS

WOMEN'S RIGHTS
The law is an ass (male).
N. Hentoff. 84:49-51+, Nov
'70.

WOODMAN
[cartoon] 76:82, Mar '70;
79:90, Je '70; 85:63, Dec '70.

WOODSTOCK WEST
Revolution in the Rockies:
Woodstock West. J. Bishop.
80:71-2, Jl '70.

WOOLF, Douglas
Bank day [story] 14:14-27,
Sept/Oct '60.
The Flyman [story] 6:81-92,
autumn '58.
One of the truly good men
[review] 8:194-6, spring '59.
Quadrangle [story] 27:93-
4, Nov/Dec '62.
Who's afraid of Leonard
Woolf? [autobiographical essay]
31:111-4, Oct, Nov '63.

WOOLHISER, Jack
[illus] 47:62, 65, Je '67.

WORDS and music [play] S.
Beckett. 27:34-43, Nov/Dec
'62.

The WORDS behind the slogans
[essay] W. Höllerer. 21:119-
26, Nov/Dec '61.

The WORLD of sex [autobi-
ographical essay] H. Miller.
17:21-31, Mar/Apr '61.

WORLD WAR, 1939-45 - Poland
see
SIKORSKI, WLADISLAW (General)

WREN, CHRISTOPHER S.
see
SHEPHERD, Jack and Chris-
topher S. Wren.

WRIGHT, Jay
The end of an ethnic dream
[poem] 47:41, Je '67.

WRITERS
see
AUTHORS
BLACK AUTHORS
DRAMATISTS
POETS

WRITING
Essentials of spontaneous
prose. J. Kerouac. 5:72-3,
summer '58.
Should I assume America is
already dead? S. Krim. 68:
19-21+, Jl '69.
see also
DRAMA--TECHNIQUE
ESKIMO LITERATURE
FICTION--TECHNIQUE

WRITING for the theatre [essay]
H. Pinter. 33:80-2, Aug/Sept
'64.

WRITTEN address to an Italian
judge [essay] J. Kerouac. 31:
108-10, Oct/Nov '63.

- X -

XARAS, Theodore
[illus] 80:37, Jl '70.

- Y -

YACOUBI, Ahmed

The night before thinking
[story] 20:18-30, Sept/Oct '61.

YACOUBI, AHMED - CRITI-
CISM AND INTERPRETATION
The night before thinking
Comments on The night be-
fore thinking. W. Burroughs.
20:31-6, Sept/Oct '61.

YADOYA, No Meshimori [pseud]
Two poems. 31:90, Oct/Nov
'63.

YEATS, WILLIAM BUTLER -
CRITICISM AND INTERPRE-
TATION
Recordings of William Butler
Yeats [review] D. Greens. 8:
200-1, spring '59.

YESENIN-VOLPIN, Aleksander
The raven [poem] 20:69-71,
Sept/Oct '61.

A YIPPIE manifesto [essay] J.
Rubin. 66:41-3+, May '69.

YIPPIES
A Yippie manifesto. J.
Rubin. 66:41-3+, May '69.
see also
HOFFMAN, ABBIE
RUBIN, JERRY

YOU [poem] M. Rumaker. 35:
71, Mar '65.

YOU too can be john wayne
[poem] G. Briggs. 77:43, Apr
'70.

YOUNG, Al
On dancing [poem] 76:34-5,
Mar '70.

YOUNG, Dan [photos]
see
NEUBERG, Paul and Dan Young

YOUNG, LESTER - CRITICISM
AND INTERPRETATION

Lester Young: originality beyond swing. M. Williams. 39:
71-3, Feb '66.

YOUNG men waking at daybreak
[poem] T. Williams. 50:29,
Dec '67.

YOUNG, Wayland
The excluded words [essay]
32:28-32+, Apr/May '64.

YOUTH
Hayden-Marat/Dylan-Sade:
defining a generation. J. Newfield. 52:23-5, Mar '68.
Notes from the underground:
right on with the best generation. D. Rader. 76:18, Mar
'70.

YOUTH - ADULT RELATION-.
SHIP
see
GENERATION GAP

YOUTH - BERLIN
Berlin impressions. G.
Corso. 16:69-83, Jan/Feb
'61.

YOUTH - UNITED STATES
The ability to function. N.
Hentoff. 79:45-7, Je '70.

YRRAH
[cartoon] 69:58, Aug '69.

YURICK, Sol
Hubert Selby: symbolic intent and ideological resistance
(or cocksucking and revolution)
[essay] 71:49-51+, Oct '69.

- Z -

ZABO
[cartoon] 44:73, Dec '66;
47:83, Je '67.

ZANJ [poem] J. Stowers. 65:
26, Apr '69.

ZAPPA, Frank
'50s teenagers and '50s rock
(as told to Richard Blackburn)
[essay] 81:43-6, Aug '70.

ZAR
[cartoon] 70:63, Sept '69.

ZEMANN, Hilde
[photo] 36:cover, Je '65.

ZEN BUDDHISM
Aspects of Japanese culture.
D. T. Suzuki. 6:40-56,
autumn '58.

ZILNIK, ZELIMIR - CRITI-
CISM AND INTERPRETATION
Early works
Early works: an interview
with Zelimir Zilnik. W. Van
Dyke. 75:43-5, Feb '70.
From the third eye...a
parable of rebellion. D. Rader.
78:91, May '70.

ZIP
[cartoon] 74:21, Jan '70.

The ZOO story (a play in one
scene--1958) E. Albee. 12:28-
52, Mar/Apr '60.

PART II

Lists of Contributors

(authors of essays, reviews, etc; authors of short stories, novels, etc. ; dramatists; poets; translators; cartoonists; illustrators; and photographers)

Authors of Essays, Reviews, etc.

ABEL, Lionel
AMAR, Abu
AMRAM, David
ANAND, Mulk Raj
ARNAUD, Noel
ARONOWITZ, Alfred
ARRABAL, Fernando
ARTAUD, Antonin
ASHTON, Dore

BARKER, Danny
BARNIER, L.
BARRY, Joseph
BARTHES, Roland
BECK, Julian
BECKETT, Samuel
BEHAN, Brendan
BENTLEY, Eric
BESS, Donovan
BISHOP, Jordan
BLACKBURN, Paul
BLANCHOT, Maurice
BÖLL, Heinrich
BONITZER, Pascal
BOSQUET, Michel
BOUCHÉ, H-P.
BOYLE, Kay
BRAUTIGAN, Richard
BRECHT, Stefan S.
BRENNAN, Garnet E.
BROWN, Cecil M.
BUCHWALD, Art
BURROUGHS, William S.
BUTOR, Michel

CAMPBELL, Joseph
CAMUS, Albert
CARADEC, F.
CARROLL, Kent
CARROLL, Paul
CARSON, L. M. Kit
CASTRO, Fidel
CHALUPECKÝ, Jindřich
CHESTER, Alfred

CIORAN, E. M.
CLEAVER, Eldridge
COMOLLI, Jean
CONGRAT-BUTLER, Stefan
CORNEILLE
CORSO, Gregory
CUEVAS, José Luis

DALÍ, Salvador
DAVIS, Douglas M.
DEBRAY, Régis
DÉCAUDIN, Michel
DELAHAYE, Michael
DÉMERON, Pierre
DENBY, Edwin
DESTRÉ, Sabine
DODDS, "Baby"
DOUGLAS, William O.
DRIGGS, Frank S.
DUBERMAN, Martin
DUBUFFET, Jean
DUPREE, Louis
DÜRRENMATT, Friedrich

ELISCU, Lita
ELMAN, Richard
ESPINASSE, Françoise
ÉTIEMBLE
ETIENNE, Luc

FERLINGHETTI, Lawrence
FITZSIMMONS, Thomas
FLAMMONDE, Paris
FOWLES, John
FOWLIE, Wallace
FRIEDMAN, B. H.
FUKUDA, Rikutaro
FULLER, R. Buckminster

GARA, Larry
GARDNER, Fred
GELBER, Jack
GENÊT, Jean
GINSBERG, Allen

GIRODIAS, Maurice
GLEASON, Ralph J.
GOLDBERG, Joe
GONZALEZ, Luis J.
GOODE, Erich
GOODMAN, Paul
GOTTLIEB, Saul
GRAFE, Frieda
GREEN, Maurice
GREENBERG, Clement
GREENE, David
GREER, Herb
GREGORY, Horace
GUEVARA, Ché
GUSTAITIS, Rasa
GYSIN, Brion

HAINES, William
HAYDEN, Tom
HELD, Jean-François
HENDRICKS, Jon
HENTOFF, Nat
HERNTON, Calvin C.
HIGGINS, Aiden
HOCHHUTH, Rolf
HODEIR, André
HOFFMAN, Abbie
HÖLLERER, Walter
HOLLO, Anselm
HOLMES, John Clellon
HOWARD, Kenneth
HOWARD, Richard

IONESCO, Eugène

JAMES, Jud
JASPERS, Karl
JEFFERIS, G.
JOHNSON, Uwe
JONES, LeRoi
JORDAN, June

KAROL, K. S.
KARP, Ivan C.
KEMP, Lysander
KEROUAC, Jack
KISTING, Marianne
KOCH, Kenneth
KOLAKOWSKI, Liszek
KOTT, Jan
KRIM, Seymour
KUNITZ, Stanley

LABARTHE, André
LAHR, John
LALL, Anand
LEARY, Timothy
LEIRIS, Michel
LÉON-PORTILLA, Miguel
LESTER, Julius
LIEHM, Antonin
LU, Ch'iu-Yin
LYND, Staughton

McCLURE, Michael
McCOY, Esther
McREYNOLDS, David
MALCOLM X
MANCEAUX, Michèle
MARKOPOULOS, Gregory J.
MAROWITZ, Charles
MARSHALL, John
MARTIN, Lionel
MASSIN
MAURICE, Bob
MENDÈS-FRANCE, Pierre
MICHAUX, Henri
MICHELSON, Annette
MILLER, Charles
MILLER, Henry
MILLS, C. Wright
MINER, John W.
MOLLET, Jean
MORIN, Edgar
MORRISSETT, Ann
MORRISSETTE, Bruce
MYERS, John Bernard

NABOKOV, Vladimir
NARBONI, Jean
NATHAN, John
NERUDA, Pablo
NEUBERG, Paul
NEWFIELD, Jack
NEWLOVE, Donald
NICHOLS, F. L.
NORRIS, Hoke

O'DOHERTY, Brain
O'DONOGHUE, Michael
OGLESBY, Carl
O'HARA, Frank
OLSON, Charles
OZICK, Cynthia

PATALAS, Enno

PAZ, Octavio
PEKAR, Harvey
PETTERSEN, Will
PHELPS, Donald
PHILBY, Kim
PIA, Pascal
PIERRE, Sylvie
PINTER, Harold
PONIATOWSKA, Elena
PORTER, Fairfield
POTTER, Jeffrey
PRICE, James
PROUST, Marcel

RADER, Dotson
RANDALL, Margaret
RAPHAEL, Lennox
RAPOPORT, Louis
RAYFIELD, Fred
RECHY, John
RECK, Michael
REXROTH, Kenneth
REYNOLDS, Frank
RIVERS, Larry
ROBBE-GRILLET, Alain
ROCHE, Paul
ROSSET, Clement
ROTH, George Andrew
RUBIN, Jerry
RUDD, Mark
RYAN, John Fergus

SAILLET, Maurice
SALE, J. Kirk
SALZMAN, Eric
SÁNCHEZ SALAZAR, Gustavo
SANDLER, Irving
SANDOMIR, I. L.
SAROYAN, William
SARTRE, Jean-Paul
SAWYER, Kenneth
SCHECHNER, Richard
SCHICKEL, Richard
SCHLEIFER, Abdullah
SCHNEIDER, Alan
SCHORER, Mark
SCHULTZ, John
SCHUYLER, James
SCHWOB, Marcel
SEALE, Bobby
SEAVER, Richard
SEGAL, Abraham
SELBY, Hubert

SELDON, E. S.
SELIGSON, Tom
SERREAU, Geneviève
SEYMOUR, Alan
SHAINBERG, Lawrence
SHATTUCK, Roger
SHEPHERD, Jack
SKIR, Leo
SLATER, Philip E.
SNOW, C. P.
SNYDER, Gary
SONTAG, Susan
SPELLMAN, A. B.
SPIKE, Paul
STEINGESSER, Martin
STEWART, Rex
STROMBERG, Robert
SUTHERLAND, Elizabeth
SUZUKI, Daisetz T.

TAGGART, William
TALBOT, Daniel
TALLMAN, Warren
TALLMER, Jerry
TAYLOR, Simon Watson
TERRELL, Robert
TORMA, Julien
TOWARNICKI, Frédéric de
TROCCHI, Alexander
TURNER, Frederick W.
TYLER, Parker
TYNAN, Kenneth

ULLERSTAM, Lars
UNTERECKER, John

VAN DYKE, Willard
VERTOV, Dziga
VIAN, Boris
VOGEL, Amos
VOZNESENSKY, Andrei

WAIN, John
WAINHOUSE, Austryn
WALFORD, Roy L.
WATTS, Alan
WILLIAMS, Heathcote
WILLIAMS, Martin
WILLIAMS, William Carlos
WILLIAMSON, John
WOLF, Roger C.
WOOLF, Douglas
WREN, Christopher

YOUNG, Wayland
YURICK, Sol

ZAPPA, Frank

Authors of Short Stories, Novels, etc.

ABRAMOV, Fyodor
ADAMOV, Arthur
ALLAIS, Alphonse
ALLEN, Woody
AMIDON, Bill
AMOR, Guadalupe
ANDERSCH, Alfred
ANDERSON, Benny
ARNETT, Carroll
ATHILL, Diana

BATAILLE, Georges
BECKETT, Samuel
BIANCIARDI, Luciano
BIELER, Manfred
BORZIC, Jean
BOYLE, Patrick
BRAUTIGAN, Richard
BROOKE, Richard
BROWN, Cecil M.
BROWN, Kenneth M.
BRUNOT, James
BUKOWSKI, Charles
BULATOVIC, Miodrag
BURROUGHS, William S.

CALISHER, Hortense
CÉLINE, Louis-Fernand
CHARHADI, Driss ben Hamid
CHERRYTREE, E. F.
CHESTER, Alfred
CICELLIS, Kay
CLAIR, René
CLARKE, Austin C.
COHEN, Edward M.
CONROY, Frank
COOVER, Robert Chapin
COREY, L. G.
CORSO, Gregory
CREELEY, Robert

DAGERMAN, Stig
DAUMAL, René
DELANEY, Shelagh

DÉRY, Tibor
DI PRIMA, Diane
DORN, Edward
DUPRESS, Louis
DÜRRENMATT, Friedrich

EARNSHAW, Anthony
EASTLAKE, William
ELMAN, Richard
ELSNER, Gisela

FARGUE, Léon-Paul
FÉNÉON, Félix
FERRY, Jean
FOREST, Jean-Claude
FOSTER, Charles
FRIEDMAN, B. H.
FUENTES, Carlos

GADGIL, Gangadhar
GARIBAY, Ricardo
GARNER, Bob
GARRETT, Leslie
GASCAR, Pierre
GELBER, Jack
GENET, Jean
GOLD, Herbert
GOMBROWICZ, Witold
GOREY, Edward
GOURMONT, Remy de
GOVER, Robert
GRASS, Günter
GREY, Irene

HARDING, Gunnar
HARESNAPE, Geoffrey
HICKEY, John
HIGGINS, Aidan
HIMES, Chester
HOCHHUTH, Rolf
HÖLLERER, Walter
HUNTER, Robert
HUNTLEY, Timothy Wade

IONESCO, Eugène

JAHN, Janheinz
JARRY, Alfred
JOHNSON, Paul
JOHNSON, Uwe
JONES, LeRoi

KAMENEV, Nicolai
KAYE, Anthony
KEMAL, Yasar
KEROUAC, Jack
KLOSSOWSKI, Pierre
KUPPERBERG, Tulie

LALL, Anand
LAMBERT, Spencer
LI YÜ
LIN YATTA
LIND, Jakov

McCRARY, Jim
MADISON, Russ
MAILER, Norman
MALAPARTE, Curzio
MASON, Michael
MERWIN, William S.
MICHAELS, Leonard
MILLER, Henry
MITCHELL, Julian
MOLINARO, Ursule
MROZEK, Slawomir
MYERS, Lou

NEWLOVE, Donald

O'CONNOR, Philip
OE, Kenzaburo
OPPENHEIMER, Joel

PAPALEO, Joseph
PARISE, Goffredo
PAZ, Octavio
PIEYRE DE MANDIARGUES,
    André
POZAS ARCINIEGA, Ricardo
PRÉVERT, Jacques
PRICE, Bill
PURDY, James

QUENTEAU, Raymond

RADAR, Dotson

REAGE, Pauline
RECHY, John
REVELLI, George
RICHIE, Donald
ROBBE-GRILLET, Alain
ROEHLER, Klaus
ROSENTHAL, Irving
ROUECHÉ, Berton
RULFO, Juan
RUMAKER, Michael
RYAN, John Fergus

SADE, Marquis de
SALAS, Floyd
SANDERS, Ed
SCHULTZ, John
SELBY, Hubert
SELVON, Samuel
SHUFFLER, Jack C.
SINGH, Krushwant
SKIR, Leo
SKVORECKY, Josef
SOUTHERN, Terry
SOUTHGATE, Patsy
SPIKE, Paul
STEVENS, Shane
STOPPARD, Tom

TANINO, Aki
THACKER, Eric
THOMAS, John
THOMAS, Mack Sheldon
TROCCHI, Alexander
TUTUOLA, Amos

UEDA, Akinari

VIAN, Boris

WALFORD, Roy L.
WALTER, Otto
WARHOL, Andy
WEBER, David O.
WELCH, Lew
WEST, Anthony C.
WILLIAMSON, John
WOOLF, Douglas

YACOUBI, Ahmed

161

Dramatists

ADAMOV, Arthur

ALBEE, Edward

ARNAUD, Georges

ARRABAL, Fernand

ARTAUD, Antonin

BECKETT, Samuel

BEHAN, Brendan

BRECHT, Bertolt

CORSO, Gregory

DE GRAZIA, Edward

DUBERMAN, Martin

EÏCH, Günter

GARCÍA LORCA, Federico

GARRO, Elena

HOFMANN, Gert

IONESCO, Eugène

JARRY, Alfred

KOCH, Kenneth

McCLURE, Michael

O'DONOGHUE, Michael

ORTON, Joe

PINGET, Robert

PINTER, Harold

SOUTHGATE, Patsy

STOPPARD, Tom

SWAN, Jon

WILLIAMS, Heathcote

ANDREWS, Lyman
ANTONINUS, Brother (William
 Everson)
ANZAI, Hitoshi
ARCHILOCHOS
ARP, Hans
ARREOLA, Juan José
ASHBERY, John
AUSTIN, Robert
BACHMANN, Ingeborg
BARNES, Lakenan
BECK, Julian
BECKER, Paul
BECKETT, Samuel
BERGER, Patricia
BERRY, Fred
BLACKBURN, Paul
BLASER, Robin
BLOK, Alexander
BORGES, Jorge Luis
BOYD, Bruce
BRECHT, Bertolt
BROUGHTON, James
BROUGHTON, W. S.
BROWN, P. (Pete) R.
BUGGS, George
BUKOWSKI, Charles
BURNS, Jim
BURROWS, E. G.
CALVILLO, Manuel
CANADA, Stephen
CARROLL, Paul
CATENACCI, Edward N.
CELAN, Paul
CENDRARS, Blaise
CHUMACERO, Alí
CLIFFORD, Joan
CORSO, Gregory
CREELEY, Robert
CREWS, Judson
CROUCH, Stanley
CROZIER, Andrew
CRUZ, Victor Hernandez
CUMMINGS, e. e.

CUNLIFFE, Dave
DAHL, Ronald
DARTON, Eric
DAVIS, Hank
DELANEY, Shelagh
DENT, Thomas
DE OCA, Marco
DOOLITTLE, Hilda (H. D.)
DORN, Edward
DOWDEN, George
DUNCAN, Robert
DUPREE, Louis
DÚRAN, Manuel
EASTLAKE, William
ENZENBERGER, Hans
ESHLEMAN, Clayton
EVERSON, William (Brother
 Antoninus)
EVTUSHENKO, Evgeny
FARGUE, Léon-Paul
FERLINGHETTI, Lawrence
FIELD, Edward
FIOFORI, Tam
FOWLER, Gene
FRUMKIN, Gene
GARCÍA LORCA, Federico
GARCÍA TÉRRES, Jaime
GINSBERG, Allen
GINSBERG, Louis
GLEESON, Patrick Shannon
GRADY, James
GRAHAM, Henry
GRASS, Günter
GRAY, Pat
GREGORY, Horace
GROSS, John
GUEST, Barbara
H. D. (Hilda Doolittle)
HAMILL, Pete
HANDKE, Russell
HAN-SHAN
HAVEL, Vaclav
HEISSENBÜTTEL, Helmut
HENDERSON, David

HERBERT, Zbigniew
HERNTON, Calvin C.
HO-CHI-MINH
HOCHMAN, Sandra
HOFF, Rowell
HOFFMAN, Phil
HOLLO, Anselm
HOROVITZ, Michael
HUBBELL, Lindley Williams
  (Hayashi Shuseki)
HUIDOBRO, Vincente
JACKRELL, Thomas L.
JACKSON, Richard
JARRY, Alfred
JONES, LeRoi
JONES, Roy
JULIAN THE APOSTATE
KANDELL, Lenore
KENWORTHY, Stephen
KING, Franklin
KNOX, Hugh
KOCH, Kenneth
KOOSER, Ted
KRIM, Seymour
KROHN, Herbert
LAMANTIA, Philip
LEE, Don L.
LEVERTOV, Denise
LEVINSON, Michael S.
LIMA, Frank
LOGAN, John
LOWELL, Robert
LYTTLE, David
McCLURE, Michael
McKAIN, David
MADONIA, Gail
MALANGA, Gerald
MALINA, Judith
MAYAKOVSKY, Vladimir
MAYES, R. Inskip
MEDNICK, Murray
MENG-LUNG, Feng
MENKITI, Ifeanyi
MERRILL, James
MERWIN, William S.
MILES, Josephine
MOFFETT, Cleveland
MONDRAGON, Sergio
MORAFF, Barbara
MORGAN, Edward
MORSE, Carl
MYERS, David
MYERS, Paul E.

NERUDA, Pablo
NORSE, Harold
NUTTALL, Jeff
O'CONNELL, Richard
O'DONOGHUE, Michael
O'HARA, Frank
OLSON, Charles
OPPENHEIMER, Joel
PALCEWSKI, John
PASTERNAK, Boris
PATTEN, Brian
PAZ, Octavio
PENDEL, Dale
PLYMELL, Charles
POSNER, David
PRÉVERT, Jacques
PROPPER, Dan
RANDALL, Margaret
RAWORTH, Tom
REAVIS, Charles S.
REVERDY, Pierre
REXROTH, Kenneth
RICE, Stan
RICKERT, Richard
ROCHE, Paul
ROSTEN, Norman
ROUECHÉ, Berton
ROZEWICZ, Tadeusz
RUKEYSER, Muriel
RUMAKER, Michael
RUSSO, A. P.
RYAN, Pat M.
SABINES, Jaime
SAGGESE, Robert
SANDOMIR, I. L.
SARGENT, Elizabeth
SEIDEL, Frederick
SHAPIRO, Karl
SHARAT CHANDRA, G. S.
SHARKEY, John J.
SHUSEKI, Hayashi (Lindley
  Williams Hubbell)
SIMPSON, Joseph W.
SMITH, Herbert
SMITH, William Jay
SNYDER, Gary
SOUTHGATE, Patsy
SPICER, Jack
STANFORD, Herbert W.
STEINGESSER, Martin
STOWERS, J. Anthony
STUCKEL, Eugene
SURGAL, Jon

THEROX, Paul
TIPTON, David
TOMLINSON, Charles
TROCCHI, Alexander
VALLEJO, César
VAN BUSKIRK, Alden
VIAN, Boris
VOZNESENSKY, Andrei
WALCOTT, Derek
WEBB, Charles Graham
WELLS, Robert
WHALEN, Philip
WIENERS, John
WILBUR, Richard
WILLIAMS, Jonathan
WILLIAMS, Tennessee
WILLIAMS, William Carlos
WRIGHT, Jay
YADOYA, No Meshimori
YESENIN-VOLPIN, Aleksander
YOUNG, Al

Translators

BARNSTONE, Willis
BECKETT, Samuel
BENTLEY, Eric
HOLLO, Anselm
LEVERTOV, Denise
NIMS, John Frederick
ROTHENBERG, Jerome
SNYDER, Gary
TANINO, Aki
WALEY, Arthur
WATSON, Burton

Cartoonists

ALEX
AMI
ARUEGO
ASPINWALL
B. U. S.
BLAKE, Quentin
BLECHMAN, R. O.
BORN, A.
BOWSER, Larry
BRANDRETH, R.
CABALLERO
CALDWELL, John
CALMAN
CANZLER
CAZ
CESC
CLAUDE
CORK
COSPER
CRANE, Jim
CURSAT
CURTIS
DANILO
DAWSON
DE CARLO
DESCLOZEAUX
EFBÉ
ENIF
FEHR
FERGUSON, A.
FLORA, Paul
FOX
GOOGIE
GRUS
HARDER, Kelsie
HARRIS
HATCHFIELD
HOSKIN
HUFFAKER, Sandy
JEFFERY
JON
K. E. D.
KAJAN, Tibor
KANE, John

KAPLAN, Ervin
KLIBAN
KRAHN, Fernando
KRISTOFORI
LEE, Bill
LEON
LETTICK, Dave
MACK, Stan
McKEE, Jon
MAL
MARTIN, Jerome
MENA
MENDELSON, Ed
MEYEROWITZ, Rick
MUNZLINGER, Tony
MURRAY
MYERS, Lou
NORDENSTRÖM, Hans
NUÑO
O'BANNON
OLSEN
PARÉ
PASCAL, David
PICHA
POUZET
RAUCH
RINCIARI, Ken
ROBINS, Ted
RODRIGUES
ROSS, Larry
SALTZMAN, Tony
SAXON, Charles
SEMPÉ
SENS, A. G.
SINCLAIR, Bill
SINÉ
STAMATY
TREZ
UNGERER, Tomi
VAL
VAN WOERKOM
VASCO
WENDE, Philip
WESSUM

WOLINSKI
WOLTZ
WOODMAN
YRRAH
ZABO
ZAR
ZIP

Illustrators

ALCORN, John
ARIKHA, Avigdor
BECK, Jack W.
BERTRAND, R.
BOBBER, Richard
BONNARD
BONUS, Jack
BRAMLEY, Peter
BROWN, Donna
BRUNOFF, Laurent de
CHWAST, Seymour
CONDAK, Cliff
DALY, John
DAUMAL, René
DAVIS, Paul
DI GRAZIA, Thomas
DUHEME, Jacqueline
DUMARCAY, Philippe
FAUST, Jan
FEIFFER, Jules
FOREST, Jean-Claude
FRITZ, Virginia
GORDON, Bonnie
GRASHOW, James
GREEN, Norman
GREEN, Peter
GROSSMAN, Robert
GROSZ, George
GUTZEIT, Fred
HAYS, Philip
HEDDA
HOLLAND, Brad
HUFFAKER, Sandy
HUFFMAN, Tom
IVANOV, S.
JAMIESON, Douglas
JARRY, Alfred
JENKYNS, Chris
JOHNSON, Guy
JON
KANAREK, Michael
KARLIN, Eugene
KATZ, Alex
KUHL, Jerome

LEE, Bill
LEVIN, Arnold
LEWIS, Tim
LIPPMAN, Peter
LOGRIPPO, Robert
LONIDIER, Lynn
MACK, Stan
McLEAN, Willson
McMULLEN, Jim
MAFFIA, Daniel
MARTIN, Jerome
MATTELSON, Marvin
MAX, Peter
MEYEROWITZ, Mickey
MEYEROWITZ, Rick
MIKUWAIA
MILLER, Steve
MOSCHELLA, Michelle
MURAKAWA, Gennosuke
MUSIALOWICZ, Henryk
NESSIM, Barbara
PASSALACQUA, David
QUAY, Stephen
RINCIARI, Ken
RIVGAUCHE, Michel
ROWE, William
RUBINGTON, Norman
SAROYAN, William
SARTAIN, Gailard
SCHAUMANN, Peter
SCHREITER, Richard
SCHULENBERG, Robert
SELIG, Sylvie
SELTZER, Isadore
SINCLAIR, Bill
SLACKMAN, Charles B.
SMITH, Richard
SOMSKY, John
SPINA, Paul
SPRINGER, Frank
STEIR, Pat
SUMNER, Bill
SWANSON, Karl W.
TOMLINSON, Roger

TOPOR, Roland
UNGERER, Tomi
WAGNER, John
WEISMAN, Ann
WEISS, Chicago
WHITE, Charles
WHITESIDES, Kim
WILCOX, David
WOOLHISER, Jack
XARAS, Theodore

Photographers

ADAMS, George
ADELMAN, Bob
ARBUS, Diane
AVEDON, Richard
BACH, Eric
BAURET, Jean-François
BERKSON, Bill
BISCHOF, Werner
BOISE, Ron
BOKELBERG, Werner
BRASSAÏ
BROWN, Dean
CADOO, Emil
CARTIER-BRESSON, Henri
CHARLES, Don
CHAZ
CROSS, Elizabeth
CROSS, Guy
DE VINCENT, George
DOUGLASS, Ann
FEINSTEIN, Harold
FRANK, Robert
FREED, Arthur
FRIEDMAN, Benno
GHNASSIA
GOLD, Michael
HALSMAN, Philippe
HARRISON, Howard
HENNESSEY, Brian
HORN, Paula
HOSOE, Eikoh
JANAH, Sunil
JONVEL, Jean
KIRSTEL, Richard
KRAFT, Lee
KRAUSS, Lester
LAFFERTY, Thom
LAGARDE-LIAISON
LARCHER, David
LEE, James
LYON, Fred
McCOY, Dan
MAISEL, Jay
MARK, Mary Ellen

MITCHELL, James
MITCHELL, Julio
NAKAMURA, Masaye
NAMUTH, Hans
NEIDE, Peter
NEVELSON, Susan
NIBLOCK, Phil
NOBLE, Richard
PAPADOPOLOUS, Peter
REDL, Harry
RIEMENS, Henny
ROSSET, Loly
ROTH, Sanford
SAMETH, Martin
SANTOCE, Charles
SCHLESINGER, Steven
SCHLITTEN, Don
SCHWERIN, Ron
SHINOYAMA, Kishin
SILKE, James R.
SWOPE, Martha
TORRE, Lou de la
VELTRI, John
VIGNES, Michelle
WALDMAN, Lester
WALLACH, Richard
WAREING, William
YOUNG, Dan
ZEMAN, Hilde